D0965849

BOOKS BY

CLIFFORD H. POPE

THE REPTILE WORLD 1955

TURTLES OF THE UNITED STATES AND CANADA 1939

THESE ARE BORZOI BOOKS

PUBLISHED BY ALFRED A. KNOPF IN NEW YORK

THE REPTILE WORLD

Arizona coral king snake *(Lampropeltis pyromelana)* from the Chiricahua Mountains of southeastern Arizona. This beautiful species occurs from extreme northern central Mexico through the southeastern corner of New Mexico, all of Arizona but its southwestern desert region, and on northward well into Utah and Nevada. *(Courtesy The American Museum of Natural History and Charles M. Bogert; photograph by George M. Bradt)*

THE REPTILE WORLD

A NATURAL HISTORY OF THE
SNAKES, LIZARDS,
TURTLES, AND CROCODILIANS

CLIFFORD H. POPE

NEW YORK ALFRED A KNOPF
1964

L. C. catalog card number: 54–12979

© *Clifford H. Pope, 1955*

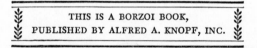

THIS IS A BORZOI BOOK,
PUBLISHED BY ALFRED A. KNOPF, INC.

PUBLISHED NOVEMBER 14, 1955
REPRINTED TWO TIMES
FOURTH PRINTING, FEBRUARY 1964

TO MY WIFE

Introduction

✣

FEW LAYMEN realize how rapidly our knowledge of animal life is being increased by research. In the field of herpetology, the study of reptiles and amphibians, about one thousand new titles appear every year. Nearly all of these are brief technical papers, and only a few are books and monographs. It is patent that a short book cannot begin even to summarize the vast reservoir of knowledge of reptile life. The proper selection of material and its well-organized presentation can, nevertheless, arouse interest and act as water poured into a dry pump to prime it. The facts to be found in the pages that follow have been carefully sifted from hundreds of papers and books; references to the most important of these will be found in the five bibliographies. The works of the following living herpetologists have been drawn upon most frequently: Bogert, Carr, Dunn, Loveridge, Mertens, A. S. Romer, Rose, K. P. Schmidt, H. M. Smith, M. A. Smith, and Taylor. I also wish to acknowledge my lifelong indebtedness to the late Raymond L. Ditmars, whose works, now classics, first stimulated my interest in reptiles.

It might well be asked what organizations sponsor and support the researchers who write these innumerable technical papers and books. Broadly speaking, the study of animals may be divided into three great categories: function, or what makes them tick; anatomy, or how they fit together; and classification, or how they are related. The study of function has been carried on chiefly in university laboratories, that of classification in large museums, that of anatomy in both university and museum. Zoology undoubtedly would progress more rapidly if each institution pursued all three types of research; segregation tends to create antagonistic groups that work at odds rather than co-operatively. The eleven contemporary herpetologists just named are about equally divided between universities and museums; three of them are from the Old World, the rest from the United States. This geographical distribution roughly reflects the relative amount of herpetological interest to be found in the parts of the world concerned.

In an effort to avoid technicalities and simplify the writing, I have faced the danger of being called unscientific. Students of animal behavior have developed a whole vocabulary that enables them to avoid teleological language, but their terminology, in my opinion, would be inappropriate for this book. The reader need simply remember that, for instance, when I write of a snake as a "bluffer" I do not imply that it surveys a particular situation and decides: "Ah, now is the psychological moment to pull that nice little trick of mine." No doubt the bluffing is entirely unpremeditated and even unconscious; calling it a bluffer is merely a way of getting the idea across with the least complexity of language. The literal-minded specialist might well argue that the layman must be taught to think less anthropomorphically some day, so why not begin now. I admit the validity of this argument, but do not want to be the pioneer teacher.

In general I have divided my treatment of each reptile group about equally between function and classification. Anatomy or structure has been subordinated to, though closely correlated with, function, whereas geographical distribution and classification have been intimately joined; in fact, I have emphasized distribution because most readers will have the greatest interest in a local animal, and it is only fair to let them know which are local. The treatment of the different groups has been purposely varied to some degree, not only to avoid monotony but to give wider scope to the work as a whole; the necessity of drastic selection has already been dealt with.

The snakes have been placed in advance of the lizards, an order contrary to that of evolution. I have done this arbitrarily and offer no excuses; the act is purely one of whimsy.

It is unfortunate that two of the four most important terms in classification are confusing because of irregular plurals. These four are *species* (same in singular and plural), *genus* (plural: genera), *family*, and *order*. In plain English these would be, kind, group of closely related kinds, and so on up. The species is the basic unit, and so basic and important is it that modern statistical research (a great percentage of modern biological work is statistical) has enormously complicated the concept of a species. Basically, it is a population of animals in nature, the individuals strongly resembling one another and breeding only among themselves. To the average person it is usually a "kind." The fact of reproductive isolation is important because, once a species begins to interbreed freely with others, it soon loses its special characteristics and therefore its identity as a species.

Studies have shown that frequently species may be divided into subspecies, which are geographical subdivisions. Thus eastern individuals of a species widely distributed over this country may differ noticeably from western individuals, while those from the central part of the country may combine the characteristics of the eastern and western ones. These turncoats are called "intergrades." The studies of subdivisions of species have become so involved, and frequently the differences between them are of such a technical nature, that I have decided to use the species as the basic unit, almost always either ignoring its subdivisions or merely mentioning them.

The inclusion of scientific names is a necessity, if to some readers an unpleasant one. For some species no suitable common name exists. In certain cases I give alternative technical names, though only one is really correct; the others have been in use for a long time and are thus the more familiar. This practice helps those not up with the latest song and dance in taxonomy.

A clear exposition of the modern concept of species, their origin and subdivision, may be found in *Systematics and the Origin of Species*, by Ernst Mayr (New York; 1942).

A few words on geographical terminology: the terms "Malay islands" and "Malay Archipelago" are used synonymously and do not include the Philippine Islands or New Guinea.

Acknowledgments

✾

I AM DEEPLY INDEBTED to my wife, Sarah H. Pope, for a vast amount of fact-checking, criticizing, and editing. As I alone am responsible for the selection and presentation of material, all deficiencies and errors must be blamed on me.

Dr. Karl P. Schmidt read part of the section on snakes; he also gave advice and much encouragement. Dr. Bernard Greenberg went over the treatment of lizard courtship and mating, offering much constructive criticism. Dr. Frederick Medem read the entire section on crocodilians and contributed the account of hunting crocodilians for scientific purposes. Charles M. Bogert has given encouragement and information. Miss Lillian Ross clarified many editorial difficulties. For all this invaluable aid I am sincerely grateful.

Numerous other friends have helped me. Dr. Robert F. Inger and Hymen Marx found books and papers and gave information. Robert Snedigar, Dr. Laurence M. Klauber, and Dr. James A. Peters also supplied information. Dr. and Mrs. Donald A. Boyer listened while I read the account of geckos. Lucy P. Cullen allowed me to use the African folk story about the chameleon. Mr. and Mrs. Richard S. Cutler held one copy of the manuscript in their house for safekeeping. Dr. Arnold A. Zimmermann read much of the galley proof, making many helpful suggestions.

The Zoological Society of Philadelphia kindly granted permission to quote part of Archie Carr's article on sea turtles (*Fauna*, June 1948). I took the quotation directly from Carr's "Handbook of Turtles" by permission of Cornell University Press.

Chicago Natural History Museum has been most co-operative

in allowing use of their manifold facilities and in granting leave of absence for work on this book. To Director Clifford C. Gregg I am indebted for sympathetic interest.

The illustrations have been drawn from varied sources. A great many were acquired through the courtesy of The American Museum of Natural History and the kindness of Charles M. Bogert of that institution. Mr. Bogert took several of these photographs. Through the kind offices of James A. Oliver and William Bridges, the New York Zoological Society likewise contributed a large number. My gratitude to these persons and organizations is unbounded.

Several excellent photographs taken by Isabelle Hunt Conant were presented by her and Roger Conant. Walker Van Riper contributed interesting action pictures made with elaborate high-speed equipment. Through the kind co-operation of Charles E. Shaw, the Zoological Society of San Diego gave some unique photographs. To these, as well as to the following, I am indeed grateful: Howard K. Gloyd, Frederick Medem, Bernard Greenberg, William G. Hassler, and Richard C. Snyder.

I am indebted to the following friends and institutions for one or two illustrations or assistance with illustration work: Violet Wyld, Theodore D. Steinway, Hymen Marx, Park Phipps, Fred R. Cagle, Charles W. Dawson, Laura Brodie, Margaret Bradbury, Anne Hessey, T. Paul Maslin, Ivo Poglayen, the Chicago Zoological Society, The Chicago Academy of Sciences, and Chicago Natural History Museum.

Contents

Contents

Contents

Contents

Contents

xvii

Contents

Illustrations

Illustrations

Illustrations

PLATE   FOLLOWING PAGE 258

xxiii

THE REPTILE WORLD

Reptiles

(Class Reptilia)

EVERYONE KNOWS that turtles, snakes, lizards, alligators, and crocodiles (crocodilians) are reptiles, and that reptiles, along with fishes and amphibians (frogs, toad frogs, salamanders, and the rare cæcilians), are vertebrates, or animals with backbones. Recognition of turtles and crocodilians presents no problem. Snakes are too readily confused with worms, legless salamanders, and elongated, finless fishes; even limbless lizards can be troublesome. This difficulty is largely obviated by the knowledge that snakes and lizards have dry skin covered with scales. The general resemblance in form between salamander and lizard is also a cause of constant confusion, especially in the eastern United States where both abound, and where salamanders are commonly called "lizards." The salamander, however, never has scales, and its skin is nearly always noticeably moist.

The adjective "cold-blooded" is commonly applied to reptiles and other lower vertebrates. The implication of this term is that the reptile, being content with almost any temperature, simply takes on that of its surroundings. Prolonged investigations by Cowles and Bogert [1] have shown that, though the reptile does have the temperature of its environment, it is by no means indifferent to changes. Instead of having a built-in heating system, the reptile controls matters by seeking out a spot that will enable it to assume a comfortable temperature. This explains the constant moving about that is characteristic of reptile behavior.

[1] These authors have written many papers on temperature regulation in reptiles, but two by Charles M. Bogert adequately explain their findings: "Reptiles Under the Sun," *Natural History Magazine*, Vol. 44 (1939), pp. 26–37; and "Thermoregulation in Reptiles, a Factor in Evolution," *Evolution*, Vol. 3 (1949), pp. 195–211. The later paper is technica

3

Crocodilians

(Order Crocodilia or Loricata)

ALLIGATORS

CAIMANS

CROCODILES

FALSE GAVIAL

GAVIAL

General Account

✺

A GROUP of animals without a name is like a kitchen pot without a handle. Before we can even begin to consider the alligators, crocodiles, and their relatives, we must give them a handle, and the best one by far is "crocodilian." This name comes from a Greek word and is not hard to remember when its similarity to "crocodile" is kept in mind. In technical books these reptiles may be called either "Crocodilia" or "Loricata."

Among the major groups of reptiles the crocodilians number fewer kinds than any other, yet these few include the largest reptiles, and, in fact, no really small species exist. There are many small turtles, lizards, and snakes, but no one has ever seen a pocket-size crocodilian that was not simply an infant. It is not surprising that in such a small assemblage there is no great difference in the general appearance of individual species, and because of this it is easy to draw a word picture of a "typical" crocodilian. This cannot be done with the lizards, snakes, or turtles, as all of those major groups include at least hundreds of species instead of the mere twenty-five that comprise the crocodilians.

The body of the crocodilian is joined to the powerful tail so inconspicuously that, were it not for the hind legs, you might have trouble telling where the body ends and the tail begins. The tail is far from being a mere ornament, for without it the crocodilian would be unable to move about in its favorite element, water. The tail is all-important in the undulatory swimming motions. The legs are large, though not powerful like the tail. They are folded against the body when the animal swims, and are used only in carrying it about on land, where it can make some speed for a short distance.

Contrary to general belief, the crocodilian does not drag itself about, but raises the body high off the ground when moving on land (Plate 3). The belief in the dragging process probably arose from the sight of frightened crocodilians sliding into the water. At such times the animal may slide down a slippery, sloping bank without getting up on its legs. The tail is also a powerful weapon of defense, as anyone who stands near an enraged crocodilian will soon find out. A swift sideswipe of the heavy tail knocks a man down at the moment when a similar sideswipe of the open jaws has put them in a position to take the best advantage of the blow by the tail.

In addition to an ability to take care of itself by using the jaws and tail, the crocodilian is well protected on the back by a tough coat of hard, horny scales reinforced by little plates of bone. The horny scales are set in rows, and have keels that form continuous ridges. The resulting armor is so tough that it might be described as impenetrable, remembering, of course, that all such terms are relative. In some crocodilians, even the belly scales are reinforced with bone, and the massive skull is so bony that no vulnerable spot can be found by an enemy.

In spite of this formidable armor, the crocodilian, like the turtle, has a weak link in the chain of its existence. While developing in the egg and just after hatching, it is dependent on its mother for protection. The eggs are easily found and are relished by various mammals, and the hatchlings are comparatively defenseless.

The crocodilian is amphibious—that is, it lives both on land and in the water. It takes to water for protection and gets most of its food from water, though it must have land on which to lay its eggs. Sunny banks are a favorite haunt, and no doubt the habit of sunning is of importance to its health.

The great importance of water to the crocodilian is shown by the shape and form of its head, especially the bones of the skull. The openings of the nose are on top of the snout and near its tip. This is of course a very convenient place for the nostrils of an aquatic animal. In most reptiles the air passes through the nostrils and into the mouth, allowing the shipping of water into the air supply when the head is submerged and the mouth is not kept tightly closed. The mammals avoided this difficulty by developing in the mouth a roof (the palate) above which the air passes to the throat. The crocodilians did the same thing much better and long before the mammals. The air that enters the nostrils at the tip of the long crocodilian snout must pass above the palate and into the throat, which can be closed by a flap of mucosa. If a crocodilian seizes an animal below the water, the necessary opening of the mouth does not interfere with breathing. The position of the eyes high on top of the head enables the almost completely submerged crocodilian to keep a watch on its surroundings while it breathes comfortably by means of the elevated nostrils at the tip of the snout.

Experiments have shown that at least the American alligator can remain under water as long as five hours before drowning. The length of time for drowning probably differs from species to species and depends on the water temperature and the activity of the animal.

The crocodilians as a whole had their heyday during the reign of the dinosaurs and give us a glimpse of the life of the Age of Reptiles when gigantic scaly creatures were the most conspicuous forms of animal life. The few crocodilians alive today, remnants of a glorious past, may be thought of as living fossils. In contrast to this, the crocodilian's body is not without its modern developments. The heart, for example, has four chambers, the teeth are in separate sockets, and the body is divided by a diaphragm or muscle that is used in breathing. These "living fossils" can thus look down their long noses at other reptiles and justly claim to be ahead of them in these important improvements that were only later developed by the mammals themselves.

LIST OF LIVING CROCODILIANS

As THERE are so few crocodilians, we can give a list of all the kinds or species that are known and then, after discussing the group as a whole, consider in detail almost every kind. (It would take volumes to treat the innumerable lizards, snakes, and turtles in similar detail.) What the crocodilians lack in numbers they make up for in size and romantic appeal. Among reptiles the man-eating crocodile holds a unique place in its relation to the human being. The venomous snake may be thought of as a killer though not an eater of man, and the giant constrictors are man-eaters only in the human imagination. Note that the list that follows includes a brief indication of the range of each species.

ALLIGATORS AND CAIMANS
(Family Alligatoridæ)

Broad-nosed Caiman   Paraguay and Brazil
   (*Caiman latirostris*)
Paraguay Caiman   Paraguay River System
   (*Caiman yacare*)
Spectacled Caiman   Amazon and Orinoco Basins
   (*Caiman sclerops*)
Central American Caiman   Mexico, Central America, and
   (*Caiman fuscus*)   Colombia
Black Caiman   Amazon Basin and Guianas
   (*Melanosuchus niger*)
American Alligator   Southeastern United States
   (*Alligator mississippiensis*)
Chinese Alligator   Eastern China
   (*Alligator sinensis*)
Smooth-fronted Caiman   Amazon Basin
   (*Paleosuchus trigonatus*)
Dwarf Caiman   Amazon Basin
   (*Paleosuchus palpebrosus*)

CROCODILES AND FALSE GAVIAL
(Family Crocodylidæ)

West African Dwarf Crocodile   West Africa
   (*Osteolæmus tetraspis*)
Congo Dwarf Crocodile   Upper Congo Basin
   (*Osteolæmus osborni*)
Nilotic Crocodile   Africa and Madagascar
   (*Crocodylus niloticus*)

African Slender-snouted Crocodile (*Crocodylus cataphractus*)	Congo Basin to Senegal
Mugger or Marsh Crocodile (*Crocodylus palustris*)	Southern Asia
Siamese Crocodile (*Crocodylus siamensis*)	Southeastern Asia and Java
New Guinean Crocodile (*Crocodylus novæ-guineæ*)	New Guinea
Australian Crocodile (*Crocodylus johnstoni*)	Australia
Mindoro Crocodile (*Crocodylus mindorensis*)	Philippine Islands
Salt-water Crocodile (*Crocodylus porosus*)	Southern Asia, Malay Archipelago, and Australia
Cuban Crocodile (*Crocodylus rhombifer*)	Cuba
Morelet's Crocodile (*Crocodylus moreleti*)	Mexico and Central America
American Crocodile (*Crocodylus acutus*)	Northwestern South America, Central America, Mexico, West Indies, and Florida
Orinoco Crocodile (*Crocodylus intermedius*)	Orinoco Basin
False Gavial (*Tomistoma schlegeli*)	Malay Peninsula and Archipelago

GAVIAL
(Family Gavialidæ)

Indian Gavial (*Gavialis gangeticus*)	Southern Asia

The average person in traveling through wild country is always struck by the sight of large animals, and is apt to think that they must be rare and of special interest. Certainly they are of special interest, although the chances are they are extremely well known. It is the small, inconspicuous animal that is vastly more apt to be a rarity. There are hundreds of small snakes and lizards as yet un-

11

known to science, whereas it is probable that scarcely a gigantic reptile remains unknown.

The crocodilians, with their great size, illustrate this point admirably. By 1825 three fifths of the twenty-five crocodilian species listed above had been formally introduced to science. In this century only three of the twenty-five species have been introduced to science and all of these by the same man, Dr. Karl P. Schmidt, who in a lifelong study of crocodilians has proved to be a sort of crocodile Sherlock Holmes, detecting new kinds overlooked by others. To his credit is the discovery of the Congo dwarf crocodile (1919), the New Guinean crocodile (1928), and the Mindoro crocodile (1935). By way of contrast, the introduction of new species of lizards and snakes is at least a weekly occurrence in the annals of technical herpetology.

ALLIGATOR AND CROCODILE

IN THE United States at least, the question most often asked about crocodilians is: "What is the difference between an alligator and a crocodile?" It is not surprising that this question has become so popular in a country with but one crocodile and one alligator. Yet even in the United States the question has little practical point, as the natural ranges of these two crocodilians approach each other only in extreme southern Florida—the American crocodile, like other crocodiles, being a tropical reptile in contrast to the American alligator, which lives in a temperate region. Because of this difference in ranges, these two animals can almost never be confused by the hunter.

Looking at the matter from a scientific point of view, we see that the alligators and crocodiles are placed in separate families, and therefore must have many differences in the way they are put together, so to speak. To point out these differences would take us beyond the scope of this work, but a glance at an American alligator placed next to an American crocodile will show that we need only remember that the alligator's snout is much the broader. With a little practice anyone can tell one from the other instantly. To carry the matter still further, it can be pointed out that in agreement with the more narrow snout of the crocodile, the fourth tooth of the lower jaw fits into a groove of the upper; in the broad snout of the alligator this tooth slips into a pocket of the upper jaw.

SIZE, AGE, GROWTH

THE QUESTION of greatest size is as annoying to the specialist as it is fascinating to the layman. The trouble with it is that facts are almost impossible to get, and the larger the animal concerned the harder the problem. Moving very large reptiles about is hard enough in any case, but when one of these creatures is of gigantic proportions the difficulty becomes truly formidable. Everyone knows the temptation to stretch measurements, and what chance is there for even a professional reptile man to encounter one of these enormous individuals? Skinning the carcass does not help because skins are always much longer than the body from which they came.

The scientific student of reptiles is prone to exaggerate these stumbling-blocks and to avoid the question of greatest size. But this attitude is not reasonable because size is important from the scientific as well as from the lay point of view. The experience of Dr. Schmidt at Lake Ticamaya, Honduras, well illustrates the point. The average size of the numerous American crocodiles at this lake was reported as 15 feet, and an alleged 12-footer had just been shot by a "gringo" hunter. The tape measure applied to this specimen proved it to be only 8 feet 9 inches long. Dr. Schmidt remarks at this point that the naturalist who carries a steel tape is sure to be discouraged. The largest specimen encountered during the week of hunting at Ticamaya measured only 11 feet 2 inches.

By measuring many skulls of crocodilians of known length Dr. Schmidt has come to some sobering conclusions for the lover of record sizes. For example, a notorious man-eating salt-water crocodile that lived on Luzon in the Philippine Islands was shot by two hunters, who recorded its length as 29 feet, its girth as 11. Fortunately, the skull was brought to this country, where it is considered to be the world's largest crocodilian skull. On the basis of its measurement (about thirty inches), the possessor could not have been more than 22.5 feet long.

Strangely enough, the most reliable record measurement made by a scientist was taken more than a century ago by the famous explorer Alexander von Humboldt. This measurement was of an Orinoco crocodile 22 feet 4 inches long. The following summary of approximate crocodilian dimensions is taken from Dr. Schmidt.

When the crocodilians are arranged in order of size they may be roughly divided into three groups—giant, large, and small. The difference between the average and greatest lengths is often very marked. This probably means only that measurements have been taken on too few individuals; if hundreds of specimens were measured, the gap would be much smaller.

The measurements of the two alligators included below call for comment. The American alligator has been slaughtered so ruthlessly that gigantic individuals are no longer found. The Chinese alligator, now all but extinct, has lived for thousands of years in a populated area, and certainly does not now reach the length that it formerly did. Unfortunately, we have no way of knowing to what size it once grew.

LENGTH OF CROCODILIANS IN FEET

Giant Species (*Maximum length 19–23*)

American Crocodile	greatest: 23	average: 10–12
Orinoco Crocodile	greatest: 23	average: 10–12
Indian Gavial	greatest: $21\frac{1}{2}$	average: 12–15
Salt-water Crocodile	greatest: 20	average: 12–14
American Alligator	greatest: $19\frac{1}{6}$	average: 8–10

Large Species (*Maximum length 12–16*)

Nilotic Crocodile	greatest: 16	average: 12
False Gavial	greatest: 16	average: 9–10
Black Caiman	greatest: 15	average: 10–12
Mugger or Marsh Crocodile	greatest: 13	average: 10
Siamese Crocodile	greatest: 12	average: 10
Cuban Crocodile	greatest: 12	average: 6–8

Small Species (*Maximum length less than 10*)

New Guinean Crocodile	greatest: $9\frac{1}{3}$	average:	8
Spectacled Caiman	greatest: $8\frac{2}{3}$	average:	5–6
Morelet's Crocodile	greatest: 8	average:	6–7
Australian Crocodile	greatest: 8	average:	6–7
Paraguay Caiman	greatest: 8	average:	6–7
African Slender-snouted Crocodile	greatest: 8	average:	6
Mindoro Crocodile	greatest: 8	average:	5–6
Broad-nosed Caiman	greatest: $6\frac{3}{4}$	average:	6
Chinese Alligator	greatest: $6\frac{1}{2}$	average:	$4–4\frac{1}{2}$
West African Dwarf Crocodile	greatest: 6	average:	5
Central American Caiman	greatest: 6	average:	4–5
Smooth-fronted Caiman	greatest: $4\frac{2}{3}$	average:	4
Dwarf Caiman	greatest: 4	average:	$3\frac{1}{2}$
Congo Dwarf Crocodile	greatest: $3\frac{3}{4}$	average:	3

One large alligator farm in the southeastern part of the United States keeps its alligators in pens, and each pen has a label giving the age of the animals in it. The largest individuals are alleged to be hundreds of years old. Such exhibits, seen as they are by thousands of tourists every year, only help to further the false belief that crocodilians live for centuries. If we think the matter over, we realize that an alligator 500 years old would have been well grown when Columbus reached the New World. Just how could the owner of such an animal know its age? As there is no way of determining the age of an old crocodilian, these claims at once appear ridiculous.

What then is the answer to the question: "How long does a crocodilian live?" In the first place, this is not a simple question. Suppose we ask: "How long does a human being live?" Do we mean how long does the average man or woman live, or what is the greatest age attained by a human being? The answer to the first of these questions must be multiplied by two or three to get the answer to the second. In the case of a wild animal, only very careful and prolonged study will reveal the average length of its life; even the maximum, if great, is not easily determined.

No one knows how long crocodilians live in a state of nature, but the late Major Stanley S. Flower made an investigation of the duration of life in animals living in captivity (chiefly in zoos), and the results of his work give us our best information. Among fifty-five kinds of reptiles definitely known to have lived 20 or more years, Major Flower lists thirty-one turtles, eleven crocodilians, ten snakes, two lizards, and the tuatara. The three kinds of crocodilians that lived more than 30 years were: an American alligator (56 years); a Chinese alligator (50 years); a marsh crocodile (31 years). All of these three were still alive when the records were made. In the face of what is actually known, the alleged great length of life of the crocodilian shrinks considerably. So far there is no evidence that crocodilians live even as long as man himself.

It might be added parenthetically that the famous American alligator "Jean-qui-rit" of the Jardin des Plantes, Paris, died on April 4, 1937, after a possible 85 years of captivity. Apparently there is no way of proving or disproving the validity of this record, and Major Flower refused to accept it.

No one knows just how fast most crocodilians grow. Dr. Malcolm A. Smith states that the Siamese crocodile is about 39 inches long at the end of its third year, that the usual rate of growth of crocodilians in a state of nature probably is some 10 to 12 inches per year. So much more is known about the rate of growth of the American alligator than about any other kind of crocodilian, that I have given some details of its growth rate on page 25. All the known facts about the growth of crocodilians refute the widespread belief that the gigantic reptiles grow very slowly. Slow growth is, however, often characteristic of individuals living in captivity on unsuitable food, a fact that no doubt gave rise to the false belief.

DISTRIBUTION

WITH THE exception of the two species of alligators, the American and the Chinese, all of the crocodilians are typically animals of the tropics. Taking the limits of the tropics literally as the Tropic of Cancer on the north and the Tropic of Capricorn on the south, it can be said that the two true alligators are never found in the tropics. As to the other crocodilians, their distribution as a whole cannot be so precisely defined by these same limits; where tropical climates prevail beyond these limits, crocodilians may be found a few degrees to the north or south. It goes without saying that such lovers of warmth do not ascend into mountains. The low temperature of air and water in mountainous country is probably the chief condition that would keep crocodilians from thriving.

A few other interesting points about the distribution of these reptiles should be mentioned. In spite of the few species that have survived to the present day, almost every tropical region has at least one kind of crocodilian. In all of Africa (including Madagascar) there are but four kinds, and in Asia six. Australia has but two. When we come to tropical America, matters change; South America alone has nine or even ten kinds (the tenth not yet formally described for the scientific record). Colombia, with its seven (or eight) species, might be thought of as the world's crocodilian headquarters. Thus it is seen that crocodilians are thinly spread about the waist of the world.

The continuous distribution of the tropical crocodilians does not arouse curiosity, whereas the presence of one alligator in China and another in the United States does. But a glance at the fossil record removes the mystery by showing that alligators were once widely distributed. For example, two kinds of extinct alligators have been found in Nebraska alone, and fossils of the alligator family have been discovered in South America and Europe as well. It is not unusual in other groups of animals and plants to find in the eastern United States and in eastern China species that are much alike.

FOOD AND FEEDING

THE FEEDING habits of crocodilians do not vary greatly from species to species except that some kinds are much bolder than others in occasionally attacking large prey, including man. All of these reptiles are meat-eaters that normally kill their prey and devour it at once. Carrion may be eaten, and there are reports of the burying of food, presumably to "ripen" it. Animals of all sizes from insects to large mammals fall victim to the rapacious crocodile; undoubtedly the vast majority of its victims are small and would not weigh more than a pound. This statement may come as a surprise to those who have read reports, *some* of them no doubt true, about large mammals being dragged into the water and quickly devoured. Detailed studies of the stomach contents of American alligators show that the basis of the diet is a small animal of one kind or another, and surely the same holds true for the other crocodilians.

The ability of the crocodilian to see above the water while concealed in it enables it to capture animals floating on the surface, or to seize by the snout those that come to drink at the water's edge. The broad jaws of most species readily secure the aquatic creatures; the slender snout of the gavial is a special device for catching swift-swimming fishes. Another group of reptiles, the extinct phytosaurs, had slender snouts and presumably were fish-eaters like the gavial. But the ancient phytosaurs had one disadvantage when compared with the modern long-snouted crocodilian: the nostrils opened back near the eyes. The nostrils of some phytosaurs were elevated, and possibly the disadvantage was thus overcome.

By far the most interesting thing about the feeding habits of crocodilians is the way they overcome large prey and reduce it to pieces that can be swallowed easily. This method is also used by crocodilians struggling over the same object. Once the jaws get a firm hold on the animal, the body of the crocodilian turns over and over, revolving rapidly on its long axis, so that one of two things happens: either the victim is turned over and over until it is rendered completely helpless, or it is simply twisted into two pieces. I have seen the photograph of a man who was given this treatment and had his arm torn from the socket. Oddly enough, he lived and was able to sit up to be photographed the day after the accident. The twisting action kept him from bleeding to death by closing the ends of the blood vessels instead of allowing them to remain open, as would have been the case if the arm had been cut off by a sharp knife.

After the prey has been overpowered and reduced to pieces small enough to be swallowed, it is literally gulped down. If a piece includes big bones, these may be crushed by the jaws. Mouthfuls beyond a certain length may be tossed about until they will start end-first down the throat. The head is held high and tilted backward during this preliminary process, and is lifted above the surface if the crocodilian is submerged. Although large objects are always wolfed out of water, very small ones may be swallowed when the head of the crocodilian is under it and the jaws are tightly shut.

Some lizards deal with their food in much the same way and may even twist in contending for it, but it is the crocodilian that has developed to their highest state the twist and the gulp. For a water animal with teeth and flat jaws that have no shearing or grinding action, the twist is a highly efficient way of overcoming prey.

REPRODUCTION

CROCODILIAN LIFE histories are obscure at best, and when it comes to reproduction, we are truly in the dark. The evasive word "reported" must be used all too often. Frequently we must fall back on casual observations of sportsmen who may or may not be trained in scientific observation.

As far as is known, all crocodilians reproduce by means of eggs laid in nests that are usually guarded by the female. The life history of these giant reptiles is simple when compared to those of the other reptile groups with the exception of the turtles: all turtles lay eggs that are buried in the ground by the female and then deserted. The life histories of lizards and snakes are much more varied; in both groups some species may lay eggs, others bring forth young more or less after the fashion of mammals. In some snakes the eggs are carefully guarded, in others they are deserted, and so on.

Several kinds of crocodilians are reported to add one maternal touch that puts them ahead of the other reptiles: the mothers, when attracted by sounds made by the hatching young, open the nests to let the offspring escape.

Both sexes of all crocodilians have two pairs of sex or scent glands that secrete most actively during the mating season. One pair is in the lips of the cloaca, the other opens to the outside on the right and left halves of the lower jaw. It is presumed that these glands secrete stuff that helps the individuals find one another during the mating season.

More information about reproduction is given below under the accounts of some of the species.

HUNTING SOUTH AMERICAN CROCODILIANS
FOR SCIENTIFIC PURPOSES

DR. FREDERICK MEDEM, of the Universidad Nacional, Bogotá, Colombia, has kindly given me information on his method of hunting South American crocodilians for scientific study.

Harpoons are used because bullets damage the skulls, and specimens shot in the body frequently escape. Besides the harpoon and its thirty-foot rope, one needs a stick, a small boat (Medem used dugouts; Plate 15), a light, and a machete or two. The harpoon is loosely attached to a stick so that the two readily separate when the former becomes buried in the animal. Three men are required: a harpooner, a paddler, and a general assistant.

The hunting begins about two hours after dark. The harpooner sits in the prow and tries to shine the light in the eyes of the crocodilian. The expert can tell the species by the color of the eyes. After a caiman or crocodile has been found, the boat must be quickly brought to within six feet of it and the harpoon sunk into its side where the skin is not heavily reinforced. Once struck, the victim leaps out of the water and then dives. It swims first in one direction and then in another, so that the rope, as it is played out, is prone to get twisted around the prow of the boat. The animal finally becomes exhausted and is brought to shore for killing; if the shore is not handy, it is killed in the water. Killing is accomplished with great difficulty, especially in the water, because cutting through the heavy armor of the neck to sever the spine requires both strength and skill; the crocodilian struggles even after its spine has been cut. Sometimes the brain has to be destroyed by piercing it with a stick or wire; it is advisable to tie the jaws shut before attempting this.

Dr. Medem says the danger in hunting crocodilians is not great, as few *caimaneros*, or hunters, are killed; but it is likely that he underestimates the possibilities of being hurt, or even killed, unless one is highly expert. A spectacled caiman five feet long once bit him severely after he had severed the head! Moreover, the hunter has to know his animal: the spectacled caiman, for example, uses the jaws rather than the tail, whereas the smooth-fronted and dwarf caimans strike savagely with their tails as well as with their jaws. On two occasions a harpooned caiman actually leaped into Dr. Medem's dugout and gave the barefoot occupants a lively time, and once a "dead" individual over five feet long struck him twice with its tail and almost upset the dugout before jumping back into the water. The American crocodile is able to break the strongest canoe with a blow of its tail.

ECONOMIC IMPORTANCE

CROCODILIAN HIDES furnish excellent leather that is used extensively in the manufacture of such items as shoes, trunks, traveling bags, pocketbooks, and various novelties. Great waste is unavoidable because, with the exception of small individuals whose entire hides are made into novelties, only the skin of the belly and sides is processed. The plates of bone in the skin of the back make it valueless, and for the same reason even the belly skin of some species cannot be used.

The United States has been a good market for crocodilian hides since the early part of the last century; by 1850 the trade was still extensive, and even as late as 1902 some 280,000 skins were tanned annually, about half of them coming from Mexico and Central America. It is estimated that the annual take in the 1920's had fallen off to 50,000 a year. It need scarcely be added that the slaughter of literally millions of alligators has greatly reduced the population; in 1929 the species was still abundant over only about half of its original range. The tropical crocodilians hold their own better. An extremely interesting report by Dr. Remington Kellogg on the economic importance of alligators was published by the U.S. Department of Agriculture in 1929.

Account by Species

✧

FAMILY ALLIGATORIDÆ

BROAD–NOSED CAIMAN
(*Caiman latirostris*)

THE BROAD-NOSED caiman is found in Paraguay and over much of eastern and southern Brazil. Early travelers wrote many descriptions of this and other caimans of the Amazon Basin, but the difficulty of being certain as to which species was being described makes it advisable to disregard most of these accounts. Dr. Schmidt found the remains of a marine toad (*Bufo marinus*) and of a bird in the stomach of one broad-nosed caiman. The marine toad does not live in the sea, as its misleading name implies. Dogs have been known to die a few minutes after merely biting this gigantic toad with a highly venomous skin.

PARAGUAY CAIMAN
(*Caiman yacare*)
PLATE 1

SPECTACLED CAIMAN
(*Caiman sclerops*)
PLATE 2

CENTRAL AMERICAN CAIMAN
(*Caiman fuscus*)

THE PARAGUAY, spectacled, and Central American caimans are closely enough related to be currently classified as mere geographical variations of one species. Although such variants are disregarded elsewhere in this book, I am making an exception here because the ranges of these three are so great and, for the most part, so discrete geographically. It must be borne in mind that the current classifi-cation, through the combination of these three into one, reduces by two the crocodilian species of the world. The three caimans in question are distributed as follows: Paraguay caiman—Paraguay and near-by territory (with one puzzling record for distant eastern Brazil); spectacled caiman—the island of Trinidad and South Amer-ica north of the range of the Paraguay caiman, and east of the An-des but at relatively low altitudes; Central American caiman—from the Atlantic coast of Colombia through Central America (at rela-tively low altitudes) to the extreme southwestern coast of Mexico. There is some indication that the Central American caiman also lives on the Pacific coast of Colombia as well as a little farther north than the *extreme* southwestern Mexican coast.

Dr. Medem, who has devoted more time than anyone else to the study in the field of New World crocodilians, has observed in Colombia that the spectacled caiman prefers lakes and the quiet parts of rivers, avoiding currents, whirlpools, and the like. Dr. Schmidt, who was able to examine thirteen stomachs of the Para-guay caiman, found fishes and their remains in eight, crabs and re-mains in six, snails and remains in five, and remains of a water snake in one. There were no stomach stones in spite of the fact that most crocodilian stomachs contain them. Dr. Medem found mollusks and crabs in stomachs of the Central American caiman, and noted that it enters the brackish-water swamps of the Magdalena River, Co-lombia.

BLACK CAIMAN
(*Melanosuchus niger*)

THE BLACK caiman is found in the Amazon Basin and the Guianas. It is the one caiman known to exceed nine feet in greatest length, and is, in fact, the only dangerous member of the alligator family. The American alligator, as noted elsewhere, once reached a greater length but was never a threat to human life.

AMERICAN ALLIGATOR
(*Alligator mississippiensis*)
PLATE 3

THE AMERICAN alligator is found all over peninsular Florida and thence northeastward through the Okefenokee Swamp and along the South Atlantic coast to Albemarle Sound, North Carolina. Westward from Florida it occurs along the coast to Louisiana, where its range expands inland to cover nearly all of that state, the Mississippi Valley well into Arkansas, the Pearl River Valley into Mississippi, and all of the lowlands of eastern Texas.

The giant reptiles of the United States are of course the American alligator and crocodile and the sea turtles. Among these the sea turtles may be rated as harmless to man and seldom encountered. The crocodile is by far the more dangerous of the two crocodilians, but it too is seen in the wild by few because of its small range. This leaves us with the alligator, whose extensive range frequently brings it into contact with man. Just how dangerous is an alligator? The answer is that, in spite of its size, an alligator is not dangerous. But, like most general statements, this one has its exceptions. A female alligator guarding its nest will attack, but its movements on land are clumsy and an active man can easily avoid it. The other exception applies to less than one per cent of the encounters between alligator and man. On these rare occasions an alligator not defending a nest will attack, and a few authentic cases are on record.

As an illustration, let us take the experience of the late E. A. Mc-Ilhenny, as related in his fascinating book (see bibliography). As a boy in southern Louisiana, he and his young friends used to amuse themselves by swimming among alligators and teasing them. This close association continued throughout a long life, and on only one occasion was he convinced that an alligator actually attacked him. This individual, eleven to twelve feet long, slid off a bank as Mr. McIlhenny approached and waited in the water until it was able to strike his pirogue with the tail, hurling its occupant against the bank. Luckily, he quickly regained his balance and shot the attacking reptile. Mr. McIlhenny followed up several cases of persons who supposedly had been drowned or bitten by alligators in the water; all of these proved to be the victims of the alligator gar, a kind of fish.

It is indeed remarkable that so large and formidable an animal proves to be so inoffensive. A man who wrestles alligators as a stunt for the entertainment of tourists can easily render the animal harmless by holding its jaws shut with his hands. One of the difficult parts of the act is to shake the alligator unobtrusively so as to give it the appearance of fighting hard. That the jaws of the crocodilian are powerful is shown by Mr. McIlhenny's experiment of getting one to bite a steel plate. The long ninth tooth on either side, instead of penetrating the steel, was pushed up through the skull, and had to be pulled out from the top with heavy pliers. The jaws of a big alligator are able to crush the larger bones of fully grown cattle.

It might be concluded with reason that so large and powerful an animal would have few enemies. Such a conclusion is justified when alligators three or more feet long are in question. But, as in the case of the turtle, the crocodilian has its period of vulnerability, and that is before and just after hatching. Raccoons, opossums, skunks, hogs, and bears are fond of the eggs, while the young in water are devoured by large fishes. A nest unguarded by the mother is almost certain to be devastated. It goes without saying, of course, that man is the alligator's archenemy.

Information on the length of life of the American alligator is given on page 16.

In nature, and under the best of captive conditions, the American alligator grows rapidly. Mr. McIlhenny marked individuals and turned them loose. Upon recapture he found that the average length at two years was 40.7 inches; at four years, 62; at six years, 72. During the sixth year the males begin noticeably to outstrip the females in growth until at the age of ten they are some two feet longer (9 feet 2 inches on the average), and about two and a quarter times as heavy (251 pounds).

The maximum size of the American alligator has been somewhat reduced along with its population. Early travelers described rivers teeming with so many individuals that a man might have walked across on their backs. This may or may not be an exaggeration, but we do know that some of the early measurements of alligators 18 or 19 feet long were reliable. During the late years of the last century Mr. McIlhenny secured authentic measurements of three specimens more than 18 feet long, the longest being 19 feet 2 inches from tip to tip. Today one is fortunate to see a 12-foot alligator. The weights of three males kept by Mr. McIlhenny were:

Grandpa	591 pounds	(11 feet 6 inches)
Jim	486.5 pounds	(11 feet 9.5 inches)
Big-boy	460 pounds	(12 feet 1 inch)

Alligators dig deep holes or dens, which may be forty feet long. They usually have water in them at least part of the year, although in the dry season the dens are often far from water. The winters are spent in the dens, which are also used as retreats from danger.

The alligator's first sounds are made before the escape from the egg, and apparently have the important purpose of letting the mother know that it is time to open the nest. This sound is best described as an "umph" repeated several times, and is even made by the adult. An angry adult when frightened makes a quavering hiss; the males or bulls bellow or roar, especially during the mating season. The deep, booming bellowing of many enclosed alligators is an alarming sound that causes a strong vibration of the air and often frightens visitors in zoos.

Dr. Kellogg gives the results of the examination of the stomach contents of 149 alligators, all but twelve of which were taken in the tidal marshes of Louisiana. The food of the entire lot was made up of forty-seven per cent crustaceans (shrimps, crabs, crawfishes); twenty-three per cent insects and spiders; twenty-nine per cent animals with backbones (chiefly fishes, snakes, turtles, birds, and mammals). If the alligators had been taken in another type of country, the results would have been noticeably different; these percentages at least show what takes place in one typical region. For example, the almost total absence of frogs is certainly due to the scarcity of frogs in tidal marshes rather than to the alligator's dislike of frogs, which are one of the staples of the diet.

An alligator has a big stomach. Mr. McIlhenny once found three whole pigs in a specimen that measured just under twelve feet, each pig weighing about thirty pounds. He also witnessed the killing of a three-year-old cow by a blunt-tailed alligator ten feet ten inches long.

One item is conspicuously absent from the alligator's menu: man. This is interesting, as many other species of crocodilians no larger than ours do not hesitate to attack human beings.

The alligator is an indiscriminate feeder that will eat any animal from a deer or hog to a beetle, the food depending on the size of the alligator, the season, and the locality. It is safe to say that most of the animals of suitable size that walk, swim, or fly in the alligator's territory fall victim to it at one time or another. Little or nothing is eaten by alligators from early October to late March. During the summer they are heavy feeders, and undoubtedly an increase in appetite late in the season causes them to eat a surplus, which is stored as fat to offset the long period of abstinence.

The act of mating in alligators takes place in water and is not unlike that of other reptiles, the male mounting the female and twisting his tail under her while her tail is raised and her body turned a little to one side. Ten to fifteen minutes are required for completion of copulation. From twenty-nine to sixty-eight eggs are laid at a time during the period from late May through most of June, and an average of nine weeks is required for incubation. The nest measures from five to seven feet at the base, and is from two and a half to three feet high. The female guards it and also tends it by smoothing it with her body in wet weather, watering it with water from her body in dry spells. She helps the young escape by biting off the top of the nest at the proper time.

The actual building of the nest by the female alligator is so complex that I shall outline the process by numbered steps. Mr. McIlhenny has described at length the behavior of one female, and from his description I have made the following condensed account. First: clearing an area approximately eight by ten feet in a brier patch by biting off, pulling up, and mashing down all the vegetation

27

there. Second: making a pile of trash and fresh vegetation in the center of the cleared area by use of her mouth and backward movements of her body. Third: working this material into a well-packed, flat-topped mound by crawling over it and pulling the loose material toward the center. Fourth: making a hollow in the center of the mound by pushing her hind feet one at a time outward from the center, her front legs braced in the outer edge of the nest-mass and her body slowly revolving about it. Fifth: filling the hollow with mouthfuls of mud and water-plants taken from the bottom of the water near by. Sixth: smoothing and shaping the whole mound by moving around and around it and over its top. Seventh: making another hollow in the mound much as in step four. Eighth: depositing the eggs in the cavity, turning the body while doing so. Ninth: covering the eggs, first with the wet material taken from the nest rim with her mouth, and then with fresh mud and water-plants from the water; pressing down and smoothing with her belly all this material while depositing it. Tenth: making the nest into a smooth-surfaced, cone-topped structure by crawling around and around on its slopes. This particular female worked on the nest off and on for three days and two nights.

In all the records of natural history it would be hard to find a more fascinating picture than this of the clumsy alligator making a nest with mud, trash, and fresh vegetation as material, her great belly and broad mouth as tools.

Hundreds of thousands of young alligators have been used in the tourist and novelty trades. For example, in 1890 about 8,400 of them were sold to tourists in Jacksonville alone, and, more recently, one Florida dealer was disposing of three thousand a year. Many of these are bought as pets. Although this trade in live alligators has been greatly reduced, I am still often asked just how a young individual should be cared for.

An alligator does not make a permanent pet for the average home because it will become much too large in too short a time if cared for properly, and will be unhealthy and unhappy if it is not. The Brookfield Zoo near Chicago has built up a great herd of alligators from the infants left by disconsolate owners. The zoo once negotiated with a Florida dealer to reverse the direction of alligator traffic.

A young alligator should be kept in an ordinary aquarium or tank with a sand beach rising out of water about three inches deep and the tank at least as wide as the 'gator is long. Most important of all is the temperature, which at all times must be 75° F., or even a little higher. Direct sunlight should reach the tank for an hour or two a day. A lamp giving ultraviolet light may be substituted. The sunlight should never completely cover the aquarium because it may become too hot in such a confined place, and kill the pet. In nature the little alligators eat all kinds of small creatures; unfortunately, few persons are able to provide such a variety for a pet. Small whole fishes or the internal organs of larger ones are best, but generous amounts of liver with a little raw beef will do. The alligator likes to take its food by sideswipes; this fact must be kept in mind and the food presented from one side. The timid keeper may prefer to use a small stick for the purpose. Food may have to be forced into the mouth at first. It is always well to add to the diet some concentrated form of cod-liver oil, and three good feedings a week should suffice. Food may be refused for weeks on end in winter, or if the temperature is low. An infant alligator should be handled as little as possible, at least until it has begun to feel at home and grow rapidly.

CHINESE ALLIGATOR
(*Alligator sinensis*)
PLATE 4

FROM THE point of view of animal geography, the presence of an alligator in eastern central China would not be too unlikely, but the survival of one there would be considered highly unlikely. Few parts of the world have been more thickly inhabited for a greater length of time by people with so varied a diet and an ancient habit of using parts of many rare animals as medicine, and the value of crocodilian skin when made into leather would scarcely be overlooked by them.

It is probable that this oriental alligator was once found over a large area, and that the few living individuals are a bare remnant of a once enormous population. But how is it possible under any conditions for such a large animal to survive in the lower Yangtze Valley? The explanation is simply this: the rivers of this region have always been so unruly that their large flood plains are uninhabitable and give refuge to countless millions of wild animals. During much of the year these uninhabited plains are covered with rank grasses and it is in this dense cover that the alligators hide. It should also be observed that before the introduction of modern hunting guns the difficulty of shooting animals was very great; the bag was not worth the powder and shot required to get it, and, moreover, primitive guns were expensive and anything but common. Visitors were always astonished at the vast flocks of wild fowl that darkened the skies over the rivers and valleys of China. Game was trapped in many ingenious ways, but the catch could not keep up with the natural production, and the alligators escaped extermination along with the other wild life. It has been conjectured that the Chinese alligator may very recently have met its end on the plains of China, but I doubt this.

So little is recorded about the life history of the Chinese alligator that an account of its unusual history and pursuit will include most of what is known about its habits. Although the Chinese have written about this reptile for more than fifteen hundred years, western science did not recognize its existence until 1879; the first specimen did not reach a museum collection of the United States until 1910. In that year a skull and mounted skin were received by the Museum of Comparative Zoology of Harvard University.

I was fortunate in being the first westerner to visit the home of this reptile and to secure a series of individuals for scientific study. As a member of the Third Asiatic Expedition of The American Museum of Natural History, led by Dr. Roy Chapman Andrews, I was sent to Wuhu, a city a short distance up the Yangtze River from Nanking. It was from the region of Wuhu that most of the alligators appeared to come. Being strongly advised that the presence of a foreigner would make prices soar, I remained in the city and on March 14 sent out two scouts. Late on the nineteenth one of the scouts proudly strode in ahead of a rickshaw loaded with five securely bound alligators. Their sluggishness showed that they had been aroused from hibernation; the most active made feeble movements and roared a little.

Our series of nineteen specimens was soon complete and I decided to visit the dens. Less than half a mile from a large village, the specimens had been dug out of burrows, each a foot in diameter and about five deep. A wildcat that dashed out of one was chased until exhausted and caught; Chow, my assistant, dressed in his long robe, had joined the chase. The ground was so bare that not even a cat could find a hiding place.

If the conception of the ubiquitous Chinese dragon is based on this alligator, it is in China that a crocodilian has attained its peak of respect and adoration. The dragon has been not only an imperial symbol but an omen of good fortune. It is also credited with great and wide power over the affairs and environment of man. A displeased dragon may withhold the rain or even make the earth quake.

SMOOTH–FRONTED CAIMAN
(*Paleosuchus trigonatus*)
PLATES 5 AND 6

DWARF CAIMAN
(*Paleosuchus palpebrosus*)

THE SMOOTH-FRONTED and dwarf caimans are not only much alike in form and size, but they occur together over the Amazon Basin and the low regions north of this basin and east of the Andes. They are the smallest of the alligators and their relatives. Surprisingly little is known about their life histories. In Colombia Dr. Medem observed that they are very powerful swimmers and live in creeks and in the parts of the rivers where the current is swift, while the spectacled caiman, as we have seen, likes lakes and the quiet parts of rivers. The smooth-fronted and dwarf caimans appear to violate the general rule that two very similar species are not found closely associated in nature (see page 36). No doubt further field studies by

Dr. Medem will bring out some interesting differences in habits that have so far escaped notice.

Dr. Medem has noted that the black mark running along the middle of the head of the smooth-fronted caiman makes it very hard to find as it lies quietly on the river's bottom during the day. This mark may be of great value in helping the crocodilian to avoid its enemies. In the stomachs of this caiman Dr. Medem found remains of fishes, frogs, birds, mammals, and aquatic insects.

FAMILY CROCODYLIDÆ

WEST AFRICAN DWARF CROCODILE
(*Osteolæmus tetraspis*)
PLATE 7

THE WEST African dwarf crocodile, the smallest but one among the true crocodiles and their relatives, lives in the coastal streams of the West African rain forests, and in savannas of this region. It does not stray more than nine or ten degrees north or south of the equator, and, therefore, is a true native of the hot tropical lowlands. The small size of the two dwarf crocodiles of Africa keeps them from being dangerous to man.

CONGO DWARF CROCODILE
(*Osteolæmus osborni*)

THE CONGO dwarf crocodile, the smallest of living crocodilians, is a denizen of the uppermost tributaries of the Congo River of central Africa. This is a region of rain forests at relatively high altitudes. It is not surprising that so little is known about the habits of this rare animal, which was not introduced to science until 1919, soon after its discovery by an expedition of The American Museum of Natural History. It is so much like the West African dwarf crocodile

32

that some have held the two to be one and the same species. Recent studies have shown that they differ in structure and live in different types of country, their ranges not even overlapping. The discoverer of the Congo dwarf crocodile, Herbert Lang, reported that its nest is constructed of vegetable matter.

NILOTIC CROCODILE
(*Crocodylus niloticus*)

THE NILOTIC or Nile crocodile is found in Africa from the Cape of Good Hope in the south to Tunisia in the north, and it even strays up the eastern coast of the Mediterranean to enter rivers that flow into the sea on this coast. It is abundant in places. Major Flower made frequent counts of individuals seen in a day along the Nile and its branches, and his record was 123 noted on December 7, 1906. He often saw as many as thirty during one day's travel. In 1922 a bounty was offered for crocodile eggs brought in to Mwanza on Lake Victoria, eastern central Africa. During the first six months more than one hundred thousand eggs were turned in and the expensive experiment had to be discontinued. This figure gives some idea of the crocodile population in the region of Mwanza.

After spending much of his life in Egypt, Major Flower came to appreciate the feeling that the peoples of Africa have for the crocodile. To them the toll of human lives that it takes and the destruction of domestic animals for which it is responsible are inevitable results of natural laws. Moreover, the crocodile is useful in many ways: the flesh and eggs are eaten; the skin is made into helmets and shields; the teeth and bony scutes are used as ornaments and charms; and, above all, the contents of the musk sacks are highly valued. The crocodile also has ethical and spiritual significance. In the discipline of youth it takes the place of witch or goblin of the West, and for adults it may be a sort of lie-detector: a man suspected of adultery is forced to swim a crocodile-infested river to prove his innocence.

The destruction of human life wrought by this crocodile is hard to determine. One report leads us to believe that it is slight, whereas

33

another points to the opposite conclusion. Here are some examples. One explorer who worked in the Congo for six years and hired more than thirty-eight thousand porters did not see a single case of death by a crocodile. During seven years of travel in the Sudan another observer learned of only one case. In contrast is the report of the killing or mauling in five years of fourteen persons of one village in the region of the Fourth Cataract of the Nile. It might be concluded that local conditions determine the destruction that takes place. The Nilotic crocodile appears to attack human beings wherever conditions are strongly in its favor. When a villager is taken, the other inhabitants become very careful for a while, approaching the water cautiously and even tying their buckets to the ends of long sticks; after a time their wariness relaxes and the crocodile gets another chance.

The attitude toward destruction of life by crocodiles in rural Africa and Asia is probably very much like the attitude toward the toll taken by traffic in a modern city of any part of the world: there is much talk about prevention, and various precautions are taken, but everyone knows in the bottom of his soul that the destruction will continue and that nothing really effective can be done about it.

Here are a few miscellaneous but interesting facts about this crocodilian. The eggs are buried in sandbanks. The young kept in captivity will grow, on the average, nine inches a year. A captive specimen seven feet eight inches long weighed 160 pounds.

AFRICAN SLENDER–SNOUTED CROCODILE
(*Crocodylus cataphractus*)
PLATE 8

THE AFRICAN slender-snouted crocodile is one of the four species of crocodilians with a narrow snout, the others being the Australian crocodile and the Indian and false gavials (the snout of the Orinoco crocodile is only comparatively narrow). As already stated, this type of snout is adapted to fish-catching, and the African slender-snouted crocodile, like the Indian gavial, is indeed a fish-eater. It

(*Photograph by Frederick Medem; courtesy Chicago Zoological Society*)

1. Paraguay caiman (*Caiman yacare*). Attains a length of eight feet.

2. Spectacled caiman (*Caiman sclerops*). This head was taken from an individual about five feet long, killed in the region of the Cienaga Grande, Colombia. Two spines of catfish fins have penetrated the floor of the mouth; the catfish was found in the stomach.

(*Photograph by Frederick Medem*)

(*Courtesy The American Museum of Natural History*)

3. American alligator (*Alligator mississippiensis*) on its way.

4. Chinese alligator (*Alligator sinensis*). Attains a length of six and a half feet.

(*Photograph by Frederick Medem; courtesy Chicago Zoological Society*)

5. Smooth-fronted caiman (*Paleosuchus trigonatus*) three feet five inches long, killed on the Rio Apaporis, Colombia. Young male.

6. Head of a smooth-fronted caiman, killed on the Rio Apaporis, Colombia.

7. West African dwarf crocodile (*Osteolæmus tetraspis*).
Attains a length of six feet.

8. African slender-snouted crocodile (*Crocodylus cataphractus*).
Attains a length of eight feet.

9. Mugger or marsh crocodile (*Crocodylus palustris*).
Attains a length of thirteen feet.

10. Siamese crocodile (*Crocodylus siamensis*).
Attains a length of twelve feet.

(*Zoological Society of Philadelphia*)

11. Salt-water crocodile (*Crocodylus porosus*). Attains a length of twenty feet.

12. Cuban crocodile (*Crocodylus rhombifer*). Attains a length of twelve feet.

(*Zoological Society of Philadelphia*)

13. American crocodile (*Crocodylus acutus*) at home in Lake Ticamaya, Honduras. Habitat group in Chicago Natural History Museum with plastic crocodiles and foreground by Leon L. Walters.

(*Photograph by Isabelle Hunt Conant*)

14. Young American crocodile (*Crocodylus acutus*).

15. American crocodile (*Crocodylus acutus*) from the Rio
Palenque, Colombia, with professional hunters or caimaneros.
This adult male measured ten feet five inches. The hunting boat
is about twelve feet long, and the hunters must sleep in it.

(*Photograph by Frederick Medem*)

16. False gavial (*Tomistoma schlegeli*). Attains a length of sixteen feet.

17. Tuatara (*Sphænodon punctatum*). Most lonesome of reptiles.

ranges from the Congo Basin westward through the tropical coastal region of Africa's great western bulge as far as Senegal. The eggs are deposited in a nest made of vegetable matter.

MUGGER OR MARSH CROCODILE
(*Crocodylus palustris*)
PLATE 9

THE MUGGER or marsh crocodile is the common crocodilian of the fresh waters of the region extending from Baluchistan in the west to Assam in the east and Ceylon to the south. It lives in swamps, reservoirs, and rivers, and may even be kept in semi-captivity. For example, near Karachi a reservoir or "tank" surrounded by a high wall contains many muggers that live there and breed in a sandy corner of the enclosure. Centuries ago the area of this reservoir was in the midst of a large swamp inhabited by hundreds of these crocodilians, whose descendants have been protected because of the presence of the tomb of a holy hermit. The noted authority on crocodilians, Dr. P. E. P. Deraniyagala of Ceylon, records the mugger also from the salt lagoons of Ceylon.

If its natural home dries up, the mugger either buries itself in the mud or goes in search of another home. In more technical language, it either estivates or migrates. The eggs, usually fifteen to twenty in number, are buried in sandbanks at the time when the rains begin. The young hatch in about fifty days; the hatchlings are approximately ten inches long. Fishes are the mainstay of the diet, although birds and other backboned animals are eaten.

On the mainland of Asia the mugger has a good reputation, for it seldom attacks man. Dr. Deraniyagala states that such is not invariably the case on Ceylon, where the mugger may become ferocious. He believes that ferocity develops after a crocodilian has devoured a corpse or seized a bather by mistake. He points out that one might expect the mainland muggers to be man-eaters because they are said to eat the corpses washed off burning ghats into the rivers.

SIAMESE CROCODILE
(*Crocodylus siamensis*)
PLATE 10

THE SIAMESE crocodile chooses to live in rivers above tidal limits as well as in the quiet water of inland swamps. It eats chiefly fishes and is not dangerous; the country people are not afraid to bathe in waters where it is common. Dr. Smith found that the young made good pets and would respond when he imitated their high-pitched croak. The rate of growth has already been dealt with on page 16. The range includes southern French Indochina, Thailand (Siam), the northern part of the Malay Peninsula, and the island of Java, where it is rare.

NEW GUINEAN CROCODILE
(*Crocodylus novæ-guineæ*)

THE FRESH-WATER crocodile of New Guinea seems to be a case parallel to the Mindoro crocodile. That is, both of these fresh-water species live on islands also inhabited by the salt-water crocodile, and avoid competing with this monster by living inland rather than in the river mouths so dear to the salt-water species. This may sound strange to some readers: are not the jungles of the Philippine Islands, let us say, big and wild enough to have two kinds of crocodiles living together in them? Certainly they would seem to be, but modern studies of animals have shown over and over again that something called "competition" does exist and makes it next to impossible for two kinds of animals much alike to live closely together. Two species often appear to do so, but exact studies nearly always show that in some way they are actually separated; one may live in the trees, the other on the ground; one may eat food entirely different from the food of the other, and so on. The very fact that the salt-water crocodile is so successful, as shown by its wide range and its abundance, suggests that other crocodiles much like it would

36

be unable to live with it. Additional examples of competition among reptiles will be discussed from time to time.

Crocodiles have long been said to hide large animals that they have captured, and return to eat them later. Presumably this habit not only makes for the conservation of food, but allows it to soften through aging and thus to be more readily divided for swallowing. Dr. Wilfred T. Neill, Jr., gives recent evidence that the New Guinean crocodile has this habit. In 1943, in the region of Port Moresby, he came upon a five-foot individual lying by a mound of dried grass in some dense vegetation. The animal fled, and an investigation of the mound revealed the remains of a young wild hog. Farther on Neill saw a second mound with similar contents and the tracks of a crocodile near by. As the salt-water crocodile also lives in New Guinea where these observations were made, it is possible, though improbable, that this larger species had made the caches.

AUSTRALIAN CROCODILE
(*Crocodylus johnstoni*)

THE AUSTRALIAN crocodile ranges over tropical (northern) Australia. It is another slender-snouted species little feared by man. In this respect it is sharply contrasted with the salt-water crocodile, which is also found in northern Australia. In accordance with its docile nature, the prey is relatively small. The nest mound is made of "leaves, grass, and sand."

MINDORO CROCODILE
(*Crocodylus mindorensis*)

THE MINDORO crocodile, of the Philippine Islands, as noted above, is one of Dr. Schmidt's recent discoveries. It is also found on Luzon, and Mindanao, and in the Sulu Archipelago. This species seems to live inland, in contrast to the wide-ranging salt-water crocodile of the coastal areas. The Mindoro crocodile must be, or at least once

37

was, extraordinarily abundant: Dr. Robert Mertens received a report that in 1932 one American hunter bagged on Mindanao more than twelve thousand specimens for the leather industry in half a year. This is another example of the kind of slaughter of crocodilians that goes on all over the world. It is poor conservation of natural resources, but, of course, legislation to protect a potentially dangerous animal is hard to secure.

SALT–WATER CROCODILE
(*Crocodylus porosus*)
PLATE 11

THE SALT-WATER crocodile has the most extensive range among crocodilians, occurring from the eastern coast of India to the Philippines and northern Australia. It is also known from the Fiji and Solomon islands, and formerly lived in extreme southeastern China. The explanation of this far-flung occurrence is the type of territory frequented: the mouths of muddy rivers and canals near the sea. The delta of a large river with an extensive flood plain within tidal limits is a paradise for this crocodilian, which may even be seen miles from the shore.

Among the twenty-five living crocodilians, the salt-water and the Nilotic crocodiles are the champion man-eaters. This is due to great size and ferocity as well as to wide range. But the compliment is returned to the salt-water crocodile by the peoples of the Irrawaddy delta, who are fond of its flesh and catch it by means of hooks and a duck or puppy for bait. The Nilotic crocodile is also considered a table delicacy.

On Ceylon the destruction of life may be great; in one district, government records showed that fifty-three persons were devoured in twenty-five years. Dr. Deraniyagala writes of an individual only nine feet long that ate two persons. Such a small specimen may squeeze in between displaced stakes protecting a bathing area. Destruction is often wrought in well-inhabited places; for example, a crocodile seized a girl near a bridge with heavy traffic and swam down the river, occasionally exposing the victim at the surface but successfully avoiding the bullets that were fired at it from shore. These incidents happened on Ceylon.

The salt-water crocodile is often called the largest living reptile. The dimensions of all the crocodilians given above and taken from Dr. Schmidt do not bear this out even for the crocodilians, and doubt may again be raised when we consider the leatherback turtle, which occasionally weighs three quarters of a ton. The difficulty is that, whereas turtles are often weighed, crocodilians of great size seldom are. It seems to be a question of shape as well as location. How much easier it is to weigh a turtle (with its convenient shape) on a boat than a crocodile in a swamp. An American alligator nine feet long weighed only 320 pounds. In contrast to this, a leatherback but eight feet long weighed 1,286 pounds.

The female salt-water crocodile constructs a nest of vegetation. This crude structure, guarded by its maker, which sometimes basks on top of it, may contain from twenty-five to sixty eggs. Incubation probably takes two and a half months, and is helped by the heat of decay of the mass. Thus the breeding habits of this species do not differ in general from those of the other kinds that construct nests of vegetation. Differences surely do exist, but would be brought out only by prolonged and detailed studies.

CUBAN CROCODILE
(*Crocodylus rhombifer*)
PLATE 12

THE CUBAN crocodile is now exceedingly rare on Cuba except in the great Zapata Swamp of the southern coast. It is also found in the Lanier Swamp of the near-by Isle of Pines. The life history has not been studied in any detail; to do so would be hard because the crocodilian, persecuted by hunters, has retreated to the most inaccessible parts of these swamps. One item of the diet is the Cuban freshwater gar pike.

MORELET'S CROCODILE
(*Crocodylus moreleti*)

ALTHOUGH MORELET's crocodile was introduced to science in 1851, its distinctness was doubted by most students of crocodilians until Dr. Schmidt rediscovered it in the great jungle area known as the Sibun Swamp. Here, just west of Belize, British Honduras, he found in fresh water hundreds of small specimens, but few large ones. The young of the season must have been hatched a short time before his arrival in late January 1923. A study of stomachs showed that these young specimens were living almost entirely on water insects, snails, and crustaceans. Remains of very few backboned animals were found in the stomachs.

AMERICAN CROCODILE
(*Crocodylus acutus*)
PLATES 13, 14, AND 15

THE AMERICAN crocodile is the only true crocodile that is found in the United States, and it is also one of the two crocodilians of this country, the American alligator being the other. The differences between these two reptiles have been discussed on page 12 and the fact pointed out that they now occur together in an extremely limited area of southern Florida.

Although early records prove that the American crocodile once ranged over much of the southern part of peninsular Florida, the species is now known to survive only in the region of Biscayne Bay, the tip of the state southwest of this bay, and the Keys. From Florida it ranges through the West Indies, southern Mexico, Central America, and Colombia to Ecuador.

Dr. Medem's Colombian *caimaneros*, or crocodile-hunters, reported seeing repeatedly two white or albino specimens in the Palenque River. Such crocodilians are very rare. These hunters said that the American crocodile bellows during thunderstorms and earthquakes, and that its bellow sounds like a dog's. The eggs, according to them, are buried in sandy banks, often near the trunks of fallen trees.

Dr. Schmidt in 1923 visited a veritable crocodile paradise of northern Honduras. The object of his visit was to collect material for an exhibit of the American crocodile in Chicago Natural History Museum. This paradise was Lake Ticamaya in northern Honduras, and here all the advantage lay on the side of the collectors. It is an interesting example of how man may upset the balance of nature-minus-man. The crocodilians of this lake seemed to live under ideal conditions, but with the arrival of man all was changed and the reptiles were doomed.

Lake Ticamaya, only one to five feet deep, has a layer of muck on a firm bottom; its water is green and soupy because of the growth of microscopic plant life in it. This algal growth produces so much gas that an animal walking under the surface can be followed by the rows of bubbles that arise. Crocodiles were so numerous in 1923 that seventy-five individuals were counted at one time in one bay, and all those seen were of medium to large size, the very largest being from eleven to twelve feet long. A hunter could scarcely dream up more suitable conditions.

Dr. Schmidt and his co-worker, Mr. Walters, found that the local method of hunting the crocodiles was with a harpoon, and after watching a harpooner in action they used the method themselves. Early in the morning they would set out in a dugout canoe, the harpooner standing in front. When an alarmed crocodile took to the bottom, they followed his line of bubbles until a throw was possible. If the first try missed, as it usually did, the animal was apt to double on its trail or turn suddenly and thus escape. A direct hit was frequently ineffective because the bony head and the plates of the back turn a harpoon. Then there was the danger that the bubbles raised by the paddles would obliterate the trail of a near-by crocodile. But the greatest difficulty was with the crocodile that simply came to rest on the bottom and refused to move. The end usually came when a closely pursued victim, deciding to give up underwater tactics, swam at the surface and made a perfect target. A harpooned animal, once hauled in, put up surprisingly little fight; it could only rush about on the surface with the jaws open; it had no effective way to resist capture.

Hunting at night with a light and gun was easy if one wanted only to kill; the crocodiles are readily lost after being shot. They must be killed outright because usually they come to the surface only once. The skulls are often damaged by the bullets, and the specimens are of little use for scientific study. In waters less favorable to man, a baited set line can be used with good results.

At Lake Ticamaya sunning crocodiles were occasionally flushed, and their surprisingly quick dash for the water was always enjoyable to see. The hips of a walking or running individual were held much higher than the shoulders, and the observers were reminded of four-footed dinosaurs in museum exhibits. A single nest with fresh eggs was found. It was in a shelving gravel beach and held twenty-two eggs. The parent had dug a hole a foot deep by sixteen inches across at the top and laid the eggs in two layers without regular arrangement. In spite of local advice that the eggs are inedible, they proved to be much like ordinary hens' eggs, if a little tougher. The food of the young crocodiles seemed to be chiefly fishes, that of the larger ones fishes, turtles, and mammals. There were signs of cannibalism.

ORINOCO CROCODILE
(*Crocodylus intermedius*)

THE ORINOCO crocodile lives at low altitudes all over the Orinoco drainage. This means that it is found east of the Andes over much of Venezuela and parts of adjacent Colombia. The eggs are buried in the ground.

FALSE GAVIAL
(*Tomistoma schlegeli*)
PLATE 16

THE FALSE gavial, discovered on Borneo, was introduced to science as long ago as 1838. It has since been found on the southern part of the Malay Peninsula, and shown to be relatively common on Sumatra. As indicated by the slender snout, it is chiefly a fish-eater, and it lives in the fresh waters of rivers. Although the shape of the head is much like that of the true gavial, the false gavial is classified as an unusual crocodile rather than a gavial.

FAMILY GAVIALIDÆ

INDIAN GAVIAL
(*Gavialis gangeticus*)

THE LIFE history of the gavial has not been studied carefully, though Dr. Smith gives some information on its habits. Fishes are the mainstay of the diet; birds and mammals are also eaten. The use of the slender jaws as fish-catchers has already been noted. Man is seldom attacked by this shy reptile in spite of the not infrequent discovery of ornaments in the stomachs of slain individuals; such objects are devoured along with human corpses, which they may commonly encounter in the rivers of their habitat. Forty or more eggs are laid in sandbanks, and the young appear in March and April.

Range: The Indus, Ganges, Mahanadi, Brahmaputra, Kaladan, and probably the Irrawaddy river systems of the Indian region of southern Asia.

Bibliography

Deraniyagala, P. E. P.: "The Tetrapod Reptiles of Ceylon." *Ceylon Journal Science*, Vol. 1 (1939), pp. 1–412.

De Sola, C. Ralph: "The Cuban Crocodile: An Account of the Species *Crocodilus rhombifer* Cuvier, with Notes on Its Life History." *Copeia*, No. 3 (1930), pp. 81–3.

Flower, Stanley S.: "Notes on the Recent Reptiles and Amphibians of Egypt, with a List of the Species Recorded from That Kingdom." *Proceedings, Zoological Society London*, Part 3 (1933), pp. 735–851.

——: "Further Notes on the Duration of Life in Animals.–3. Reptiles." *Proceedings, Zoological Society London*, Series A, Part 1 (1937), pp. 1–39.

Inger, Robert F.: "The Systematic Status of the Crocodile *Osteoblepharon osborni*." *Copeia*, No. 1 (1948), pp. 15–19.

Kellogg, Remington: "The Habits and Economic Importance of Alligators." *U. S. Department of Agriculture*, Technical Bulletin 147 (1929), pp. 1–36.

McIlhenny, E. A.: *The Alligator's Life History*. Boston: Christopher Publishing House; 1935.

Medem, Frederick: "*Palæosuchus trigonatus* (Schneider) en Colombia (Noticia Preliminar)." *Lozania, Acta Zoologica Colombiana*, Número 5 (1952), pp. 1–12.

Mertens, Robert: "Die Rezenten Krokodile des Natur-Museums Senckenberg." *Senckenbergiana*, Vol. 26, No. 4 (1943), pp. 252–312.

Neill, Wilfred T., Jr.: "Notes on *Crocodylus novæ-guineæ*." *Copeia*, No. 1 (1946), pp. 17–20.

Pellegrin, Jacques: "Mort d'un Alligator Présumé Avoir Vécu 85 Ans à la Ménagerie des Reptiles." *Bulletin, Muséum National d'Histoire Naturelle*, 2nd Series, Vol. 9 (1937), pp. 176–7.

Reese, Albert M.: *The Alligator and Its Allies*. New York and London: G. P. Putnam's Sons; 1915.

Rooij, Nelly de: *The Reptiles of the Indo-Australian Archipelago. I. Lacertilia, Chelonia, Emydosauria*. Leiden: E. J. Brill; 1915.

Schmidt, Karl P.: "Notes on Central American Crocodiles." *Field Museum Natural History Zoological Series*, Vol. 12 (1924), pp. 79–92.

——: "A New Crocodile from New Guinea." *Field Museum Natural History Zoological Series*, Vol. 12 (1928), pp. 205–31.

——: "Notes on South American Caimans." *Field Museum Natural History Zoological Series*, Vol 12 (1928), pp. 205–31.

Bibliography

——: "Notes on New Guinean Crocodiles." *Field Museum Natural History Zoological Series*, Vol. 18 (1932), pp. 167–72.

——: "Crocodiles." *Fauna*, Vol. 6 (1944), pp. 67–72.

Smith, Malcolm A.: *The Fauna of British India, Including Ceylon and Burma. Reptilia and Amphilia.* Vol. 1.—*Loricata, Testudines*. London: Taylor and Francis; 1931.

Tuatara

(Order Rhynchocephalia)

PLATE 17

General Account

☼

THE TUATARA is interesting for three reasons: It is the most lonesome of reptiles; it lives only on small islands off the coast of New Zealand; it looks like a chunky lizard, whereas it is only a lizardlike reptile. The name "tuatara" means "bearing spines," and is borrowed from the language of the Maori of New Zealand. The tuatara is known to science as *Sphænodon punctatum*, the sole surviving member of the order Rhynchocephalia. Thus we see that we go from bad to worse in trying to get a simple name for this "living fossil." The long scientific name of the tuatara's order means "beakhead."

After reading in the press about this reptile whose closest known relative lived in Europe 135,000,000 years ago, the visitor to a zoo may be disappointed and ask: "Well, why don't you just call it a lizard and make things easier?" A complete answer would be out of place here, but it can be said that no lizard has two openings on the side of the skull as the rhynchocephalians do. It is not hard to believe that such a big difference in the skull is of great importance in classification.

Much publicity has been given to the so-called "third eye" of the tuatara, whereas this extra eye is found in many lizards and does not set the tuatara off from them. It is located on the top of the head and is easily seen in the young as a translucent scale, but becomes covered with skin in the fully grown individuals. Although it has a lens and retina, and a nerve that may connect the retina to the brain, there is no iris. The crude structure of this eye and its tendency to degenerate with age indicate that an appreciable amount of light does not reach even the retina.

49

The discovery of the tuatara was just as startling to the scientific world as the capture of a dinosaur would have been. In fact, the ancestors of this little reptile reached their highest development before the reign of the dinosaurs; the rhynchocephalians never became so large or so numerous, and therefore cannot be said to have had a glorious past like that of the dinosaurs. As these giants among reptiles came to their own, the little fellows with the long name faded out but managed to hang on in one corner of the world, whereas the dinosaurs went out with a bang. But when we try to descend the tuatara family tree, we come to a gap that lasted well over a hundred million years and takes us back beyond the time when the dinosaurs flourished; countless generations of tuataras and their close cousins died without leaving a fossil record in the rocks.

Incidentally, just to prove that the tuatara is important to science, it can be said that about one hundred technical papers have been written on it. All parts of the animal have been examined, minutely described, and compared with similar parts of other types. The rate of oxygen intake and the amount of heat produced by its body have been studied. Most college textbooks on animals mention this "ghost out of the past."

How did the tuatara reach New Zealand? The details are not known, but the fact that rhynchocephalians once lived in Africa, Europe, Asia, and North and South America takes away much of the mystery. With so wide a distribution it is not surprising that they reached even such a remote place as New Zealand. They possibly went via Australia, but there is an alternate route through the islands to the north and east of Australia. When the Europeans first arrived, tuataras were living on the main islands; the introduction of domestic animals and rats accounts for their extinction there.

More interesting by far are two other questions: why is this creature a lone survivor, and why does it survive on those islets of New Zealand? Some reasonable guesses have been made by Charles M. Bogert, of The American Museum of Natural History, New York.

The life processes are lower and slower than those of any other living reptile, and are even lower and slower than those of any other vertebrate or animal with a backbone. One tuatara showed no signs of breathing for an hour even though its temperature was a suitable 48° F.! This rate of living is probably correlated with activity at the unusually low temperatures that prevail in New Zealand and may have prevailed back in the Age of Reptiles when the dinosaurs flourished. Here, perhaps, is a part of the explanation of the slow-living tuatara's survival on New Zealand, its extinction elsewhere, and the absence of dinosaurs everywhere except in museum fossil exhibits.

The difficulty that the tuatara encounters in competing with mammals has already been pointed out; obviously the slow rhynchocephalians were no match for the rapidly rising mammals of the Age of Mammals that followed the Age of Reptiles. The ancestors of the tuatara took the only way out: the boat for New Zealand, which, fortunately for them, the early mammals missed.

Here is an excellent example of how the scientist builds up his theories. A visitor to a laboratory might ask a physiologist just why he is keeping that poor "lizard" shut up in such an odd-looking box. The physiologist's answer would be that, in the first place, it is not a box but a respiratory chamber; that the animal is not a lizard but a tuatara; that he is keeping it shut up to study its respiratory exchange of oxygen and carbon dioxide. From this he hopes step by step to build up a theory of the rise and fall of the rhynchocephalians and even the dinosaurs, as they, too, perhaps had mammal trouble and temperature difficulties like those of the tuatara. Thus a physiologist shut up in a stuffy laboratory may have his mind on places thousands of miles away and eras millions of years ago.

The tuatara's greatest total length is thirty inches and the maximum weight a little over two pounds. Snakes, turtles, lizards, and crocodilians all grow much larger. The tuatara is active chiefly at night, when it feeds on such animals as earthworms, slugs, snails, insects, and even small backboned animals. The prey is stalked, and is caught by a sudden lunge. The age it attains is unknown; one individual kept in the Dublin Zoo was known to have lived at least thirty-three years.

In sharp contrast to other living reptiles, the male has no copulatory organ, and mating must therefore be accomplished as in birds: by direct contact of the cloacas. The eggs, about an inch in length, are relatively small—only half the size of those of the Gila monster of similar proportions. The incubation period is long and begins in the spring (November). The clutch of fourteen or fewer eggs does not hatch for approximately a year.

Much has been written about the association between the tuatara and the petrels that live on the same islets. The reptile usually lays its eggs in the sand of abandoned petrel burrows; bird and reptile often share a burrow. The tuatara can, however, dig its own hole.

The tuatara, known to science since 1831, has been exhibited in several European zoos; before 1952 it had been seen in only one zoo of the United States: the National Zoo in Washington. A few living individuals had reached the universities and museums of this country. In 1952 the New Zealand government permitted three specimens to be sent to American zoos, but one of these soon died. The New York Zoological Park prepared, at great expense, a special cage with temperature controls. Dr. James A. Oliver, the curator in charge there, reports that his specimen refused food at first, and croaked "softly like a frog whenever it was picked up." It soon learned to come to the keeper and climb on his hands, sometimes even taking food from them: strips of raw meat, raw fish, worms, and insects. The food is worked slowly into the mouth and chopped into a fine pulp by the shearing action of the teeth.

Much also has been written about the danger of the tuatara's extinction. Thanks to the foresighted New Zealand government, this danger appears to have been eliminated, the future of the most lonesome of reptiles assured. Recent observations have shown that the original vegetation of the tuatara's islets is quickly restored when grazing animals are removed, and studies have proved that the best way to preserve a population of animals is to keep its home or habitat intact. The removal of a few or even many individuals has no permanent ill effect, whereas the destruction of the natural environment will quickly bring decimation. The tuatara population is now large enough to hold its own indefinitely if the vegetation of the islets remains undisturbed.

Bibliography

Bogert, Charles M.: "The Tuatara: Why Is It a Lone Survivor?" *Scientific Monthly*, Vol. 76 (1953), pp. 163–70.

Oliver, James A.: "The Timeless Tuatara." *Animal Kingdom*, Vol. 56 (1953), pp. 2–8, 31.

Schmidt, Karl P.: "References to the Tuatara in the Stephen Island Letter Book." *Fieldiana, Zoology*, Vol. 34 (1952), pp. 1–10.

Turtles

(Order Chelonia)

General Account

NAMES

THERE ARE snakes that look like lizards, lizards that look like snakes, lizards that look like crocodilians, and the tuatara, which is always taken for a lizard. In contrast to all this confusion, the turtles stand alone among reptiles by always looking like turtles. In spite of this, both popular and scientific names for turtles are in a state of great confusion that dwarfs the difficulties encountered in common names for the crocodilians.

The common names for turtles in England presented no problem because only the marine kinds were found there. The Englishman therefore thought of a turtle as a strictly aquatic animal, especially a marine one. Conversely, he called all the other shelled reptiles "tortoises." When the early English-speaking settlers came to America they found a confusing array of these reptiles, and applied the names "turtle," "tortoise," and the Indian "terrapin" to them more or less indiscriminately. It is not surprising that inconsistencies arose, because the turtles of the New World do not fall into sharply defined land and water groups. The term "terrapin" seems to have been reserved for certain table delicacies. In general, the strictly land species are now called "tortoises"; the aquatic ones "turtles." As a single all-inclusive name is used for each of the other major groups of higher animals, I see no reason why the turtles should be an exception, and therefore I consider all of the shelled reptiles "turtles."

Oddly enough, the difficulties with the scientific names are still more discouraging. These difficulties are due to choice-of-name technicalities that need not detain us. This order of reptiles was so long known as the Chelonia that the word "chelonian" has become a name in general popular use. More recently some technical works have shifted to Testudinata and Testudines.

The lay reader will never understand these difficulties of taxonomy or classification because such an understanding calls for years of study. Pondering the fact that the relatively few classifiers were forced to coin in less than two centuries literally hundreds of thousands of animal names may arouse some sympathy. The wonder is that the confusion is not greater.

ORIGIN AND STRUCTURE

LIKE THE crocodilians, the turtles have probably passed their heyday and are still on the decline, a decline that no doubt became much steeper with the rise of man, a comparatively recent event. It is interesting to note a rough correlation between the numbers of living species in the major reptile groups and the state of the group as a whole: whether it is prospering or declining. Multiply the number of crocodilian species (25) by ten, and you get the approximate number of turtles; multiply this by ten and you get 2,500, the approximate number of snakes, a group that is thought to be at least holding its own. The same may be said for the 2,700 species of lizards.

Turtles have been turtles since the Triassic period, or, in round numbers, for 200,000,000 years. This is a long time even for a major reptile group; in fact, turtles sprang directly from the so-called "stem reptiles," the cotylosaurs. These antiques flourished in the Permian period, which began 230,000,000 years ago. The fossil record does not give us the steps in the development of the turtle, though one ancient reptile that appears to be a turtle "missing link" is known as *Eunotosaurus;* it had teeth, a flat body, and greatly broadened ribs that almost touched one another at the edges. The top of its skull is not known, a lack that is a great handicap in making out its relationships.

This incomplete fossil record is surprising in view of the abundance of fossil remains of turtles in many parts of the world. These are sometimes numerous enough to be a nuisance for the collector. Not only the turtle's shell becomes fossilized readily, but the compact, thick skull as well. The delicate skull of a snake stands in sharp contrast; it seldom remains intact long enough to become a good fossil.

For the student of reptile structure, many parts of the turtle call for special study, yet we shall have to confine ourselves to a few of these, chiefly the jaws and the shell. The lack of teeth and the possession of a shell are characteristics that set the turtles off from other reptiles, and must have had their advantages. In the case of the teeth, it was merely a substitution of a horny ridge that served the same purpose with fewer complexities in development and maintenance, but the shell is a protective device that has real positive value. A visit to a collection of medieval armor will convince anyone that man has long been envious of the turtle's shell. A suit of armor is an impressive sight, though no more impressive than the shell of a turtle. The difference is that the complexities of the armor are obvious at a glance, whereas those of the shell have already been the subject of decades of careful study whose end has not been reached.

Superficial examination of the shell will show that it is made up of two layers, an outer one of horny material like our fingernails and toenails (the shields or laminæ) and an inner one of bone (the plates) (Plates 18 and 19). Each of these layers is broken up into sections that fit together like tiles in walls and floors. The odd thing is that the sections of the horny or outside layer do not coincide with those of the underlying bone. Presumably in the early turtles the shell was made up as follows: the broadened ribs below; a layer of independent bones next; a layer of horny scales, each with a core of bone, covering all and, of course, forming the exposed surface of the shell and strongly resembling what may be seen on the back of a modern crocodile. In the latest, or now typical, model of turtle shell, the horny scales of the surface have become separated from their bony cores to form the surface exposed to the outside, whereas the cores have disappeared and the underlying layers of bone have fused with one another. One purpose of explaining all this is to point out what complex problems students of reptile structure are able to decipher. Examination of a shell that has been divested of its occcupant will show that the ribs are involved in the structure of the shell, but a hint of the true complexity of the shell and its development was gained only through an astonishing amount of careful study by numerous workers who had at their disposal many turtles of different species.

It is necessary to explain here the terms carapace, plastron, and bridge, as they will be encountered in all descriptions of turtles (Plates 18 and 19). The carapace is the upper part of the shell that covers the back and sides, the plastron that part over the belly; carapace and plastron are joined on each side by a bridge. Carapace, plastron, and bridges are all made up of the same two layers, an outer one of horny shields, or laminæ, and an inner, complex one of bony plates.

The length of a turtle always means the length of the carapace taken in a straight line from its front to its rear edge—not following the curve, as one might suppose.

Before leaving the turtle's shell, we must pause to consider two consequences of it. One of these is the necessity of reversing the usual relationship of the girdles, the bones supporting the limbs, with the rest of the skeleton; the other consequence is the change in the manner of breathing. Almost everyone has seen enough skeletons of higher animals to know that in them the girdles are ordinarily outside the rib box; a few astute observers may have noticed that the bony box of the turtle, its shell, is outside the limb supports, or girdles. Thus evolution had a major mechanical problem to solve in making a turtle what it is and has been for so long a time. The actual steps are unknown, but a study of embryology shows us what takes place every time a turtle is formed, and the process proves to be very different from what it was long assumed to be. This assumption had the girdles taking the active part by migrating inward, whereas it is the shell that takes the situation in hand and encloses the girdles.

The shell rudiment first appears as a raised area extending along the embryo's back, and soon grows outward in all directions, this growth suggesting the flow of very thick molasses. The ribs form independently just below this rudiment and soon come so completely under its influence that their subsequent positions and relations are largely determined by its growth. One important consequence of this is that the ribs remain comparatively straight, never curving to meet on the lower side. The growth of the shell rudiment is so rapid and its influence on the ribs so great that the limb girdles are soon enclosed. The embryo as a whole grows in a side-to-side direction faster than in an up-and-down one, giving the resulting turtle its characteristic flattened shape. In becoming part of the shell, the backbone, except in the region of neck and tail, loses its identity and function. The shell is a structure far too strong for its possessor to need additional support in the nature of a rod extending through it.

Coming to the second consequence of the shell, I must point out first that one important part of breathing in most higher animals involves expansion of the chest, a fact that constricting snakes have taken great advantage of. But how can a turtle expand its chest? The answer is that it has developed its own method of drawing air into and expelling it from the lungs. This method is basically similar to the diaphragm breathing of mammals, including man, though it involves a special arrangement and use of muscles. Air is drawn in when the contraction of two flank muscles makes the body cavity around the lungs larger, and forced out when the contraction of two pairs of ventral (belly) muscles press the viscera against the lungs. The shoulder bones rotate forward while the air is being drawn in, but this movement is not a necessary part of breathing.

The clarification of turtle breathing is another example of how science may advance like the proverbial frog that, in climbing the mountain, slips back almost as much as it advances. The mechanism was described as long ago as 1863, but since then much ink has been wasted in conjectures, especially those concerning the importance of throat and girdle movements, the original account having been forgotten or overlooked. It was left for a brief note published in 1941 by Dr. Ira B. Hansen to put the matter on its feet once more.

Turtle respiration is accomplished in two other ways. Many water turtles are able to use the throat lining as a sort of gill: the little oxygen that is absorbed from water pumped in and out of the throat is enough to enable an inactive turtle to remain submerged much longer than if it depended solely on air held in the lungs. The other method is the alternate filling and emptying through the anus of two sacs that open into the cloaca; they promote the absorption from the water of a small amount of oxygen much as does the throat.

Finally, breathing in a turtle is far from the simple and regular taking in and forcing out of air as in man. There are cycles of partial and complete expirations, and periods of pause during which the lungs are only partly filled. These pauses may last from a minute or less to several hours. This ability to "hold the breath" is due to three factors: very thorough ventilation of the lungs, low consumption of oxygen, and a low unloading tension for hemoglobin, the part of the red blood cells that carries oxygen. The holding of the breath referred to here occurs in land turtles that have no chance to supplement their oxygen supply by getting any from water.

AGE, SIZE, GROWTH

THE TURTLE is generally believed to attain a great age, and this is one popular belief that does not call for "explosion"; at least the explosion would be little more than a mild pop. Turtles undoubtedly live longer than any other animal with a backbone, including man himself, the mammal with the greatest life span, but there is no evidence that they live hundreds of years.

The difficulties of determining the length of life of long-lived animals in nature is discussed in detail under the crocodilians (page 15), and the same difficulties apply to turtles. However, the hard shells of most turtles make them relatively easy to study by marking and recapturing. Nevertheless, nearly all of the longevity records that we now have are based on captive individuals. Under the crocodilians, the results of Major Flower's study of captivity records are cited. Thirty-one kinds of turtles were included by him among the fifty-five reptiles definitely known to have lived twenty or more years in captivity. Next to the turtles stand the crocodilians, with eleven kinds listed. Five kinds of turtles are listed as having lived a century or more, whereas the oldest reptile not a turtle had survived only fifty-six years. Even the little common box turtle (*Terrapene*) of the United States is credited by Major Flower with 123 years. Taking with a grain of salt his maximum figure of 152 years, I still remain convinced that a few species of turtles have a life span of well over a century. I am ready to believe that the potential longevity of many species is at least a century and a half; how often they survive this long in nature is another question (see again the discussion of the crocodilians).

Dates carved in the shells of turtles by unknown persons have no scientific value because there are so many two-legged jokers abroad. A box turtle with "1850" carved in its plastron makes one re-examine the animal for further evidence of age, and ponder the possibilities, whereas one with "10 B.C." in its shell is a good reminder of the need for skepticism in regard to carved dates.

In ages past, two kinds of turtles have distinguished themselves by growing to a great size. One of these, marine *Archelon*, whose remains are known from what is now South Dakota, reached an over-all length of twelve feet. It lived during the Cretaceous, or some hundred million years ago, and probably weighed a ton or a little more. In comparatively recent times, only a million or so years ago, *Colossochelys atlas* plodded over the hills of southern Asia inside its seven-foot shell.

Among living turtles, the leatherback outstrips all others in size, and may well be the reptile with the greatest weight and bulk, although this honor is often given to the largest of the crocodilians. The leatherback certainly attains a weight of three quarters of a ton (fifteen hundred pounds) and an over-all length of nine feet. There is evidence that the marine loggerheads reach a weight of half a ton, and a giant tortoise (*Testudo*) has tipped the scales at 560 pounds. Dr. Schmidt has the mounted foot of a Galápagos tortoise that is mistaken by most persons for that of an elephant.

For every one of these giants there is a pygmy. In the United States, with a rich turtle fauna, the average shell length of the following four kinds falls between three and four inches: striped and common mud turtles (*Kinosternon*) and Muhlenberg's and spotted turtles (*Clemmys*). Weights of small turtles are seldom taken, but a yellow mud turtle (*Kinosternon*) with a shell five inches long weighed only thirteen and eight tenths ounces.

Although the common belief about the age of turtles calls for only mild debunking, that about their rate of growth requires drastic correction. The sight of a giant tortoise in a zoo nearly always calls forth remarks that its size alone proves its great age. As a matter of fact, one of these giants weighing 350 pounds *may* be no more than twelve years old: an individual from the Galápagos Islands that was confined in California increased its weight from 29 to 350 pounds in seven years. Three others, kept in Texas, weighed from 7 to 13 pounds in 1928, from 179 to 183 in 1937, an annual increase of 21 or 22 pounds per turtle; their shells about doubled in length during this same period.

The period of development leading to sexual maturity or the ability to reproduce is surprisingly short. Dr. Carr states that the hawksbill, a large species of the sea, may reach maturity in three years, and there is ample evidence that many other species do the same in from three to seven. Rapid growth probably comes before maturity and during its first year; growth does not cease then but is continued at a much reduced rate for an undetermined length of time.

It is not correct to state flatly that the age of a turtle can be told by counting the rings on its shell, although it is correct to say that in some species living under certain conditions the age of relatively young individuals can so be determined with more or less accuracy. For instance, in the common box turtle (*Terrapene*) living in New York State, the age can be exactly told through the first five years, and with some accuracy for the next ten. As this species has a potential longevity of more than a century, the usefulness of the ring-counting may be questioned. The desert tortoise (*Gopherus*) of western North America is an example of a species in which the method in question serves no purpose. Students of turtle life histories often find ring-counting useful in their technical studies. The counting of growth rings in turtles and the segments of rattles in rattlesnakes are roughly comparable in accuracy of results.

The outer layer of the shell in most turtles is made up of rows of horny shields; anyone can understand that these shields must get larger as the area of the shell increases with growth. As the underlying bone grows, new horny substance appears around the edge of the old shield. A detailed study proves that this new substance is deposited under the old horny shield, though visible only around the edges. When growth slows down, as during hibernation, a wrinkle instead of an expanse of new substance appears around the margin of the old shield. Close scrutiny of a shell will, under the best conditions, show peripheral wrinkles alternating with broad, smooth bands of horny substance. Several factors combine to obscure the picture, the obscurity becoming more confusing with every year of the turtle's life. The chief among these annoying factors are the following: the wearing away of the older horny shields and, in many species, the loss of them through frequent shedding; the lack of alternate periods of rest and rapid growth in turtles of certain parts of the world. The way the outer layer of the turtle's shell grows may not be of much practical value in age determination, but it is an extremely rewarding process to observe; one can have pleasure watching the formation and addition of horny substance in turtles whose age is noted by other methods.

SUNNING

The habit of sunning is so common among water turtles that it is noticed by all persons who live or travel in wild country; land species also sun themselves, but not to the same extent. Regulation of body temperature is probably the chief benefit of basking in the sun. Leeches and other external parasites are banished, the growth of algæ retarded. No doubt growth is stimulated either directly or indirectly.

Sunning has its disadvantages: it advertises the presence and whereabouts of even the most shy of species, and promotes the capture of the bold kinds or individuals. The habit is given up by sea turtles that are constantly molested, but retained by those living in the most remote places. I know of no information on the persistence of the habit in molested fresh-water species.

SENSES AND INTELLIGENCE

ONE OF the most surprising facts that has been revealed by scientific studies of turtles is their lack of a sense of hearing. By this I mean the perception of ordinary air vibrations entering the ear. In view of the well-developed middle and inner ears, this fact is most unexpected, and many an owner of turtles has been convinced that they hear very well indeed. Casual observation of reptile behavior can be misleading; a turtle that is responding to vibrations of the ground—caused by the chopping of its food on a block of wood, for example—can readily be seen as responding to sound carried by the air. The behavior of reptiles is notoriously hard to study because of their apathy or slow responses. Where a bird or mammal will respond quickly, the reptile may stage a sit-down strike. It is not unusual for a captive or experimental individual to starve itself to death for no apparent reason.

Sound perception and sound production are complementary attributes of animals—that is, those that make a lot of sounds usually have a keen sense of hearing, and vice versa. The deafness of turtles, therefore, suggests a corresponding muteness. Sounds made by mating turtles are mentioned in the treatment of reproduction, and one species is credited with the ability to make itself heard for a quarter of a mile. This loud sound of the giant leatherback sea turtle has been variously called an "indescribable kind of noise," a wail, a groan, a roar, or a bellow. When these and the very few other noises that turtles are able to make are compared with the tremendously varied and complex songs and calls of birds and mammals, we conclude that turtles make no appreciable use of sound in their daily routine, and their deafness seems less surprising. Incidentally, the Biblical phrase "the voice of the turtle" refers to the turtledove.

The sense of smell in turtles has not been carefully studied, but apparently it is good at close range. Pet turtles often appear to smell objects before eating or rejecting them. If smell production and perception are complementary, as are sound production and perception, a turtle would be expected to smell well; many of them can raise a good stink, as pointed out on page 69. So far there seems to be no scientific evidence that the odor from one turtle is made use of by another.

The skin and shell of a turtle are very sensitive. I have seen a large sea turtle literally enjoy having its shell scratched lightly by my fingers, and Dr. Carr states that a "hulking horny-skinned tortoise" can feel the tip of a straw dragged along its skin. This great sensitivity accounts for certain reactions often considered to be evidence of hearing in a pet turtle. A human being can sometimes "feel" the beat of a drum.

A person who hunts turtles soon becomes convinced that they see well. Shy species sunning on logs will slide into the water when the hunter is still at a great distance. Careful experiments have shown that certain species can tell one ordinary color from another, their range of color perception approximating that of man himself. This is interesting in view of the fact that very few kinds of mammals are able to distinguish colors; a dog, for instance, is color-blind, and rage in a bull at the sight of a red rag is a myth. Among mammals, man and the apes are exceptions and, incidentally, lead to the false belief that mammals in general see colors.

The ability of the turtle to learn—here, for simplicity's sake, called its "intelligence"—has not gone unnoticed. Anyone who has watched a pet turtle try for minutes on end to climb over a book that it could much more readily go around, or get through a crack at the hinged edge of an open door for even longer, might object to the implication that it has intelligence. In defense of the turtle the conclusion of one scientific investigator might be recorded: the wood turtle (*Clemmys*) is about on a par with a rat in learning to go through a maze. A pet tortoise (*Gopherus*) from Florida that I allowed the run of my house persistently returned to the same place to hide, finding it readily from any part of several rooms, and came to the kitchen when hungry.

Casteel's classic experiments on the painted turtle (*Chrysemys*) proved that his subjects could learn to distinguish between vertical and horizontal lines of black and white, and even between such lines of different widths. He used food as the reward for success, electric shock as punishment for failure.

Interesting observations on how turtles behave when placed on a platform were made about a half a century ago by R. M. Yerkes. Land turtles were found to be hesitant about walking off even low platforms, whereas water species walked off without regard for the elevation or distance they might fall. If you have seen basking turtles drop from rock or log into the water you can readily understand this unconcern of aquatic species about falling off platforms. Owners of pet turtles will find it useful to know this difference, for the thought of a pet crashing down on a hard surface is always unpleasant even though one knows that the shell of a turtle is very tough and will not be damaged by a fall from an ordinary table.

ENEMIES AND DEFENSE

As EXPLAINED on pages 137 and 242, there are many bluffers among the snakes and lizards. The turtles stand in strong contrast as having little bluffing ability; perhaps this is because the shell has given them such good protection that there was no need for the development of supplementary methods. Be that as it may, the shell of a turtle when developed to its full extent is a marvelous protection. A box turtle (*Terrapene*), when not too fat, can close up so completely that the thinnest blade of a knife cannot be forced into any of the cracks between the upper and lower shells. A person who did not know that a reptile in a state of repose uses very little oxygen might wonder why a tightly closed box turtle would not soon suffocate.

If a turtle's shell is such a perfect protection, we may reasonably ask how this reptile fares during the stages of its life when the shell is not present. The hatchling turtle does not have a hard shell, and is a dainty morsel for many a meat-eating animal. Moreover, the turtle nest contains eggs that are even more tempting. It is stated elsewhere that the mother turtle, in contrast to the female crocodilian, never shows any concern over the fate of her eggs, which are therefore left to be dug up by any hungry animal. A sea beach that has been visited by many laying sea turtles becomes a veritable feasting-ground for mammals, birds, and reptiles, the birds taking the hatchlings as they make their way to the water, and the mammals and reptiles, such as monitor lizards (*Varanus*), digging up the eggs as well as devouring the hatchlings. The little turtles are by no means safe when they reach the water, for in it large fishes may be waiting to gulp them down.

Enough has been written about the economic value of turtles to convince anyone that man is an archenemy in spite of his weak effort to protect them. For example, the Conservation Law of New York State, Section 194, reads: "Land turtles, box and wood turtles and tortoises shall not be taken, possessed, bought or sold." This is interesting because these turtles have no market value in New York State. The propagation of the diamondback terrapins by the United States government might be cited as an example of active economic protection of turtles.

The motor vehicle is a great destroyer of chelonian life. Turtles not only have to cross roads at times, but frequently linger on them as convenient places for sunning or, in desert areas, taking advantage of accumulated warmth. Worse still is the habit of choosing as nesting-sites sandy country roads skirting lake, pond, river, or swamp. Every year in the United States alone, laying females are crushed on roads by countless thousands.

Active means of self-protection are practiced by many turtles. The very young individuals are often masters at the art of concealment, as collectors who have tried to find tiny box turtles (*Terrapene*) know. The soft-shelled turtles are astonishingly swift in flight and may claw and bite dangerously when seized. Snapping turtles (*Chelydra* and *Macrochelys*) are formidable, although never able to "bite a broomstick in two." The common snapping turtle (*Chelydra*) undergoes a sudden change of attitude when moved from land to water or vice versa: on land it will usually strike repeatedly and effectively with its long head and neck, whereas in water it thinks only of flight and cannot be persuaded to bite.

Unpleasant odors are given off by some turtles from special glands, and apparently such odors are protective, as no other function has been ascribed to them. In the musk and mud turtles (Kinosternidæ), prime among stinkers, the odoriferous substance comes from four glands that open directly to the exterior at the edges of the shell. In its extreme degree the stink from one of these turtles can be surprisingly strong. I shall never forget riding in a jeep with a freshly caught *Kinosternon;* although the sides and wind-shield were open and we were traveling through a desert area at forty miles an hour, the musky odor remained distinctly strong and unpleasant while we drove many miles. I must admit, in all fairness to musk and mud turtles, that this was an extreme case; the turtle was big, and perhaps the excretion had become more concentrated under conditions of extreme dryness. According to Dr. Carr, the Mosquito people of Nicaragua roast a species of *Kinosternon* and eat it with relish! No doubt every kind of turtle has been eaten by man at some time or place.

FOOD AND FEEDING

THE TURTLE's method of getting and swallowing food is extremely simple and shows none of the complexities found among the snakes. The lizards and crocodilians hold an intermediate position in this respect. To put it briefly, the turtle carries a pair of choppers, these being the horny edges of the jaws, which ordinarily are smooth, sharp-edged ridges. There are no true teeth, although in some spe-cies the ridges of the jaws are pointed at the tips or even serrated, the serrations resembling teeth. Turtles that live on hard food that must be crushed have inside the mouth specially developed flat or ridged crushing-surfaces and big, powerful jaws. The front legs are often helpful in tearing off mouthfuls that the strong tongue works into the throat.

After passing the mouth, the food continues along a digestive tract much like man's except that it ends in a cloaca instead of a rectum. A cloaca is not only the receptacle for the waste products of digestion, but serves as a vagina in the female and the housing of the penis in the male. The contents of the urinary bladder must also pass through this vestibule, which opens to the outside through an orifice called the anus.

Although, like other reptiles, turtles can comfortably fast for months on end, they will feed almost as often as mammals, and grow very obese. An amusing sight is a box turtle (*Terrapene*) so fat that the hind limbs stick out when the lower shell is closed in front, and the front legs project when the hind ones are drawn in. Digestion is slow and its rate varies with the body temperature, which is always about the same as that of the surroundings. An experiment with one species proved that raising the temperature of its stomach from 64° F. to 84° F. a little more than doubled the rate of digestion.

It goes without saying that a cold-blooded turtle can live on comparatively less food than a warm-blooded mammal. Dr. Francis G. Benedict gives the following example of food requirement in a turtle, the South American tortoise (*Testudo*). The standard energy need at about 63° F. of a 9.5-pound individual would be supplied for approximately four weeks by 6.5 ounces of banana (I find that a banana of average size weighs with its skin 6 ounces). The shell of the turtle measured 11.5 inches.

Specialization in choice of food is rare among turtles. Many kinds eat both plant and animal matter; not a few devour carrion. Only the tender parts of plants are consumed, obviously because the chelonian jaw is not able to deal with tough, fibrous plants. Succulent leaves and stems and delicate blossoms are always chosen. Even certain species that have powerful jaws with greatly expanded surfaces for crushing hard-shelled animals do not confine themselves to such, but eat soft-bodied animals as well. The common map turtle of the United States is a good example.

Small invertebrates like earthworms, snails, slugs, thin-shelled bivalves, crawfishes, and insects, larval or otherwise, make up the great bulk of the animal food. Young or larval fishes and amphibians (frogs and toads, including their tadpoles) fall victim to the more robust species. Young mammals and birds are devoured by the largest turtles. The sea turtles would of course consume types of small marine animals not enumerated above. In short, a turtle will probably eat any animal that it can readily capture.

REPRODUCTION

REPRODUCTION IN the turtle, as in the crocodilian, is relatively simple: all turtles lay eggs that are buried in the ground by the female and then deserted. Usually the nest is a more or less flask-shaped cavity and its depth is determined by the length of the hind limbs of the female, with which the cavity is dug. In a few cases the forelegs may be used in making a shallow basin in the center of which the nest proper is excavated. The care exercised in nest construction ranges from the great skill shown by sea turtles in digging in sand and obliterating signs of their work afterward to the casual dropping by some mud turtles (*Kinosternon*) of single eggs in shallow holes, and even leaving the eggs half buried. In strong contrast to meticulous nest construction is the female's blissful unconcern with what may be taking place while she is nesting; once the mechanism has been released, a person may sit behind and put the eggs in a bucket as they appear; later she will turn and cover up the empty nest just as thoroughly as if it were full of eggs.

Among the higher animals it is the rule, proved by few exceptions, that copulation must immediately precede each pregnancy. Recently the turtles were found to be one of the exceptions. At least it was proved that in the diamondback terrapins fertile eggs will be laid for as many as four years after copulation, and the chances are that the same holds true for turtles in general. This extremely startling and important fact stands in sharp contrast to the lack of variety in other aspects of the turtle's reproductive life cycle.

Courtship in turtles may be little more than pursuit of the female or it may take the form of harmless biting and pushing of her as well. Some of the giant tortoises violently pound their mates, using the body like battering rams, uttering resounding roars all the while. But more remarkable yet is the gentle stroking of the face of the female by the long fingernails of the male painted (*Chrysemys*) and Troost's (*Pseudemys*) turtles. This feat is accomplished in water while the male swims in front of his mate. In these turtles it is the males that have the long nails, which are present only on the fore limbs. The sexes may be about equal in size, although the female is often the larger and may even be twice as large as the male or have three times its bulk. Differences in color are rare. In a few species the old males have relatively large heads, in a few others it is the old females that have this characteristic. Sometimes the belly shell of the male is noticeably concave, that of the female flat. By far the most constant mark of the male is the longer tail, a condition obviously due to the housing of the penis in the base of the tail. Thus it may be easy for the novice to separate several individuals of the same species into males and females, whereas he would not be able to sex a lone specimen. The tail is so large in male sea turtles that the picture of a male with tail outstretched has a decidedly odd appearance. But one has to search far and wide for such a photograph; the females are so easily photographed when they come out to lay that no one ever bothers to take a picture of a male.

In thoroughly aquatic turtles copulation takes place in the water, whereas in land species it takes place either on land or in the water. The male mounts the female and may grasp the front of her shell with his claws, or contact may be made only posteriorly, by the insertion of his hind limbs under the female's shell. Frequent sounds may be emitted by the male during the act. Little is known about the duration of copulation.

Female turtles usually deposit only one clutch a year, although the green turtle (*Chelonia*) lays as many as seven in one season. Incubation takes two or three months, with allowance for the considerable variation due to differences in temperature and humidity. Overwintering of the eggs or hatchlings is not uncommon in northern regions.

Most turtle eggs are elliptical in shape, but some are spherical or nearly so. The common snapping turtle of the United States, for example, lays eggs surprisingly like Ping-pong balls although a little smaller. The snapper's eggs even bounce well. The sea turtles also lay spherical eggs. No turtle eggs are colored; color would serve no good purpose in an egg that is always buried. The shell is either flexible or brittle. The number in a clutch ranges from one in Tornier's tortoise of Africa to at least two hundred in some sea turtles.

73

The common snapping turtle of the United States may lay as many as eighty, although this is much more than twice the number in its average clutch.

In the course of evolution the reptiles were the first of the higher animals to free themselves from the bondage of water. The fishes were of course completely dependent on it, whereas the amphibians got three feet on land, so to speak: they lived on land much of the time, but were bound to the water by the necessity of reproducing in it.

In order to get entirely independent of water the reptiles had to develop a "closed-box" type of egg, one that could be laid on land. The most familiar closed-box egg is found in the barnyard, but the hen has gone a step further in egg construction: its egg will withstand drying in the air and has a better shell. It is interesting to compare a sea-turtle egg with that of a hen. A good egg must have a shell to hold it together and keep it from drying; for the embryo, a supply of food (the yolk) and a supply of water (the white). Taking these three parts of the egg and comparing them by weight, we see that the turtle made a very good start even though it did not come up to the hen.

The shell: 11 per cent in the hen, 6 in the turtle. Obviously an egg that incubates in the air by heat from the mother's body must have a strong shell that resists pressure and drying. The buried egg of the turtle is protected from drying and uneven pressures; in fact, it must absorb moisture from the surroundings; many turtles even moisten the nest soil by liquid from their bodies.

The white: 56 per cent in the hen, 40 in the turtle. Unlike the turtle's, the hen's egg must have with it all its water supply.

The yolk: 33 per cent in the hen, 55 in the turtle. Thus the turtle egg provides relatively more nourishment than does that of the hen. Presumably the more rapid development of the latter makes a large supply of nourishment unnecessary.

One essential part of the closed-box egg has, for the sake of clarity, been left out so far; this is the air chamber, a part more essential to the hen's egg with its relatively tight shell.

RELATIONS TO MAN

MYTHOLOGY AND folklore being beyond the scope of this work, I shall give only random samples of the numerous mythical concepts of turtles. It is little wonder that these strange reptiles have aroused much interest. If they were known only from fossils, they would be counted among the great curiosities of animal life, and many conjectures would be made as to how they managed to breathe.

Perhaps in no other country of modern times has the turtle been granted such a high position as in China. The *Book of Rites*, an ancient classic, listed the tortoise as one of the four benevolent spiritual animals, and ever since it has been considered an emblem of longevity and a symbol of righteousness. Turtles carved in stone may be seen in temples throughout the land. In strong contrast to this, the turtle, in vulgar thought, is a symbol of sexual promiscuity, and a term of abuse. It is a bald insult to call a man a "turtle egg," a subtle one to tell him to "roll away."

The ancient Hindus conceived of the earth as a hemisphere with its flat side resting on the backs of four elephants that in turn stood on a colossal turtle. Even the Greek gods held the turtle as sacred, and Pan was its custodian. Many American Indians venerated this reptile and made ceremonial rattles out of its shell.

In modern rural United States, turtles do not arouse fear or stimulate the imagination to the extent that snakes do. It is commonly believed that a biting snapping turtle (*Chelydra*) won't let go until it thunders, or, if beheaded, die until sundown, but such beliefs are mild compared to stories of hoop snakes killing trees. Few individuals are greatly frightened by turtles, and few object to their presence enough to kill them. In our large cities pet turtles are abundant; no doubt the turtle population of the cities is as great as that of many country areas equal in size. The story of the hare and the tortoise has made the latter a symbol of plodding determination.

Man has been eating turtles ever since he was man, and he certainly inherited the habit from pre-humans. The sea turtles stand at the head of the list of gastronomically important kinds because of their almost world-wide distribution, their size, and their convenient habit of coming ashore in great numbers to lay on open beaches where their capture and the gathering of their eggs is mere child's play. The virtual impossibility of exterminating the sea turtles is another factor; they will be available for centuries to come.

In sharp contrast to the sea turtles with their boundless home stand the giant tortoises of the Galápagos and other islands. When discovered by the Spaniards early in the sixteenth century, the Galápagos Islands were swarming with millions of gigantic tortoises of several kinds, and were named "Tortoise Islands" ("galápago" means tortoise in Spanish). The early whale-hunters soon saw in them a valuable and free supply of fresh meat, for a tortoise turned on its back remained alive without attention for weeks if not months. A single vessel would take away hundreds of animals, all but exterminating the population. Those who do not appreciate the need of conservation laws should ponder well the history of the giant tortoises of the Galápagos.

In the United States the turtles of real commercial value are the diamondback terrapins (*Malaclemys*) of the brackish waters of the eastern coasts. The government has spent large sums of money in a successful effort to rescue them from extermination. Next to these come the two kinds of snapping turtles, the alligator and the common. The former has a limited distribution and is therefore of lesser importance. In Philadelphia the common snapping turtle is much esteemed; certain restaurants there specialize in snapper dishes. The soft-shelled turtles are relished the world over, especially in China, Japan, and the United States. In this last country they are not commonly seen in city markets but are frequently eaten locally. In southern China, on the island of Hainan, I found a sharp distinction between two kinds of soft-shells; one, Steindachner's soft-shelled turtle, was worth several times as much per pound as the common soft-shell that lives throughout the country. Unfortunately, I failed to detect the difference in quality between the two meats.

The eggs of sea turtles are relished the world over. In Sarawak, Borneo, for example, the gathering of turtle eggs is under control of the government; some seventeen thousand clutches of eggs were taken on one island during a single year. The revenue, which may be as much as thirty thousand dollars in a year, is used for research and education in science. Dr. Carr cites many instances of the culinary uses of sea-turtle eggs in the southeastern United States and the Caribbean region. Loggerhead eggs were long sold by hucksters on the streets of Savannah, Georgia, and Charleston, South Carolina, where they were used in making cakes of high quality.

After the use of the turtle's meat and eggs as food comes the use of its shell as material for the arts and crafts. Although the shells of various turtles have been put to countless more or less practical uses, the shell of the hawksbill, a kind of sea turtle, is the material that has been used more than any other taken from the turtle's back. This is the familiar "tortoise shell" of commerce. Its use was introduced to the ancient Romans from the Far East by way of Egypt; the Romans valued it chiefly as a veneer for furniture. In modern times it is mainly used in making toilet articles, ornamenting buhl furniture, and as veneer for small boxes and frames. It is worked like horn, by heat and pressure. The shells of other sea turtles are employed commercially, but they cannot be compared with true tortoise shell.

There are many other ways in which turtles serve man. A high-grade machine oil is extracted from their fat; in the United States thousands are sold as pets, and more thousands sent to school and college laboratories for student dissection. No doubt some turtles are useful in destroying harmful insects and other invertebrates; this aspect of their relation to man is not well understood.

The snapping turtles of the United States are disliked because of their alleged slaughter of game fishes and waterfowl. Recent studies have shown that this attitude is unwarranted except under certain conditions where a concentration of fowl or fishes would make the presence of snappers undesirable. Under more ordinary conditions the snapper's value as a source of meat and a scavenger probably outweighs any damage done. The same is probably true of other big turtles with a snapper-like appetite. Small kinds of turtles that happen to have an appetite like that of a game fish are a constant source of annoyance to fishermen, who somehow can find no sport in pulling a turtle out of the water. Worse yet is the habit of cleaning the hook without jerking the line. The common musk turtle of the United States arouses the special ire of the fisherman by its interest in the baited hook.

CARE OF TURTLES

In the United States thousands of baby turtles are sold as pets. These come largely from the Gulf states and are, for the most part, either map or Troost's turtles. The traffic is deplorable from the point of view of conservation (for obvious reasons), and because the infants seldom live healthy lives in captivity. A hatchling turtle needs a special diet that it rarely gets when it is a pet. The fact that almost any reptile starves to death in months rather than days deceives many owners; food is put in the aquarium or terrarium and disintegrates or dissolves, the false conclusion being that it was eaten.

One who wants a pet turtle had best secure a fully grown individual, one that has passed the critical stage of growth and is no longer subject to childhood shell-building difficulties. As this advice will be taken by few, I shall give directions for the care of these victims of the traffic in hatchlings.

If a little turtle has had its shell painted, remove the paint by carefully flaking it off with a razor blade or a sharp knife. Plastic paints are the most harmful as well as the hardest to remove; it may be found necessary to use nail-polish remover, a process that requires extraordinary care.

A glass tank or aquarium arranged so that it has about equal areas of water and dry "land" is suitable for turtles; the water should be deep enough to let the turtle swim under the surface. A floating object and stones made into a miniature cave are good additions, as most reptiles like to get out of sight part of the time. The tank must of course be kept clean.

The temperature should be maintained at about 80° F. A fifteen- or twenty-watt light bulb and a blanket (at night) will help under many conditions. Only lukewarm water should be added. Sunlight is extremely important and should be direct, although sunlight that passes through ordinary glass is better than none. A sun lamp is often helpful in winter. It must not be forgotten that any reptile will die if subjected to sunlight too long.

In the city, chopped raw liver, lean beef, or fish will do for food; in the country, only live worms and other soft animals such as insect larvæ should be given. Tender leaves, like those of lettuce, are relished by some turtles. For bone growth powdered milk, the crushed backbone of a raw fish, bone meal or "bonedust" (from a butcher) should be mixed with the food as often as possible, and cod-liver oil, preferably in concentrated form, added. Do not use dried "ant eggs" and other preparations sold in pet stores, or try to raise your turtle on houseflies. Feeding should take place about twice a week, and all food remnants carefully removed. If this is inconvenient, the food may be given in another vessel with the same depth of water. Reptiles seldom feed as regularly as do mammals, so a healthy baby turtle may occasionally refuse a meal, especially in winter.

Many baby pet turtles become blind, a condition believed to be the result of poor food or starvation. Obviously, low temperature and lack of sunlight may be secondary causes. The eyes may be washed with warm boric-acid solution, or some eye ointment applied, but such treatment will probably help the owner's feelings more than the turtle's eyes. The best remedy is an improvement of the diet and other living conditions.

DISTRIBUTION

FROM THE point of view of distribution, the turtles should be divided into two lots, the few marine species on the one hand, the many land and fresh-water kinds on the other. A limited number of the latter enter brackish water, and at least one marine turtle habitually does so. Only along this fringe do the ranges of the two groups overlap.

The sea turtles are at home throughout the tropical and subtropical regions of the world, but breed largely within the tropics. They also wander far into the temperate seas or are carried there habitually by warm currents. Thus the extreme range is extended to approximately fifty degrees north and forty south of the equator, the warm northern currents apparently accounting for the difference.

The land and fresh-water turtles, the vast majority of living kinds, are found in abundance on all the continents but Europe. Although six species are listed for Europe, only one of them is confined to that continent; this is proof that Europe has no appreciable turtle fauna all its own. In passing, it is interesting to note that no species occurs on the British Isles. The richest turtle faunas are found in Africa, eastern North America, and southeastern Asia. Africa should be thought of as the headquarters of the tortoises or land turtles, eastern North America and southeastern Asia as headquarters of the fresh-water groups. South America and Australia (together with New Guinea) have fresh-water turtle faunas that are of considerable importance. If we consider the Galápagos Islands as part of South America, the rich tortoise fauna of those islands gives to the South American fauna an element otherwise almost lacking.

River systems are followed by the most aquatic of the fresh-water turtles. This relationship between water drainage and distribution is unusual among reptiles.

The necessity of burying the eggs in the ground has profoundly affected the distribution of turtles. It goes without saying that they cannot live in regions of permanently frozen subsoil; northern Asia, northern North America, and the southern tip of South America are uninhabitable to them. This egg-laying necessity does not hold as a limiting factor for the sea turtles; their breeding area extends little beyond the tropics, and is probably limited by some effect of temperature other than freezing.

CLASSIFICATION

THE FLY in the ointment of turtle classification has always been the leatherback. Although consistently treated as a family in itself, it has been badgered about, now considered as an equivalent and close relative of the other seagoing species, now set aside as a major division of a much higher rank. I treat it as an equivalent of all the other living species of turtles, as explained in some detail on page 121.

The remaining turtles—that is, all but one of the species alive today—are usually divided into four groups, and these may be briefly listed as follows:

The sea turtles, circumglobal in distribution, few in number of species, and readily recognizable by their flipper limbs.

The soft-shelled turtles, distributed in North America, Africa, the Asiatic region, and New Guinea, and readily recognizable by their flexible shells covered with soft skin.

The side-necked and snake-necked turtles (Pleurodira), found in South America, Africa, Madagascar, Australia, and New Guinea, and recognized by the habit of drawing the head and neck into the recess of the shell by bending the neck to one side.

The rest of the turtles (Cryptodira), found on all the continents but Australia, and, almost without exception, recognized by their hard shells, limbs that are not like flippers, and the habit of drawing the head straight back into the recess of the shell. Six families are included, two of them (Emydidæ and Testudinidæ) enormous, including together some two thirds of all living species of turtles.

The foregoing classification is as simple as it can be made, almost all technical terms having been omitted; yet anyone could, with a little thought, put a turtle in hand into one of the major groups. It is patent that a few wrong identifications may result, but the inclusion of more technicalities is beyond the scope of this work. Dr. Ernest E. Williams of Harvard University published in 1950 a highly technical classification of turtles, both living and fossil. No doubt this classification will be widely accepted. It again reduces the leatherback to a subordinate position under the Cryptodira, and differs in other, but minor, ways from the scheme presented above.

The living crocodilians are so few in number that it was possible to consider them species by species. The turtles, with roughly ten times as many species (about 250), have to be treated group (genus) by group.

Account by Families

✳

SNAPPING TURTLES
(Family Chelydridæ)

Until a few years ago the snapping turtles were credited with an unusual distribution: two small genera in the Americas and a single species in New Guinea; the latter was made known to science in 1905. Suspicions developed by Dr. Phil Darlington, a specialist in insects, culminated in the discovery that the alleged New Guinean snapping turtle (*Devisia*) was merely a common snapping turtle of North America that had been wrongly labeled. Thanks to the complexity of scientific literature, such errors are all too common. Now that this annoying specimen has been put in its proper place, the snapping turtles have a reasonable distribution from extreme southern Canada southward through the United States east of the Rocky Mountains and on through eastern Mexico to Ecuador.

No turtles are more familiar in the United States than the snapping turtles. The reasons for this are not far to seek. The snappers are notorious for their ferocity, reach a great size, have a palatable flesh, and one of them is common and widely distributed. Only two species are known, but they are so different that each has its own generic name and warrants its own account here. In Europe many Miocene fossils have been found that are much like our common snapper; they have been put in the same genus but named as different species. Thus the snapper group has been much more widely distributed within the last thirty million years than it is today. The very earliest snapper fossil is from the Upper Oligocene of Europe.

ALLIGATOR SNAPPING TURTLE
(*Macrochelys temmincki*)
PLATES 20 AND 21

In spite of being the larger of the snapping turtles, the alligator snapper, for which the generic name *Macroclemys* is sometimes used, is the less familiar because of its occurrence only in the eastern central and the southeastern parts of the United States. Until very recently little was written about the habits of this giant, the biggest of our fresh-water turtles. Thanks to studies made by E. Ross Allen and Dr. Wilfred T. Neill, the major aspects of its life history are now known (see bibliography).

I would not say whether the ferocity of this animal or its size has aroused the more interest. The usual statement about the strength of its jaws is sadly exaggerated. Instead of being able to "bite a broomstick in two," it can, when weighing some forty pounds, scarcely do this to an ordinary pencil. This does not mean that large individuals should be handled carelessly; an enraged alligator snapper will retain its grip on the human hand, for example, and pull and chew until a painful wound has been inflicted. In proportion to size, the alligator snapper is less aggressive and far less dexterous in biting than is the common snapper. If the reverse were true, this passive giant would indeed be a formidable fighter.

The alligator snapper is no exception to the rule that the greatest size reached by the largest species is next to impossible to determine accurately. One hundred pounds might be given as the weight of a fully developed individual. At this weight the shell measures about twenty-four inches, and the animal is strong enough to walk around with a large man on its back. Two hundred pounds is usually considered to be the greatest weight ever attained, but accurate measurements of such big specimens are not available. The whole matter has been greatly complicated by the recent publication of an astounding record measurement: a snapper from Kansas that tipped the scales at 403 pounds. How long we must wait for confirmation of this remains to be seen.

The shell of a typical hatchling measures 1.75 inches in length, and the turtlet weighs eight tenths of an ounce. An alligator snapper lived in the Philadelphia Zoological Garden for fifty-seven years.

The size and biting ability of this turtle are not nearly so interesting as its lure. Place a very young individual in an aquarium with a few small fishes and watch with great patience; you may be rewarded with one of the truly exciting events of turtle life. The turtlet, upon noticing the fishes, will open its mouth and remain absolutely motionless save for a slight movement on the floor of the lower jaw. Close observation will reveal a tiny red object there constantly undulating in a way that suggests a worm. Even the most skeptical will be convinced that the turtle is attempting to lure the fishes, and, with luck, a capture will be witnessed. Allen and Neill actually saw two inquisitive fishes seized at one snap.

Two points in regard to the lure remain to be brought out. First, it is much more wormlike in the small than in the adult turtles. Second, the sluggish behavior of this species seems to be correlated with its lazy but clever way of securing its lunch. This lethargy, especially noticeable in the very small turtles, has method in it.

COMMON SNAPPING TURTLE
(*Chelydra serpentina*)
PLATES 22, 23, 24, AND 25

The foregoing statement that there are only two species of snapping turtles requires a little qualification here. For some unknown reason, snapping turtles become extremely rare in Mexico and in Central and South America. The relatively few specimens from these southern areas have long puzzled students; they have been considered as very similar to the snapper of the United States as well as different enough to be named as two additional species. The question has not been settled; Dr. Carr treats all of them as mere variants of one species, and I follow him because he is familiar with the turtles of tropical America at first hand. Here we have an example of how scarcity of an animal makes its accurate classification next to impossible; if snappers were abundant in Mexico and in Central and South America, the problem would have been solved long ago.

North of Mexico, the common snapper ranges over the United States east of the Rocky Mountains, and it also occurs in extreme southern Canada. The snappers of peninsular Florida appear to differ slightly and therefore have a subspecific name.

The ferocity of the snapper is proverbial. Hatchlings not yet free of their shells will bite, and an aroused adult, the very picture of impotent rage, will even advance to the attack. The forward thrusts of the head may be violent enough to lift the turtle from the ground if the target is missed. Once the jaws close on a victim, they retain their grip until the thunder rolls or the sun sets; at least that is the folk belief, which of course must be taken with a grain of salt.

If anyone wants to witness a remarkable phenomenon of turtle behavior, let him pick up by the tail an enraged snapper and hold it in water. The minute it becomes submerged, all the ferocity will vanish and it will think only of escaping. Here is evidence that a snapper has a dual personality, one for the land, the other for the water.

Large snappers weigh about 30 pounds, although gigantic individuals occasionally weigh from 60 to 70 pounds. They live in almost any aquatic situation, especially those with mucky, plant-grown bottoms. The female digs her nest in open areas, beginning early in the morning; most nests are made in the early summer. The majority of them contain from 20 to 30 eggs, but the number may be much greater (between 70 and 80). The eggs are spherical or nearly so.

The appetite of the snapper is broad: it eats both plant and animal matter, the latter consisting partly of carrion. The animal prey includes many fishes as well as many invertebrates. I have already discussed the snapper as an enemy of game fishes (page 77). The economic value of the snapper as a source of food is great, for they are caught by tens of thousands annually and sent to city markets. Dr. Karl F. Lagler reports that in Michigan during the late 1930's snappers were sold retail at ten to twenty cents per pound live weight, twenty to thirty dressed.

MUSK AND MUD TURTLES
(Family Kinosternidæ)

About twenty species of turtles are found from extreme south-eastern Canada southward through the United States, Mexico, Central America, and northwestern South America to Ecuador. These species are always divided into four groups or genera, but there is much difference of opinion as to the closeness of relationship among the groups. Two small ones, sometimes even put in a family (Staurotypidæ) by themselves, live only in southern Mexico and Central America, and can be dismissed after a brief description.

One of these genera (*Claudius*) comprises a single species, which has a lower shell or plastron lacking a movable front section; there are three keels or ridges extending along the back. The other genus (*Staurotypus*), with two species, has the keels, but the front lobe of the plastron is movable.

Having summarily dismissed the strictly tropical and little-known turtles of the family under consideration, we have yet to deal with the familiar musk and mud turtles. Without getting too technical it is hard to distinguish these from all other turtles, but they do have one characteristic that should enable anyone to recognize them: on the chin there are a few paired, short, fleshy appendages or barbels; other turtles of the United States with which they could be confused lack such appendages.

MUSK TURTLES
(*Sternotherus*)

There are two species of musk turtles, one of them found only in the southeastern part of the United States, and known as the keel-backed musk turtle (*Sternotherus carinatus*) because of the high, ridged shell. It differs enough from one part of the range to another to have received three subspecific names. Adults usually have a shell four to five inches long. They live in a variety of aquatic situations. By far the more familiar is the common musk turtle, or stink-pot. I shall give a brief account of it to serve as a sample of musk-turtle life history.

This turtle has duly impressed mankind by an ability to make a smell; even the scientific name, *Sternotherus odoratus*, which it received about a century and a half ago, refers to this ability. But an annoyed stink-pot not only raises a bad, musky odor; it bites viciously and effectively enough to remove a piece of skin from a careless hand, and this in spite of the fact that the largest specimen has a shell only five inches long. In addition to the viciousness, the odor, and the barbels or chin appendages, the common musk turtle, along with the keel-backed musk turtle, may be recognized by the wide areas of bare skin that separate the horny shields or laminæ of the lower shell, a condition more pronounced in the male.

The common musk turtle is found over almost all of the eastern half of the United States and a little of adjacent southeastern Ontario. It lives in permanent water of many types, and prefers it deep and quiet with a muddy bottom. It is so aquatic that the sun-basking habit is not developed. In feeding habits this turtle is carnivorous, with a tendency to eat some plant matter and to be somewhat of a scavenger. Although it eats a few fishes, any harm that it might do in this way is probably outweighed by the eating of fish enemies.

Most turtles show a remarkable uniformity in selection of a nesting site, but not the common musk turtle. Any place may be good enough; the female makes a crude nest or just places the eggs, usually one to five in number, almost anywhere. Eggs have been found on top of a stump, in a cow track, in a bundle of rushes, between the buttresses of a cypress tree. The last site is a favorite one in Florida. The eggshells are brittle and have a pebbled surface. The laying season lasts from April to August, but is much more restricted in any one place.

MUD TURTLES
(*Kinosternon*)

Now we have come to the backbone of the family of musk and mud turtles, its only genus with a large number of species (fourteen) and an extensive distribution. The mud turtles range from southeastern New York southwestward through Mexico and Central America on into South America to Ecuador, Brazil, and northern Bolivia. Five species occur in the United States, but not one in its northwestern quarter. Twice as many are found in Mexico, which is really the headquarters of the group. A few live in Central America and in South America, but only one kind is known to live west of the Andes.

The musk and mud turtles can be easily confused, although the latter in general may be recognized by the relatively larger plastron, the part of the shell that covers the belly, and by its movable front and rear sections. The difficulty here is that these parts of the plastron of the musk turtles are slightly movable even if never able to close in completely the head and legs as they do in some mud turtles. In the box turtles of the United States the plastron moves on one transverse hinge that divides it completely into two parts, whereas in the musk and mud turtles there is a fixed mid-section of the plastron that does not move. In short, a box turtle has but two sections to the plastron, both movable, the mud turtle has three sections, the middle one fixed, the front and rear movable on the middle one.

Even with ample space available I could not write much about mud-turtle life histories because little is known. Three of the five species of the United States are found in the southwestern states (excepting an isolated Illinois population), one in Florida, and one in the eastern part of the country, excepting most of New England and nearly all of the territory adjacent to the Great Lakes. This last species, the common mud turtle (*Kinosternon subrubrum*), has been studied in the field more than the others, and a few facts of its life history will be given for comparison with the common musk turtle. The common mud turtle is variable enough from one part of its extensive range to another to have received three different technical names. This fact is mentioned to avoid possible confusion.

The disposition of the common mud turtle is milder than that of the stink-pot, the inclination to raise a disagreeable smell not nearly so strong, and the odor itself not so bad. (However, on page 70 I write of a member of this same genus that did raise a terrible stink.) The common mud turtle is not nearly so aquatic in habits, shunning large, deep bodies of water. It is often seen foraging in water that only half covers it, or wandering about on land. Little is known about the feeding habits. The few observations on nesting show that the female is less casual in choosing a site and making the nest; it has the unusual habit of starting the nest with the front feet. From three to five eggs are laid at a time. A specimen once lived in captivity for thirty-eight years.

FAMILY DERMATEMYIDÆ

THIS FAMILY has no commonly used name in English, nor does the single species (*Dermatemys mawi*) that belongs to it. A relative of the musk and mud turtles (Kinosternidæ), this fresh-water reptile is found in rivers of the Atlantic coast from central Veracruz, Mexico, to Guatemala.

BIG–HEADED TURTLE
(Family Platysternidæ)

THE FAMILY Platysternidæ has a single species, *Platysternum megacephalum*, and this name, though long, is truly descriptive, giving the species its common English name.

While on the island of Hainan, China, I noted the habits of big-headed turtles. When annoyed, they hiss, assume a threatening pose with the mouth open, and may follow up with ferocious bites; the big head and sharp beak allow them to bite effectively though not dangerously. Among turtles in general they are unusual in frequenting mountain streams and in laying few eggs (two at a time). The ability to climb has been ascribed to them; actually, they merely clamber up rocks or trees to reach good sunning-places. It is easy to see that this would be a useful ability in the type of country that they like: streams bordered by forests. The large head, flattened shell, and long tail give this species, which is without close relatives, an odd appearance. The shell of a large one is seven inches long, the tail slightly longer than this. This turtle lives in southern China, southern Burma, Thailand, and French Indochina.

FRESH–WATER TURTLES
(Family Emydidæ)

ABOUT THIRTY per cent of all the living turtles belong to this family of predominantly fresh-water and marsh inhabitants. The family of true tortoises (Testudinidæ), with almost as many species, is the only rival. The fresh-water or emydid turtles, as we may call them for the sake of brevity, are broken up into twenty-four groups or genera, and average only about three species to a genus, which indicates that they are varied in structure. In fact, only two of the genera are relatively large, one of these having twelve, the other fourteen species.

The emydids are typical turtles, as they constitute the common types over great areas of the turtle-inhabited countries of the northern hemisphere. In correlation with their way of life, they have toes at least a little webbed, and their shells are nearly always streamlined for swimming. The exception to the rule of aquatic life is the group of box turtles of the United States and Canada. These not only are largely land-living in habit but tortoise-like in appearance.

There are two parts of the world where the fresh-water turtles abound. One of these extends from the southern United States southward to Central America with a spillover (region of much less abundance) in the north to extreme southern Canada, another in the south through most of South America. The West Indies must also be included as a minor spillover. The other area of abundance is in tropical and subtropical Asia from the Indian region eastward into the Malay Archipelago. The spillover here extends into central China and even Japan, where the main islands are reached by one species. The warmer parts of Europe might be thought of as an area of secondary abundance, for here three species live and extend the collective range to adjacent western Asia and extreme northern Africa.

In order to deal with this and the following family, the hatchet must be used in a drastic manner; space will permit but a very brief treatment of most of the genera involved. I shall divide the twenty-four genera into three lots on a geographic basis: the exclusively New World lot of six genera, the three cosmopolitan genera, and the fifteen genera exclusively of Asia, the Malay Archipelago, and the Philippines. Oddly enough, each lot has roughly the same number of species in it.

Fresh-water Turtles Found Only in the New World

As all of the six exclusively New World genera include familiar species of the United States, I shall deal with each genus under a heading of its own. Two of the six are found only in this country, two in this country and Mexico, one in Canada, the United States, and Mexico, and one on both continents and in the West Indies.

BOX TURTLES
(*Terrapene*)
PLATES 26, 27, AND 28

Our knowledge of the six species of box turtles is extremely uneven. The only two really familiar ones live in the United States, and are treated in more detail below. Both of these have been known to science for more than ninety-five years. In contrast are three Mexican kinds, two of which were discovered since 1942, and none of which is known from more than two places; their life histories have not been studied at all. Two of this trio are from extreme northern Mexico, which, together with adjacent parts of the United States, seems to be the present center of distribution of the group. The remaining or sixth species is found in eastern Mexico and has been taken in several places, but neither is its life history known. That box turtles once flourished in Florida is proved by the fossil record there carrying them back some ten million years to the Pliocene.

The two species of the United States are the common and the ornate box turtles (*Terrapene carolina* and *T. ornata*). The former, chiefly a woodland turtle, is found over nearly all of the eastern half of this country; the latter, a prairie reptile, occurs over a large area in the central United States, and even lives in extreme northern Mexico. Their ranges overlap considerably in Oklahoma and adjacent states. The common box turtle varies so much in appearance from one part of its extensive range to another that it has been given several technical names.

As already stated, the box turtles are exceptionally land-loving for the members of their large group, the emydid turtles. The only known remnant of their aquatic life lingers in the behavior of the common box turtle; during hot, dry weather this species will soak itself in shallow water.

The docility, the daylight and land-living habits, as well as the ability to close themselves into their shells, make box turtles excellent pets that are easily cared for. Their catholic feeding habits and the fact that they live longer than man himself also help. A box-turtle keeper seldom has to worry about mourning the loss of his pet as long as it remains healthy, though he may well have to appoint his successor.

DIAMONDBACK TERRAPIN
(*Malaclemys terrapin*)
PLATE 29

There are no close relatives of this turtle except the map turtles. It is a distinctive animal that deserves a distinctive name: no other turtles are so persistently known as "terrapins." Presumably this name has been fostered by dealers who have wanted to keep the species in a class by itself to enhance the economic value based on its savory meat. There has been considerable trouble with its classification and scientific naming, as anyone who tries to read technical works about it will soon find out. The trivial or species names "*centrata*" and "*concentrata*" have, among others, long been used for it, and often it has been divided into two species.

The centers of the horny shields or laminæ of the shell are raised to an unusual extent to suggest diamonds, giving the turtle its common name. Unusual also is the choice of a home. No other species of this continent lives exclusively in tidal shore waters. The range extends along the coasts of the United States from Cape Cod to an undetermined part of the eastern coast of Mexico, possibly some point in Yucatán.

One final distinctive characteristic of the diamondback must be brought out here. In no other North American turtle is there such a difference in size between the male and female, the latter attaining a bulk that dwarfs that of the former.

MAP TURTLES
(*Graptemys*)
PLATES 30 AND 31

This group of turtles (some of them are often called "sawbacks") includes six species widely distributed over the United States east of the Rocky Mountains. One kind is also found in extreme south-eastern Canada. Three species have very small ranges in our south-eastern lowlands, whereas two other species, the only familiar map turtles, have extensive ones. One of the latter, the common map turtle (*Graptemys geographica*), has a northeastern distribution, although the species is largely absent from New England; the other, the false map turtle (*G. pseudogeographica*), lives in the central states.

The map turtles are thoroughly aquatic relatives of the diamondback terrapin, but do not live in brackish coastal waters as does the diamondback. The common map turtle is almost entirely carnivorous, with a strong preference for mollusks, which its powerful jaws with their greatly broadened surfaces are well able to crush. Crawfishes are also eaten in great numbers. The false map turtle, without such powerful jaws, is not nearly so carnivorous, and should perhaps be classed as omnivorous.

PAINTED TURTLE
(*Chrysemys picta*)
PLATE 32

The painted turtle with its bright yellow and red markings is the most familiar and the most beautiful turtle of the northern half of the United States, where it ranges almost from coast to coast and occurs in extreme southern Canada as well. Along our eastern coast, in the Mississippi Valley, and in the region of New Mexico, its range extends far to the south, even reaching that part of Mexico adjacent to New Mexico. There is so much variation in appearance from one area to another that three subspecific names have been given to it, but we shall ignore these.

There are perhaps five major reasons for its familiarity in the United States. First, the extensive range, a point that needs no further elaboration. Second, the broad habitat preference, the species living in all types of quiet permanent water, even salt marshes. Third, the great numbers of individuals that may live in a single small pond or ditch, for instance. Fourth, the habit of sunning, often in great numbers on one log or other convenient object. Fifth, wandering of the females during late spring or early summer on roads or through fields in search of a laying-site.

The painted turtle devours both plant and animal matter, including some carrion as well.

PSEUDEMID TURTLES
(*Pseudemys*)
PLATES 33 AND 34

The species of this genus, about eight in number, have no widely used collective name, although they are sometimes called "terrapins." The distribution is the most extensive of any of the exclusively New World genera of emydid turtles; beginning in New England, the pseudemid turtles range southward to Argentina, including the West Indies. Their headquarters are really in the southeastern United States, where a bewildering array of subspecies is found. Only one kind lives as far north as New England, and the generic range barely touches the region of the Great Lakes; none is known in the Rocky Mountain or Pacific coast sections of this country.

The arrangement of the pseudemid species has given the turtle students their major problem of the New World. The bewildering array of populations, each differing slightly from adjacent ones, has until recently defied satisfactory arrangement, and has been responsible for a great rash of technical names and much general confusion. The matter has been straightened out by assigning the majority of these populations to two species, *Pseudemys scripta* and *P. floridana*, both with many subdivisions or subspecies that abound in the southeastern United States. These have absorbed most of the puzzling technical names. In fact, only four full species are now listed for the United States (*rubriventris* and *nelsoni* in addition to the two just given).

The pseudemid turtles are medium to large in size, one kind (*Pseudemys floridana suwanniensis*) reaching the greatest size of any emydid turtle of the New World (16.3-inch shell in the female). The neck, except in very dark individuals of certain species, is always adorned with conspicuous light stripes, and the jaws in some kinds are "toothed"—that is, the edges are noticeably serrated. In the males, the fingernails are ridiculously long, and are used in arousing the female before copulation. The pseudemid turtles are aquatic in habits. Carnivorous as well as herbivorous preferences are evident among the various kinds.

CHICKEN TURTLE
(*Deirochelys reticularia*)
PLATE 35

The long neck and finely wrinkled shell with a large-meshed network of fine yellow lines distinguish the chicken turtle from the somewhat similar painted turtle. The range extends throughout our southern lowlands from eastern Texas to North Carolina, where this turtle lives chiefly in quiet water. A proneness to wander about on land often results in a great destruction of the species by automobiles. In Florida the laying season is extensive and may include all the months of the year. From seven to fifteen eggs are laid at a time.

Fresh-water Turtles Found in the New and in the Old World

The three cosmopolitan groups or genera will be considered next, although they have little in common except their relatively broad distributions, all occurring in the New as well as the Old World. This wide distribution bespeaks a great age, which the fossil record confirms, remains from the Paleocene having been discovered. This means that members of at least one of these genera have been on earth sixty million years or more. The accurate classification of fossils is often difficult, and there is difference of opinion about which of the three genera certain specimens belong to; in spite of this uncertainty, it is probable that a good correlation between the age of the three and their wide ranges does exist.

TURTLES OF THE GENUS CLEMMYS
PLATES 36 AND 37

The species of this genus, some eleven in number, are so varied in appearance and so widely distributed that the coining of a common group name is all but impossible.

The North American *Clemmys* are four in number: the spotted turtle (*C. guttata*), the wood turtle (*C. insculpta*), Muhlenberg's turtle (*C. muhlenbergi*), the Pacific pond turtle (*C. marmorata*). The ranges of the first three taken together cover the northeastern quarter of the United States and adjacent southeastern Canada, with a southeastern extension of the spotted turtle along the coast, and a northeastern extension of the wood turtle to Nova Scotia, an extreme northern occurrence for a land or fresh-water turtle of North America (the common snapping turtle is recorded from New Brunswick, the painted turtle from Nova Scotia). The fourth, the Pacific pond turtle, is distributed along the Pacific coastal region from extreme southwestern Canada to extreme northwestern Mexico, a region otherwise almost entirely devoid of land and fresh-water turtles, none being found from southern Oregon southward through nearly all of California.

One of the two European species of *Clemmys* is found in the Iberian Peninsula and northwestern Africa, the other in southeastern Europe and western Asia.

The purely Asiatic species are five in number; one lives in Japan and four in southern China. One of the latter is also known from Annam, French Indochina. Some of these Asiatic *Clemmys*, like their American cousins, are among the prettiest of turtles. Almost nothing is known about the life histories of the Asiatic kinds.

BLANDING'S AND EUROPEAN POND TURTLES
(*Emys*)
PLATES 38 AND 39

The two species of this small group are sometimes called the "semi-box turtles" because of the hinged lower shell that enables them to close up almost as well as can the box turtles (*Terrapene*). The European species (*Emys orbicularis*) is often known as the "swamp turtle" or "tortoise." It is found in central and southern Europe, western Asia and northwestern Africa. Blanding's turtle (*E. blandingi*), one of our strictly northern species, ranges from New England to northern New Jersey westward through the region of the Great Lakes to extreme eastern Nebraska. Both of these turtles are unusual in being at home on land as well as in the water, although they should be considered as predominantly aquatic. The American kind is more carnivorous than herbivorous, whereas its Old World cousin is described as carnivorous. Blanding's turtle lays from six to eleven eggs at a time, the European pond turtle about the same number.

TURTLES OF THE GENUS GEOEMYDA
PLATES 40 AND 41

The species of this last cosmopolitan group do not live where they would get a good English name, and therefore none exists. Fourteen species are currently recognized, six of them living in the New World. These range from the coasts of Mexico (southern Sonora, the northern limit of many other tropical animals, and central Veracruz) southward to Ecuador and the Amazon basin of Brazil. Three of the species live in Mexico, four in Central America, and four in South America, one reaching the island of Trinidad. Most of them are fairly big, their shells measuring eight or nine inches in length. They may be roughly divided into an aquatic group with webbed toes, and a terrestrial one without webs; no species appears to be purely land- or water-living, the aquatic ones often wandering far from water, the terrestrial ones showing slight aversion to entering it. The little that is known about their feeding habits indicates predominantly omnivorous appetites with no strong specializations.

The eight Asiatic species are found from Ceylon and the Indian Peninsula eastward through southern China to the Ryukyu Islands and southward into the Malay Archipelago, including the Philippines. For the most part, they are small to medium in size, although there is among them one giant, *Geoemyda grandis*, that may be the very largest of emydid turtles. A shell 17.1 inches long is on record (compare the statement on page 95). Another remarkable species is *G. spinosa*, which occurs from Burma southeastward into the Malay Archipelago. It lives in jungle mountain streams and is an eater of plant matter. In the young, each horny shield or lamina of the carapace or upper shell has a spine, those of the edge of the shell being especially pronounced, and combining with the rest to give the animal a very spiny appearance. In addition, a keel or ridge extends down the back.

One of the eight Asiatic species (*G. trijuga*) is omnivorous, nothing is known about the feeding habits of some, and those of the spiny member have been mentioned. The choice of habitats is also varied; *G. trijuga* is both aquatic and terrestrial (the young invari-

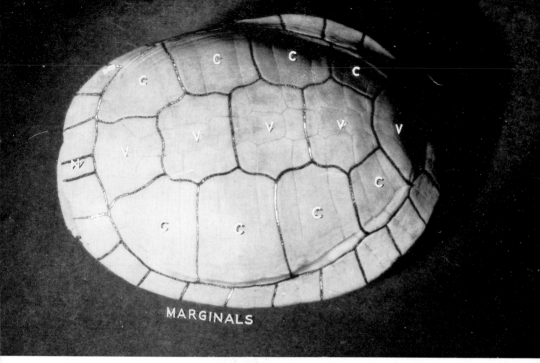

MARGINALS

(*Photograph by Mark Mooney; lettering by Edmond Malnate*)

18. Upper shell or carapace of a painted turtle (*Chrysemys*) from Michigan with the outlines of the horny shields or laminæ emphasized and their names indicated. (N for nuchal, v for vertebral, c for costal.) Outlines of the underlying bones can be made out.

19. The same shell seen from below showing the plastron. (G for gular, H for humeral, P for pectoral, A for abdominal, F for femoral, AN for anal.) Most of the outlines of the bones are obscure.

(*Photograph by Mark Mooney; lettering by Edmond Malnate*)

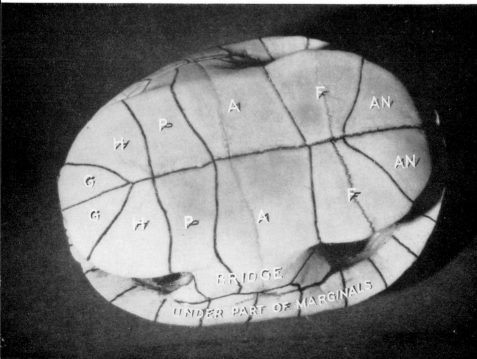

BRIDGE

UNDER PART OF MARGINALS

(Photographs by Isabelle Hunt Conant)

20. Alligator snapping turtle (*Macrochelys temmincki*).
Attains a weight of two hundred pounds.

21. Alligator snapping turtle (*Macrochelys temmincki*)
with jaws open to show lure on floor of mouth.

22. Common snapping turtle (*Chelydra serpentina*).

23. Common snapping turt(le)
(*Chelydra serpentina*)
from Plymouth County,
Massachusetts.
It weighed sixty-two pound(s)

24. Eggs of common snapping turtle (*Chelydra serpentina*) hatching. The eggs of this turtle are a little more than an inch in diameter and bounce well.

25. Snapping turtle (*Chelydra serpentina rossignoni*) from Lancetilla, Honduras.

26. Common box turtle (*Terrapene carolina*).

(*Photograph by Isabelle Hunt Conan*

27.   Ornate box turtle (*Terrapene ornata*).

28.   Klauber's box turtle (*Terrapene klauberi*) from eighteen miles
southeast of Alamos, Sonora, Mexico. This species was first described in 1943.

(*Courtesy The American Museum of Natural History*)

(*Photograph by Isabelle Hunt Conant*)

29.   Diamondback terrapin (*Malaclemys terrapin*)
from the western coast of Florida.

30. Barbour's map turtle (*Graptemys barbouri*). Note relatively big female. This species lives in the Florida panhandle and extreme southwestern Georgia.

(*Courtesy New York Zoological Society and Fred R. Cagle*)

31. A recent discovery (*Graptemys nigrinoda*). This interesting species of western Alabama (Alabama and Black Warrior Rivers) was first described by Dr. Fred R. Cagle in 1954.

32. Painted turtle (*Chrysemys picta*) from eastern North America. Male.

(*Photograph by Isabelle Hunt Conant*)

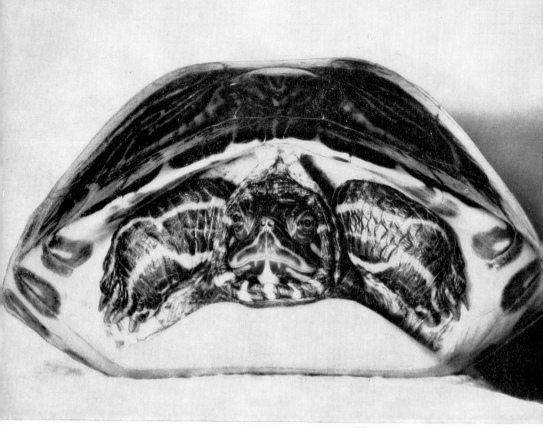

(*Photograph by Isabelle Hunt Conant*)

33. Southern terrapin (*Pseudemys floridana*)
from the Gulf Coastal Plain of the United States. Female.

(*Photograph by Isabelle Hunt Conant*)

34. Red-bellied terrapin (*Pseudemys rubriventris*).
This species ranges from Massachusetts to Virginia in the Coastal Plain. Female.

35. Chicken turtle (*Deirochelys reticularia*). Male.

(*Photograph by Isabelle Hunt Conant*)

36. Wood turtle (*Clemmys insculpta*).

(Photograph by John C. Orth)

37. Spotted turtle (*Clemmys guttata*).

(Zoological Society of Philadelphia)

(Zoological Society of Philadelphia)

38. Swamp turtle (*Emys orbicularis*).

39. Blanding's turtle (*Emys blandingi*).

(Zoological Society of Philadelphia)

(*Photograph by Isabelle Hunt Conant*)

40. American geoemyda (*Geoemyda pulcherrima*). This species has a linear range from Central America northward to the state of Sonora, Mexico.

41. Asiatic geoemyda (*Geoemyda trijuga*). This species ranges from Ceylon and southern India eastward to Burma with gaps, the range being discontinuous.

(*Zoological Society of Philadelphia*)

42.   Leopard tortoise (*Testudo pardalis*). This species is one of the two large tortoises of mainland Africa. It attains a weight of about fifty pounds.

43. West African hinged-back tortoise (*Kinixys erosa*).

(*Zoological Society of Philadelphia*)

44. Tornier's tortoise (*Malacochersus tornieri*).
This species is remarkable for its soft shell.

45. Desert tortoise (*Gopherus agassizi*).

(*Photograph by Charles M. Bogert*)

46.   Berlandier's tortoise (*Gopherus berlandieri*). Male.

47. Green turtle (*Chelonia mydas*). This is the most valuable of all reptiles.

48. Hawksbill turtle (*Eretmochelys imbricata*).
This species is the source of the tortoise-shell of commerce.

(*Photograph by Isabelle Hunt Conant*)

49. Loggerhead turtle (*Caretta caretta*). Adolescent.
A weight of at least nine hundred pounds is attained by this species.

50. Atlantic ridley (*Lepidochelys kempi*).
This is the smallest of the sea turtles.

51. Australian snake-necked turtle (*Chelodina longicollis*).

52. Matamata (*Chelus fimbriata*). Queerest of all.

53. Matamata (*Chelus fimbriata*). A noble profile.

54. South American snake-necked turtle (*Platemys platycephala*).

55. Soft-shelled turtle (*Trionyx ferox*) from the central United States.

ably aquatic, the adults predominantly terrestrial), and two other species are described as largely to entirely land-living.

Fresh-water Turtles Found Only in Asia,
the Malay Archipelago, and the Philippine Islands

Although fifteen genera, ten of them monotypic, collectively range in Asia as far to the west as the Indus River drainage, as far to the northeast as Japan, and to the southeast as the Philippine Islands and the Malay Archipelago, the whole lot is really centered on the Burma-Thailand region. Here, in the great rivers that flow into the tropics from the tableland of central Asia, exists one of the world's striking turtle faunas. Almost nothing is known of the life histories of most of these remarkable reptiles, and the very thought of studying them in such a tropical paradise makes the mouth of the field herpetologist water.

TRUE TORTOISES
(Family Testudinidæ)

The true tortoises are the slow, plodding creatures of popular fancy and fable. They are often combined with the fresh-water turtles (Emydidæ) into one huge family, the Testudinidæ, but such an aggregate, including as it would some two thirds of all living species, is most unwieldy. On the other hand, drawing a sharp distinction between the two major groups is difficult. The most distinctive characteristic of the true tortoises is found in the structure of the limbs. The column-like hind limbs remind one of the legs of an elephant, and the fore limbs are covered in front by thick scales; all the toes are without webs. The shape of the hind limbs and the lack of webs suggest land-living habits, and the true tortoises are in fact terrestrial. They are also plant-eaters. Great size is another characteristic of the group. If we except the sea turtles, the true tortoises are almost unrivaled in size; not only the giants of the tiny oceanic islands attain unusual dimensions, but several mainland kinds grow to be relatively big. *Testudo emys* of southern Asia and the Malay Archipelago may have a shell twenty-one inches long; *Testudo*

99

denticulata, the widespread South American tortoise, matches it, whereas two African species approximate these in size. A weight of fifty pounds or more is attained by some of these mainland giants.

The distribution of the whole family of true tortoises (Testudinidæ) is the same as that of the tortoises of the huge genus *Testudo* except that the gopher tortoises (*Gopherus*) extend the family range to include the southern United States and northern Mexico. The distribution of *Testudo* is considered in great detail just below. It is clear from these remarks that for those who live in the United States, recognition of a member of the family under consideration, although this family includes nearly thirty per cent of all living turtles, is mere child's play. The three gopher tortoises are so much alike that when one has been identified, the others are quickly recognized.

One more thing about this family of true tortoises should be brought out here. Africa (including Madagascar) is the tortoise heaven. Not only are more species of the massive genus *Testudo* there, but, as pointed out above, all the other genera of the family (except *Gopherus,* with a mere trio of species) live in Africa or adjacent Madagascar. Confirmation is found in one final fact: nowhere else on earth can such a concentration of tortoise species be seen. Dr. Walter Rose, a leading exponent of reptile study in southern Africa, states that as many as five species may live virtually together on one South African farm.

TRUE TORTOISES OF THE GENUS TESTUDO

PLATE 42

This enormous aggregate of species not only is the largest and most widely distributed genus of non-marine turtles, but proportionately one of the very biggest genera in any reptile group. Efforts have been made to reduce the size of *Testudo,* yet at present the consensus leaves it with some fifty species. An exact count is hard to make; there may be a few more than this number, which is such a convenient one. The complex but interesting distribution can be summarized as follows:

African region: Fourteen species are confined to Africa itself, two to Madagascar, and five more occur in the Mascarenes, the Seychelles, and other islands near Madagascar. An additional species lives in northern Africa and adjacent Asia, still another in northwestern Africa, southern Europe, and southwestern Asia.

Asia and the Malay Archipelago: Seven species are confined to Asia, the great majority of them living in the warm region from the Indian Peninsula eastward to extreme southern China and southeastward to the Malay Peninsula. One species occurs in the Malay Archipelago as well as southeastern Asia, one in southern Europe and Syria. Two additional Asiatic species are referred to in the summary of the African region. The Malay Archipelago harbors a single species that lives nowhere else; it is found in Celebes and Halmahera.

Europe: One species (*Testudo marginata*) is known only from Greece. In each of the preceding sections, a European species has been listed, making a total of three recorded from there.

South American region: Two species live in South America, one of them inhabiting Panama (near the Colombian border) and the West Indies. Fourteen species are found on the Galápagos Islands, which lie six hundred miles off the coast of Ecuador.

When we summarize this summary an odd situation becomes evident: each of the three parts of the world has its lot of *Testudo* species; Africa is well in the lead, whereas Asia and South America are about equal. Moreover, some two fifths of the species live on small oceanic islands, which in turn may be separated into a New World aggregate (Galápagos) and an Old World one (islands near Madagascar). All the truly gigantic tortoises lived on these oceanic islands, and no small kinds occurred there. What, then, is the explanation of this spread of species and how did they happen to do so well (before the arrival of man) on these isolated islands? The fossil record proves that a great assemblage of land tortoises inhabited, during relatively recent geologic times, the New as well as the Old World. These reptiles failed to survive in many continental areas, but thrived on the islands, where their size made them masters of their tiny, remote realms.

The time element in the discussion of the giant tortoises is confusing because they have been so decimated during the last few hundred years that some species of the Indian Ocean have long been exterminated (they were not included in the number of species given above) and it is hard to say in what state of near-extermination others may be. It is a problem whether the present or past tense should be used in referring to them as a whole. At about the middle of the eighteenth century, in a year and a half some thirty thousand tortoises were brought to Mauritius from other islands, many vessels being wholly employed in this traffic. This and the account on page 76 give some idea of the size of the tortoise populations and the volume of the traffic that eliminated them.

MISCELLANEOUS AFRICAN AND MADAGASCAN TORTOISES
PLATES 43 AND 44

Here we consider all of the true tortoises (Family Testudinidæ) except those just dealt with (*Testudo*) and the gopher tortoises (*Gopherus*). The seven genera live only in Africa and Madagascar and therefore form a convenient geographical unit. They are with *Gopherus* the sole members of the family that can be reasonably set off from the unwieldy genus *Testudo*. This is explained on page 100 and repeated here for emphasis.

Only one of these seven genera includes more than two species, and that is the group of hinged-back tortoises (*Kinixys*) with eight. These, widely distributed over tropical and southern Africa, are remarkable for having developed a unique way of protecting themselves with the shell. Instead of moving the plastron or belly shell, as our box turtles do so effectively, they bring the rear part of the carapace down to meet the plastron. The hind limbs are thus perfectly shielded. The hinge does not extend completely across the back, being developed only on the sides; the shell of the back is flexible enough to allow the slight movement. The hinge is not present in the young. Two of these hinged-back tortoises are well known and widely distributed: *Kinixys belliana*, typical of savanna country of tropical and southern Africa, and *K. erosa*, a reptile of the rain forests of western tropical Africa. Though terrestrial, both are fond of marshy places, and both are vegetarians.

A tortoise that has no peer lives in central Africa and was thought to be a freak until Arthur Loveridge, of the Museum of Comparative Zoology at Harvard, studied it in the field. Its name is Tornier's tortoise (*Malacochersus tornieri*), and it is a species that has all but lost a bony shell. The outside horny shields or laminæ, although well developed, are supported only by paper-thin bone, which in turn is full of holes or fenestrations—the belly shell, for instance, being mostly unsupported horny shields. The result of this loss of bone is a tortoise so soft that it can be squeezed out of shape between thumb and finger. This tortoise frequents rocky country and forces itself into narrow crevices, from which it can scarcely be extracted, especially after the lungs are inflated. Eleven individuals were found under one boulder. Loveridge also noted an ability to climb, to right itself when placed upside down, and to swim. The usefulness of the first two in rocky terrain is obvious. Tornier's tortoise lays but one egg at a time, a record that certainly will never be bettered. A second species of the genus is known.

The remaining tortoises of our miscellaneous assortment are few in number. The genera *Acinixys* and *Pyxis*, each with one species, live in Madagascar. In the latter the front lobe of the plastron is movable. The genera *Homopus* (two species), *Pseudomopus* (two species), and *Goniochersus* (one species) are found in southern Africa, although a species of *Homopus* has been taken as far north as Lake Victoria.

GOPHER TORTOISES
(*Gopherus*)
PLATES 45 AND 46

The true tortoises are represented in North America north of Panama only by the gopher tortoises. To the classifier of reptiles, these tortoises differ little from their numerous relatives of nearly worldwide distribution, but extreme geographic isolation makes it easy to consider the gopher tortoises as a separate and distinct entity. The flattened fore limbs, very efficient shovels as we shall see below, set the gophers off from their closest relatives. The three species of gophers are much alike and might even be treated as a single species, though we shall follow the usual practice of considering them apart. The desert tortoise (*Gopherus agassizi*) is found from southern Nevada southward into extreme northwestern Mexico; Berlandier's tortoise from extreme southern Texas into adjacent northeastern Mexico; the gopher tortoise (*G. polyphemus*) from the southeastern tip of Texas eastward in the lowlands through Florida and to extreme southern South Carolina. A very large specimen of either the desert or the Florida species measures thirteen inches in length, whereas Berlandier's tortoise is a somewhat smaller species.

The names and ranges give an excellent clue to habitats: the desert tortoise lives in desert country; Berlandier's tortoise in near-desert areas with well-drained, sandy soil; the gopher tortoise in regions of sandy ridges and sand dunes where the water table is not near the surface. Open woods may be inhabited by any of them. The three species are similar in being vegetarians, although it must be admitted that next to nothing is known about the feeding habits of Berlandier's tortoise. The eggs of all are spherical to elliptical and have white, brittle shells. The gopher tortoise lays from four to seven eggs at a time, and the desert species seems to lay about the same number.

Now we come to the especially interesting and characteristic thing about these three slowpokes: their digging habits, which are unique for the turtles of the United States and Mexico. Here again the information on Berlandier's tortoise is so meager that it might as well be left out even though we may feel sure that it, too, is a powerful digger. The digging processes of the desert tortoise are the more complex, as it makes two types of burrows; one type ranges in length from five to thirty feet and is made in gravel banks, whereas the other is three or four feet long and sharply inclined. The first is for hibernation, and a single burrow may harbor many individuals; the second, for protection from extremes of temperature and humidity, is individually occupied.

The gopher tortoise makes but one type of burrow, its all-purpose retreat and permanent home. The extreme length is forty feet, the greatest depth below the surface twelve. The depth is determined by the position of the water table, as this tortoise prefers a relatively dry home. In digging these long burrows, the gopher unwittingly but perhaps not unwillingly provides a permanent home for many other animals as well as a temporary retreat for still more. A burrow held at one time a pair of opossums, a raccoon, a large rattlesnake, two smaller snakes, and several rats. No less than thirty-two species of arthropods have been listed as regular inhabitants of gopher-tortoise burrows.

Although all this home construction is accomplished with their powerful fore limbs, the gophers stick to the time-honored way of digging their nests with the hind limbs.

SEA TURTLES
(Family Cheloniidæ)

OF ALL turtles the giant tortoises of remote tropical islands and the sea turtles of the warm seas are by far the most romantic and engaging. The fact that there are only five species of sea turtles makes a study of them relatively simple, and their great size helps some, too. A glance at a marine turtle is enough to convince anyone of its aquatic habits. The limbs are flippers obviously made for life in water; these reptiles move clumsily on land, which they visit only for nesting and, occasionally, sunning. This glance would also lead to the false conclusion that the shell is very fully developed. It is true that the horny shields or laminæ of the surface may be thick and strong, but, below, the construction is not as good as it is in most turtles. There has been loss of bone between the ribs, and the connection between upper and lower shells is not very rigid, either.

With only five species, the classification of sea turtles should be easy enough; actually, these few kinds have been classified with much trouble, and complete agreement has not yet been reached. Dr. Carr, whose arrangement I shall follow, fits the five species into four genera, which shows they do not for the most part closely resemble one another, and probably have had a long history. The fossil record confirms this; sea turtles have been swimming the seas since Cretaceous times, or for at least a hundred million years, and some fossil species of considerable age are much like the living kinds.

The turtles of this marine family are denizens of tropical and subtropical seas and breed only in such warm regions. Although individuals may stray into cooler seas, they cannot be considered at home there. The eggs, spherical or nearly so, are buried in the sands of open beaches. Each nest contains a relatively large number of eggs. This link with a terrestrial past is the weakest point in the turtle's existence, as the laying female, sprawled preoccupied and defenseless on the sand, is exposed to the greatest risk of its adult life. The danger does not end here, because the eggs and young must run a gauntlet of still greater dangers.

The species of this family being so few in number, we can give a brief account of each one, laying emphasis on special characteristics or those that distinguish one from the other. The ranges of three of the species encircle the globe, and are divided into Atlantic and Pacific populations or subspecies, each with its technical name. The differences between the Atlantic and Pacific turtles are in every case too slight to interest anyone but the specialist.

GREEN TURTLE
(*Chelonia mydas*)
PLATE 47

This species, by all odds the most valuable of reptiles, is the world-famous soup turtle. The fat is greenish, hence the common name. Although not in immediate danger of extinction, its numbers have been greatly reduced, and the development of modern refrigeration and transportation of foods can only increase the demand for turtle products. In spite of the circumglobal distribution of this reptile and its great value, there is little scientific information on its life history; as Dr. Carr points out with emphasis, not enough to form a sound basis for its protection and possible restoration. We still must locate the chief breeding-areas, determine the season for each and its annual egg harvest; ascertain the number of annual clutches and their size per female; discover the haunts of the young; and study any migrations of the species that may occur.

The greatest weight attained by the green turtle is about 850 pounds; in regions where it is not molested, the adult usually weighs from 300 to 500 pounds, and has a shell 38 to 46 inches long. The rate of growth has never been accurately determined, the few data available indicating sexual maturity in the female at a shell length of about 35 inches, an age of ten years at a length of 44 inches.

The disposition of the green turtle is good, although some individuals will bite when first caught. It eats chiefly marine grasses and algæ, grazing over the extensive flats of these plants. This habit largely determines its preference for shoals and lagoons of oceanic islands and continental shelves, where it often enters bays and sounds. Jellyfish, mollusks, and crustaceans are sometimes devoured. A habit apparently peculiar to this species is that of hauling out to lie on ledges or beaches for purposes of sunning or sleeping. This peculiarity raises the problem of respiration, since the weak bridges of the sea-turtle shell make breathing on land difficult. The explanation of how a sunning turtle survives much better than one on a ship's deck, for example, is not evident. Transporters of sea turtles have long had the habit of placing their turtles belly up on deck, an act often mistaken for cruelty.

HAWKSBILL TURTLE
(*Eretmochelys imbricata*)
PLATE 48

Just as the flesh of the green turtle is famous for its flavor, the shell of the hawksbill is well known for its beauty when made into ornamental objects. Some account is given on page 77 of the world-wide use of tortoise shell, or "carey," as it is called in Caribbean lands. Although the flesh has no general market value, it is often eaten locally with relish.

As indicated by the technical name, *imbricata*, the horny shields or laminæ of the shell overlap noticeably in all but the largest and oldest specimens, in which the edges come together. As to size, the hawksbill ranks next to the ridleys, the shell of a fully grown individual measuring only about two feet in length; Dr. Carr's largest one had a shell 32.8 inches long. The range embraces the warmer seas, although the species is rare in the eastern Atlantic. It does not occur north of Mexico on the western side of North America, but wanders as far north as Massachusetts on the eastern. Shallow coastal waters are the preferred haunts, and there it eats both plant and animal food. The hawksbill is a pugnacious reptile.

LOGGERHEAD TURTLE
(*Caretta caretta*)
PLATE 49

The loggerhead shares with the green turtle the distinction of attaining the greatest size of any sea turtle with a horny shell (family Cheloniidæ). The maximum dimensions of the loggerhead are unknown; there is reliable evidence of attainment of a weight of 900 pounds, and some indication of a much greater one. The usual dimensions of large individuals are: weight, 300 pounds; length of shell, three feet.

The hardiness of this species is shown by its far-flung breeding-grounds, its frequent ascent into the mouths of creeks, and its wandering into the open seas. No other marine turtle has nested as far north as Virginia, nor does any other member of its family stray northward to Nova Scotia. On our western shores, the loggerhead reaches southern California.

The disposition of this giant is bad, its diet chiefly carnivorous, its meat of inferior flavor, and its eggs an esteemed delicacy. A captive individual once attained a shell length of 24.8 inches and a weight of 81.5 pounds in four and a half years.

Imagine a dark mite of a turtlet struggling to the surface in the middle of a huge expanse of white sand over and on which numerous enemies are lurking. It behooves the mite to get to the sea as soon as possible, but how can it know which way to go? This problem has worried scientists as well as turtles, and the former, by means of elaborate experiments, have revealed an innate tendency in the loggerhead to move downhill away from a broken horizon and toward an open one. Under ordinary conditions, this will cause it to crawl seaward. The odor of the salt water was found to have no effect.

Presumably all other hatchling sea turtles have the same innate tendency.

ATLANTIC RIDLEY
(*Lepidochelys kempi*)
PLATE 50

There are several unusual things about this turtle, and not the least of these is the many names that have been given it. The most stable is "*kempi*," the trivial or species name, and by this it may always be recognized. Several generic names have been applied to it, *Caretta*, *Colpochelys*, and *Lepidochelys* being the most usual. It has been known as Kemp's turtle, Kemp's loggerhead, bastard turtle, and, currently, Atlantic ridley.

Perhaps the two most unusual things are its size and distribution. All the other sea turtles are larger; an Atlantic ridley becomes mature sexually when the shell is barely two feet long, and the record shell measures only 27.6 inches. The range, much more limited than in any other marine species, is all but confined to the Gulf of Mexico, although individuals stray northward as far as the coast of Massachusetts, and are carried across the Atlantic in the Gulf Stream to the British Isles.

Almost nothing is known about its habits except that it is astonishingly irascible, becoming hysterical with rage when captured. Dr. Carr considers it excellent for eating, an opinion with which all other connoisseurs concur, certain published statements notwithstanding.

PACIFIC RIDLEY
(*Lepidochelys olivacea*)

The name Pacific loggerhead has often been applied to this species of the warmer parts of the Indian and Pacific oceans. Along the coasts of the Americas it ranges from Chile to northern Mexico. It prefers shallow waters, and the diet is chiefly vegetarian. The size is moderate and comparable to that of the hawksbill; a fully grown Pacific ridley has a shell approximately two feet long, an extremely large shell is some six inches longer.

The laying procedure of the sea turtles is a fascinating one that has seldom been adequately described. I cannot resist quoting in full Dr. Carr's detailed description of a nesting Pacific ridley observed October 11, 1947, on Isla de Ratones in Honduranean territory of Central America.

"At 10:04 p.m. the turtle left the water at right angles and headed directly for the grass line. She crawled like a fresh-water turtle, moving alternate fore and hind flippers together. She rested three times during the fifty-two-yard traversal of the beach and stopped at 10:09 p.m. in dry sand among high-tide litter sixteen feet from the grass. Without reconnaissance she began throwing sand with fore and hind flippers, changing the orientation of her body slightly until a shallow basin had been excavated around her. Since she dug more effectively with her hind feet than with her fore feet, this pit was deeper behind than before, and the long axis of her body inclined downward toward the rear. Eventually the posterior margin of her shell had sunk about five inches below the level of the surrounding sand.

"After a short pause, during which the turtle applied her tail to several spots in apparent appraisal of the quality of the sand, she began excavating the nest cavity. The left hind flipper was lifted, brought in beneath the hind margin of the shell, and its edge pushed into the soft sand. It was then curled to enclose perhaps half a teacup of sand, which was carried out laterally and dropped with a little flip. As this fell, the other hind flipper kicked sand straight back. The process was then repeated in reverse. This was the digging procedure, and it was continued throughout with little variation.

"As the hole deepened it was made wider, and asymmetrically so, the increased dimension being that toward the turtle's head. We peered down into the cavity from time to time and saw that this asymmetrical growth was due to the fact that the fore wall received the most active scraping, not only from the curved end and edge of the flipper but also from the strong toenail which projected from the margin several inches back from the end. We determined definitely that this was frequently brought to bear against the front wall of the cavity and that it was very effective, both in removing sand and in breaking or dislodging grass roots and other obstructions. The alternate use of the two flippers with no change in the position of the body produced a hole that was noticeably square in cross section, with four definite, though rounded, corners.

"As the flippers had to reach progressively farther into the hole, digging proceeded more slowly. While the nest cavity deepened, the hind part of the turtle's shell sank lower, owing to continued gradual excavation of one side of the upper pit by the off flipper as each load of sand was removed from the lower hole by the other flipper. When the nest was as deep as the flippers could reach, digging ceased.

"The turtle slapped at her tail and cloaca two or three times with each flipper, knocking away adhering sand. The tail was dropped vertically into the hole. The cloaca, temporarily prolonged for its function as an ovipositor, extended considerably beyond the tip of the tail, its opening being about four inches below the plastral surface. The first egg fell into the nest at 10:25 p.m. Thereafter, eggs came every four to ten seconds, either singly or in groups of two, three, or four, most frequently two or three.

"The curious 'crying' by nesting females, apparently a device to keep the eyes free of sand, has been noted in other species. The present turtle began secreting copious tears shortly after she left the water, and these continued to flow as the nest was dug. By the time she had begun to lay, her eyes were closed and plastered over with tear-soaked sand and the effect was doleful in the extreme. Her behavior as the eggs were deposited heightened the melancholy atmosphere. Each time, just before eggs were laid, her head was elevated at an unnatural angle and her mouth was slightly opened, frequently allowing a loud gasp or sigh to escape. With the contraction which pushed out the eggs came a rapid lowering of her head until her chin pressed into the sand, after which she lay for a while heaving slightly. It was difficult to believe that she was not suffering acutely, but impossible to explain why.

"The last eggs were laid at 10:37 p.m. after a few somewhat increased intervals between extrusions. The turtle immediately began to fill the hole, raking in sand from the surrounding ramp with her hind flippers. There appeared to be some selection with respect to the quality of sand used, since the cloacal opening was pressed against each section of the ramp just before it was dragged into the nest, and sometimes the lot was rejected. We poured a small amount of perfectly dry sand over a part of the ramp about to be pushed into the hole. The slightly everted cloaca was touched to this and the flipper immediately shifted to another area. As sand fell into the hole it was packed by the back of first one curled flipper and then the other. When the hole was full, the turtle began to pound the sand with her plastron, at first tilting her shell to one side and the other and then, lifting herself with her fore and hind flippers, she dragged in more sand from behind and let herself fall sharply upon it. As the surface hardened, the thumping sound which these falls produced became audible from a distance of thirty feet or more. The packing operation lasted four and a half minutes and was performed with what seemed to us excessive thoroughness.

"At 10:45 the turtle stopped pounding and began flipping sand backward with her fore feet, meanwhile rotating her body laterally to bring in sand evenly from all sides. She then crawled across the nest site twice and started back to the water at 10:52."

SIDE–NECKED TURTLES
(Family Pelomedusidæ)

SINCE THERE are no widely used common English names for most of the turtles of this family, it will be necessary to rely largely on the technical ones. The English name for the group is derived from the peculiar habit of protecting the head and neck by bending the latter to one side and thus completely concealing it and the head within the shell. This method is in sharp contrast to the habit that most turtles have of simply drawing the head and neck straight back into the recess of the shell.

This is a small family of not more than fifteen species. There is some difference of opinion as to the exact number; the latest study of the African species, made by Loveridge, reduced rather than increased the number. In contrast to most chelonian families, the side-necked turtles are southern in distribution. The total range is Africa south of the Sahara Desert, Madagascar and near-by islands, and South America. All of the species are aquatic to semiaquatic in habits.

The side-necked turtles are unusual in having a family tree that would be the pride of any human blue blood. Of course every animal family has a tree, though in most cases only the tips of the highest twigs (the living species) are evident to us human beings; the fossil record is so incomplete that we cannot follow the twigs down to the branches and the branches to the trunk. There is the added difficulty that students of the living kinds usually know nothing about the fossil record, and fossil specialists are prone to neglect the living species. Thanks to the thorough study of the Pelomedusidæ, both living and fossil, by Dr. Rainer Zangerl of Chicago Natural History Museum, we have a good picture of the side-necked turtles during the last hundred million years (since the Upper Cretaceous). This picture actually includes more than three times as many fossil as living genera as well as more than three times as many fossil as living species of the family. Here is evidence of the indispensability of the paleontologist's work for a broad view of evolution.

Dr. Zangerl's monograph cleared up many technical points which we cannot go into, and brought out others which we can clearly understand. The most obvious of these is the explanation of the broken distribution. There are many fossil species from the United States and northern Africa, others from Europe, Asia, and South America. Thus it is obvious that the living kinds are merely a survival of an almost world-wide turtle fauna. More interesting still is the evidence that the one genus (*Podocnemis*), now known from a single species in Madagascar and seven in South America, has had a split lineage for perhaps a hundred million years, one line evolving in the New, another in the Old World. In contrast to the simple, one-sided distribution of living species, the total all-time distribution is as follows: seven species in Africa and Madagascar, two in Europe, one on Malta, one in Asia, two in North America, and nine in South America.

Pelomedusa, one of the three genera of the family, has a single species (long known as *galeata* but now called *subrufa*) that occurs in Madagascar and ranges over nearly all of Africa south of the Sahara. It is an aquatic reptile of open country, entering the rain forests, if at all, only along their edges. In feeding habits it is chiefly carnivorous. This reptile is often roasted and eaten with relish by the Hottentots. A quaint belief exists in the Kalahari region; its odor is said to be so much like that of a lion that cattle will stampede when they smell it.

Some account has just been given of the genus *Podocnemis*, which is conspicuous in the tropics of South America. The species are large and include a veritable giant, the arrau (*P. expansa*), the shell of which may be 31.5 inches long. Early explorers wrote fully of the hunting of the arrau and its eggs. A valuable oil is extracted from the eggs, which once were harvested annually by the millions.

The last genus, *Pelusios* (long known as *Sternothærus*), lives on Madagascar and near-by islands, and ranges over nearly all of Africa south of the Sahara Desert. There has been great difficulty in deciding just how many species exist; the result of the study by Loveridge indicates that only four live in Africa; he reduced the number by three. The species of this genus are sharply set off from those of the other two genera by the movable front section of the plastron. This device of *Pelusios* for protecting the head, neck, and fore limbs has been developed independently in a surprising number of turtle groups. Dr. Zangerl's study adds only two fossil species to the genus; the oldest one, from the Miocene of Egypt, has a geologic age of perhaps 25,000,000 years. He concludes that the *Pelusios* stock has been distinct from that of the other two genera since the Cretaceous period, which is thought to have ended 75,000,000 years ago.

SNAKE–NECKED TURTLES
(Family Chelidæ)
PLATES 51, 52, 53, AND 54

As IN the case of the preceding family, there is no well-fixed English name for this aggregate of turtles, which is often thought of as merely another lot of side-necked turtles. Actually, the two families do comprise a closely related unit set off scientifically as the Pleurodira. Even the family name is spelled three ways in technical literature: Chelidæ, Chelyidæ, and Chelydidæ. I mention this because of the possibility of confusion with the Chelydridæ, the snapping turtles. Fortunately, the family that we are about to consider is confined to South America (including the island of Trinidad), New Guinea, and Australia, and therefore not too readily confused with the snapping turtles, which are largely North American.

The thirty-one currently recognized species of snake-necked turtles are divided into ten genera, half of which are monotypic (having a single species). This extreme division indicates great differences in structure. These differences cannot be considered; distinguishing between this and the preceding family would call for more details of turtle structure than is suitable here. Suffice it to say the snake-necked turtles have long necks that, as already implied, are bent to one side like those of the side-necked turtles (Pelomedusidæ). The head and neck of the snake-necked species often cannot be completely concealed within the shell.

In Australia and New Guinea there are only two genera with more than one species apiece. In *Chelodina* the neck is very long and, together with the head, can be concealed within the shell. The jaws are so weak that the bite is little more than a harmless nip. The most familiar of the seven species is *Chelodina longicollis* of Australia, a turtle noted for its docility in captivity. The other important genus, *Emydura*, with seven of the nine species occurring in New Guinea, has a thicker, relatively shorter neck that, together with the head, cannot be concealed completely. The bite is strong. The two remaining genera of the Australian region are confined to Australia itself and have a single species apiece.

The thirteen species of South American snake-necked turtles (one kind reaches the island of Trinidad) are divided into six genera, half of them monotypic. They occur east of the Andes, and live for the most part in the Amazon and its tributaries. Only two species have been found in Colombia, although several occur in the region of the Guianas. To the south the range extends to central Argentina.

One of the New World snake-necked turtles perhaps deserves the distinction of being the queerest of all chelonians. It has been known to science since the middle of the eighteenth century, though no one has studied it under natural conditions. The matamata (*Chelus* or *Chelys fimbriata*) at first glance looks like almost anything or almost nothing, but scrutiny convinces one that it must be a turtle. The tail is short, the shell, which may exceed a foot in length, heavy and lumpy, the toes webbed, the neck thick and long, the big, broad but flattened head completely disguised by an incredible number of protuberances sticking out in all directions. The small eyes are placed farther forward than the mouth, and the nose is a proboscis. Sometimes a matamata appears to be leering or grinning, an expression resulting from the remarkable arrangement of eyes, nose, mouth, and chin.

Close examination of the jaws, a procedure always safe, shows that they are as extraordinary as the rest of this docile animal. Instead of having the usual sharp, horny edges, the jaws are fleshy and anything but sharp-edged and dangerous. This leads to suspicion that the method of eating is also odd, and so it is. Although the matamata may occasionally snap up its prey, feeding is primarily accomplished by a simultaneous opening of the mouth and enormous expansion of the neck that cause any near-by object to rush into the gape along with water. This makes a dull sound audible at a distance of several feet. Working backward, we can now understand why the head and neck are so astonishingly developed. Sluggishness plus odd appearance combine to produce a camouflage correlated with these armchair feeding habits.

The matamata is widely distributed from Colombia and the Guianas through the Amazon drainage. It lives well in captivity, making an attractive addition to any home, although the fact that it attains a weight of sixteen pounds might be considered by some a drawback.

PITTED–SHELLED TURTLE
(Family Carettochelyidæ)

THE SINGLE species of this family, among the rarest of turtles, lives in the Fly River of New Guinea. The shell, which may be twenty inches long, lacks the outer covering of horny shields, and in this way resembles that of the soft-shelled turtles. The flipperlike limbs with two claws suggest the sea turtles, but the lack of horny shields and other facts about its structure prove its close relationship to the soft-shelled turtles.

SOFT–SHELLED TURTLES
(Family Trionychidæ)
PLATE 55

THE SOFT-SHELLED turtles are well named because they live in skin-covered, flexible shells that entirely lack the horny shields or laminæ of most turtles. The term "shell" is scarcely appropriate, although well justified by usage. A soft-shell suggests a pancake with webbed feet, a long neck, and a pointed head ending in a snout or proboscis. One might jump to the conclusion that these odd creatures are ancestors of the other turtles, but studies of their structure indicate specialization. This means that they have lost the usual turtle attributes in becoming suited or adapted to life in a special environment: the soft bottoms of rivers, streams, ponds, lakes, and similar aquatic sites. Their flattened bodies are readily concealed in such places, and the long necks and snouts often enable them, while lying in mud under shallow water, to extend the snout to the surface for breathing. As already explained, at least some of them are able to supplement their ordinary breathing by getting oxygen from

117

the water (see page 61). Probably a soft-shelled turtle can indefinitely remain submerged in shallow or even deep water.

Although so specialized in structure, the soft-shelled turtles have been in this condition for a long time: from the middle of the Cretaceous, or perhaps a hundred million years. They have been successful; today about one tenth of the known turtles belongs to the group, which is well spread over the surface of the earth. To put it tersely, the soft-shells are found in abundance in the warm parts of southern Asia, with a spillover into the Malay Archipelago (one species even reaching New Guinea and the Philippine Islands), and another into Africa. A small but flourishing group of two species occurs in the United States, barely reaching Canada to the north, Mexico to the south. Australia, Europe, and South America are devoid of them.

Soft-shells are carnivorous, although not entirely so. Oddly enough, captives often show a fondness for various cooked foods of vegetable origin. The disposition of most species is so bad that large individuals must be handled with great care. The proverbial slowness of turtles does not apply to the members of this group: they not only strike with the speed of a snake, but swim and move with the rapidity of a mammal.

The species of soft-shelled turtles are divided into seven genera or groups of closely related kinds, but only one of these genera is made up of more than three species. The single large group (genus *Trionyx* or *Amyda*) has members in both the New and the Old World, whereas two of the small groups occur in Africa and the collective range of the remaining four extends from southern Asia to New Guinea and the Philippine Islands.

It will be impossible to discuss these interesting reptiles in any detail, though I shall give a brief account of every group and describe the habits of a few common species. Often technical names will be given because of lack of common ones.

The genus *Lissemys* with a single species (*punctata*) is the only Asiatic soft-shelled turtle able completely to conceal its hind limbs by two valves or flaps of skin. The species is found from the valley of the Indus River to that of the Salween, including the Indian Peninsula and Ceylon. It lives in ponds and artificial bodies of water rather than in rivers. Dr. P. E. P. Deraniyagala writes that the flesh is eaten and used as medicine; that its charred bones have been taken from ruins dating back to 4000 B.C.

The only other soft-shells with valves that allow concealment of the hind limbs are found in tropical Africa, and are known as *Cycloderma* and *Cyclanorbis*. The former genus has two species, one characteristic of the savanna or open country, the other of the forests; the three species of the latter genus are found in savannas.

One of the most remarkable and successful of soft-shelled turtles, *Pelochelys bibroni*, is found from southern China southward throughout the peninsula of southeastern Asia and the Malay Archipelago to New Guinea and the Philippines. It is a giant among turtles, an individual with a shell fifty-one inches long being on record. A specimen that I secured on the island of Hainan, China, weighed forty-two pounds although its shell was but twenty-two inches long (following the curve). Not only is the range of this reptile extensive, but its ability to live under a variety of conditions is unusual. On Hainan it was caught in small streams; elsewhere it has been found in deep, sluggish rivers as well as on seacoasts. Judging by one large Hainan specimen, *P. bibroni* appears to be a bluffer, a type of behavior rare among turtles. This individual would strike with snakelike speed, but the jaws were not brought into play, the strike being merely a punch with the snout; the hand of a fisherman struck by it suffered no injury whatsoever.

A species of soft-shell that may have a shell thirty-two inches long is found from Nepal and the delta of the Ganges to the Malay Peninsula. Its disposition is bad, and its head long, but the scientific name is easy: *Chitra indica*. Still another soft-shelled turtle, *Dogania subplana*, is placed in a genus by itself. It ranges from Burma through Thailand and the Malay Peninsula into the Malay Archipelago. Although commonly listed as part of the Philippine Island fauna, its presence there has been questioned.

About fifteen species, or considerably more than half of all the soft-shells, are enough alike to comprise a single genus, *Trionyx* (often called *Amyda*, as explained below). The distribution of this compact group is much like that of the family, most of the kinds living in southern Asia, a few in North America and the Malay

Archipelago, and one (*triunguis*) in Africa as well as western Asia.

The little that we know about the habits of these turtles indicates a general similarity, but detailed studies will surely bring out many differences. A brief summary of the life history of the spiny soft-shelled turtle will suffice and give at least a hint of the habits of the others. Perhaps no other kind has been as carefully observed.

The spiny soft-shelled turtle occurs over most of the United States as well as in extreme northern Mexico and in a small area of southeastern Canada. It is not found in the north and middle Atlantic region or in the Rocky Mountain and Pacific coastal areas. It is *the* soft-shell of the New World, the only other species, the spineless soft-shelled turtle, being smaller and much less familiar, and having virtually no commercial value.

Like many species that live over a large territory, the spiny soft-shell varies so much from area to area that it has been given six scientific names, each one used for a population showing similar characteristics and inhabiting its own area. These, the "subspecies" of science, are mentioned here only by way of warning to those who run across them in books and become confused. The name of the species is *Trionyx ferox*, and any other name used for it should be added to these two, as, for example, *Trionyx ferox spinifera*. Incidentally, the name *Amyda* is often used for the genus instead of *Trionyx*, but this fact must be accepted without question unless one wants to become involved in a most complex problem of scientific naming that is still without a satisfactory solution.

So many types of courses and bodies of water, both natural and artificial, fresh and brackish, have been given as the home of the spiny soft-shelled turtle that it is safe to describe its habitat as all permanent water. One qualification to this broad statement must be noted: swift streams of mountain forests and other heavily shaded water are avoided. It might also be pointed out that every type of water would not be used in each area; reasonable allowance must be made for individual preference of different populations.

Surprisingly little is known about the breeding habits of this turtle. In the late spring or early summer the female cautiously leaves the water during the morning or early afternoon to crawl up on an open shore. She carefully selects a site and digs with her hind limbs a flask-shaped nest the depth of which is determined by the length of her legs. She may leave without attempting to conceal the nest, or she may so carefully pack the dirt that the nest is well hidden. One observer even saw a female go a short distance and scratch around, presumably in an effort to make a decoy nest. Little is known about the incubation period. In the northern part of the range it is probable that some of the young do not emerge until the spring of the following year.

The eggs are white with a thick, brittle shell, slightly more than an inch in diameter. The shape is spherical or nearly so, and the number per clutch usually varies from ten to twenty-five.

Insects living in water and crawfishes are the mainstay of the diet, although almost any small animal will be devoured. Some plant matter is eaten and some scavenging is done. In spite of the agility of this turtle and its quick jaws, there is no evidence that fishes are preyed on to an appreciable extent. The food is swallowed whole, the front feet helping to manipulate it.

A small spiny soft-shelled turtle makes an attractive and unusual pet. Its great activity sets it off at once from other turtles, and its shape and carapace, often daintily spotted, are attractive. It should have three inches of sand under the water of its tank, and requires much less land surface than the hard-shelled turtles. In fact, it can remain in water indefinitely. Soft-shells are not seen for sale nearly so often as are the hard-shells, but they are available for the real turtle-fancier.

LEATHERBACK TURTLE
(Family Dermochelidæ)

THE LEATHERBACK (*Dermochelys coriacea*), largest of turtles, has caused the students of turtle classification more trouble than any other. This is because of the peculiar structure of its shell and its marine habits. Some have argued that it is the most primitive of living turtles, others that its shell is a secondary change correlated with its extremely aquatic life. In 1766 Linnæus, the father of the scientific naming of animals and plants, called it *Testudo coriacea* because of the leathery surface of its shell. ("*Testudo*" was then a general name for turtles.) This smooth surface had led some to believe that the leatherback has no shell, but in fact it has a shell of sorts. In the thick skin are buried countless small bones; these form a mosaic, and may well represent a part of the original turtle shell that has been lost by all other living species. The outer layer of horny shields or laminæ seen in most of them is entirely lacking in the leatherback. Complete agreement on the status of this monster has not been reached, although the consensus now regards it as primitive and at least the equivalent of all other turtles. This is why it is treated as a suborder; the fossil record does not help any. The misleading name for its suborder is Athecæ, meaning "without a shell."

Seven prominent ridges or keels extend along the back of the leatherback, five additional ones along its belly. The limbs are powerful clawless flippers, the front pair much longer than the rear. This turtle may be the heaviest of living reptiles, as a weight of at least three fourths of a ton is reached. Many individuals weighing a thousand to twelve hundred pounds are on record. The width of large specimens, flipper tip to flipper tip, is from eight to twelve feet. The young are unique among turtles in being covered with small, irregular scales that are soon completely lost. No less remarkable is the gaudy juvenile coloration that contrasts sharply with the drab, dark hues of the adult. In the infants, white or yellow spots may be more or less evident; the ridges and margins of the shell as well as the flipper margins are similarly adorned.

No other species of sea turtle wanders so far from tropical waters. Individuals occasionally appear as far south as Mar del Plata, Argentina; Cape of Good Hope, Africa; and South Australian waters; as far north as Japan; the British Isles; Nova Scotia; and British Columbia. Certainly no other reptile is found over such an extensive area.

Dr. Deraniyagala is the only herpetologist who has observed the complete nesting and laying procedure of the leatherback, and his fine account, too long to give completely, indicates that a leatherback ready to lay is little more than a gigantic animated sand-shovel.

After leaving the water in the moonlight, the female watched by him threw great loads of sand over her glistening back until she was completely coated and therefore much less conspicuous. A copious flow of tears kept her vision clear during this "sand bath." Choosing a laying-site, she swept sand about with the flippers and made a hollow by movements of the body from side to side. Next she settled to excavate, with the hind flippers, the egg cavity. The eggs, once laid, were gently covered by flipperfuls of sand. Movements of the hind parts of the body finished the covering, and then obliteration of the site began. All four limbs took part in this; sand was flung high and wide while the body gyrated and moved back and forth in the area. So effective was this sand-throwing and plowing that Dr. Deraniyagala and two helpers were unable to find the eggs by digging with the hands for an hour. Presumably what they lacked was a keen sense of smell, but even this might not have helped much because the turtle emitted a strong fishy odor that permeated the churned-up sand. Dr. Deraniyagala once disturbed a giant monitor lizard after it had made three futile attempts to find leatherback eggs.

Bibliography

✿

Allen, E. Ross and Wilfred T. Neill: "The Alligator Snapping Turtle, *Macrochelys temminckii*, in Florida." *Ross Allen's Reptile Institute*, Special Publication 4 (1950), pp. 1–15.

Benedict, Francis G.: *The Physiology of Large Reptiles with Special Reference to the Heat Production of Snakes, Tortoises, Lizards and Alligators.* Washington: Carnegie Institution of Washington; 1932.

Carr, Archie: *Handbook of Turtles. The Turtles of the United States, Canada, and Baja California.* Ithaca, New York: Comstock Publishing Associates (a division of Cornell University Press); 1952.

Casteel, D. B.: "The Discriminative Ability of the Painted Turtle." *Journal Animal Behavior*, Vol. 1 (1911), pp. 1–28.

Deraniyagala, P. E. P.: "The Tetrapod Reptiles of Ceylon." *Ceylon Journal Science*, Vol. 1 (1939), pp. 1–412.

Flower, Stanley S.: "Further Notes on the Duration of Life in Animals.—3. Reptiles." *Proceedings, Zoological Society London*, Series A, Part 1 (1937), pp. 1–39.

Hansen, Ira B.: "The Breathing Mechanism of Turtles." *Science*, Vol. 94 (1941), p. 64.

Lagler, Karl F.: "Food Habits and Economic Relations of the Turtles of Michigan with Special Reference to Game Management." *American Midland Naturalist*, Vol. 29 (1943), pp. 257–312.

Lindholm, W. A.: "Revidiertes Verzeichnis der Gattungen der rezenten Schildkröten nebst Notizen zur Nomenklatur einiger Arten." *Zoologischer Anzeiger*, Vol. 81 (1929), pp. 275–95.

Loveridge, Arthur: *Many Happy Days I've Squandered.* New York: Harper and Brothers; 1932.

——: "Revision of the African Terrapin of the Family Pelomedusidæ." *Bulletin, Museum Comparative Zoölogy*, Vol. 88 (1941), pp. 467–524.

——: *Reptiles of the Pacific World.* New York: The Macmillan Company; 1945.

—— and Benjamin Shreve: "The 'New Guinea' Snapping Turtle (*Chelydra serpentina*)." *Copeia* No. 2 (1947), pp. 120–3.

Oliver, James A.: "It Makes You Ask—What Is It? Animal? Vegetable? Mineral?" [Matamata] *Animal Kingdom*, Vol. 55 (1952), pp. 10–12.

Pope, Clifford H.: "The Reptiles of China." *Natural History of Central Asia*, Vol. 10 (1935), pp. 1–604. New York: The American Museum of Natural History.

Bibliography

——: *Turtles of the United States and Canada.* New York: Alfred A. Knopf; 1939.

Rooij, Nelly de: *The Reptiles of the Indo-Australian Archipelago. I. Lacertilia, Chelonia, Emydosauria.* Leiden: E. J. Brill; 1915.

Rose, Walter: *The Reptiles and Amphibians of Southern Africa.* Cape Town: Maskew Miller; 1950.

Rust, Hans-Theodor: "Systematische Liste der lebenden Schildkröten." *Blätter Aquarien Terrarienkunde,* 45 Jahrg. (1934), pp. 1–12.

——: *Taschenkalender für Aquarien–und Terrarienfreunde 1936.* Braunschweig: Gustav Wenzel & Sohn; 1936.

Schmidt, Karl P.: "Contributions to the Herpetology of the Belgian Congo Based on the Collection of The American Museum Congo Expedition, 1909–1915." *Bulletin, American Museum Natural History,* Vol. 39 (1919), Part I.—Turtles, Crocodiles, Lizards, and Chameleons, pp. 385–624.

Shaw, Ralph J. and Francis M. Baldwin: "The Mechanics of Respiration in Turtles." *Copeia* No. 1 (1935), pp. 12–15.

Siebenrock, F.: "Synopsis der rezenten Schildkröten, mit Berücksichtigung der in historischer Zeit ausgestorbenen Arten." *Zoologische Jahrbücher,* Supplement 10 (1909), pp. 427–618.

Smith, Malcolm A.: *The Fauna of British India, Including Ceylon and Burma. Reptilia and Amphibia.* Vol. 1.—*Loricata, Testudines.* London: Taylor and Francis; 1931.

Waite, Edgar R.: *The Reptiles and Amphibians of South Australia.* Adelaide: Harrison Weir; 1929.

Williams, Ernest E.: "Variation and Selection in the Cervical Central Articulations of Living Turtles." *Bulletin, American Museum Natural History,* Vol. 94 (1950), pp. 505–62.

Yerkes, R. M.: "The Formation of Habits in the Turtle." *Popular Science Monthly,* Vol. 58 (1901), pp. 519–29.

Zangerl, Rainer: "The Vertebrate Fauna of the Selma Formation of Alabama." *Fieldiana: Geology Memoirs,* Vol. 3 (1948), pp. 1–56.

Snakes

(Suborder Serpentes)

General Account

✻

ORIGIN AND STRUCTURE

SOME OF the chief attributes of a snake that make it a snake are obvious at a glance: slender form, and lack of limbs, ears, and eyelids. Several characteristics anything but obvious must be added to the picture to make it relatively complete: backward-slanting teeth, lower jaw halves that may be stretched apart where their tips meet, a boxlike brain case contrasted with otherwise loosely connected skull bones (Plate 58), and numerous vertebræ with their attached pairs of ribs (Plate 56).

When we consider these points one by one, we find most of them intimately associated with some snake habit: the lack of limbs, slender form, and great number of ribs and bones of the back with the method of locomotion; the backward-slanting teeth, the separable halves of the lower jaw, and the well-protected brain but loosely connected skull, with the overcoming and devouring of large prey without the aid of limbs. As our approach to anatomy is strictly functional, it will not be necessary to discuss further these characteristics; each will be considered in connection with its associated habit. A functional approach to anatomy, I repeat for emphasis, is one that refuses to separate the structure of any part of an animal from the use to which that part is put by the animal. For example, the elasticity of the attachment of the tips of the lower jaw halves appears, from the human point of view, to be useless, but the sight of a snake devouring an object that forces jaw halves several inches apart gives the character vital meaning. Much descriptive anatomy is dull merely because the mention of function is omitted.

The bones of the snake's spinal column are not only numerous but complex in structure, possessing as they do special parts that hold them firmly together. When a snake is seen to bend with such ease the assumption is that the bones of the back must be loosely joined. That such is not the case can be shown by stretching a dead snake on the ground in a straight line and twisting the tail. It will at once be noticed that at a slight twist the entire body rolls. If the same experiment is performed with the tightest chain of similar proportions, the links move independently of one another to a surprising degree, and the experimenter will realize how closely connected are the vertebræ. A snake bends readily only because there are many bones to take part in the bend, each joint contributing a little.

The stare of a snake is due to its lack of ability to close the eye —that is, to cover it with a movable lid; the eye is permanently protected by a transparent cap. This cap, being continuous with the skin covering the whole body, is shed along with the skin. At first we think how inconvenient this condition is, but further thought will bring to mind many advantages. For example, a snake enters water without the least inconvenience, and of course does not have to run the risk of getting irritating particles in its eye. It manages to sleep with the eyes open, like some human beings. Although a snake has tear glands, it cannot shed its tears the way mammals do.

A snake's ears are even harder to find than its hips; it has no external ear or eardrum. The inner ear is developed, and no doubt sounds carried through the ground are heard well enough, the contact of the snake with the ground being so extensive.

Snakes have been snakes since Cretaceous days, or for at least a hundred million years. They evolved from lizards of the type known today as monitors (Varanidæ) and are therefore the last great reptilian specialization or development. The loss of limbs was not a new idea; various groups of lizards have given up theirs, and even among some living groups of lizards the limbs have a tendency to disappear or become of little use. When the limbs of the snake vanished it was for good; the remnants of the hind limbs in a few primitive types are mere useless tokens of appendages once indispensable. Not only the front legs are gone, but all the shoulder bones that supported them. Obviously, then, it takes more than the lack of limbs to make a snake. Several other important characteristics have already been given.

In contrast to turtles and some other heavy-boned reptiles, the snakes do not leave a good fossil record. This is partly because of the simplified body skeleton, partly because of the slender teeth and delicate skull with many of its bones only loosely joined to the rest. The evolutionary tree of the extinct groups of snakes will never be reconstructed in detail.

AGE, SIZE, GROWTH

DIFFICULTIES IN finding out the length of life of long-lived animals in nature are discussed in detail under the crocodilians (page 15) and mentioned under the turtles. These difficulties are perhaps still greater with the snakes, and again we must rely on records of captive individuals, especially the work by Major Flower. Ten kinds of snakes were included among his fifty-five reptiles definitely known to have survived 20 or more years of captivity. Although five kinds of turtles are included as having lived a century or more, the first snake, an anaconda (*Eunectes murinus*), appears at the relatively low figure of 28 years. The appearance of snakes in the list after this is odd:

At 22 and 23 years the following four species are given:

Boa constrictor (*Constrictor constrictor*)
Reticulate python (*Python reticulatus*)
European leopard snake (*Elaphe situla*)
Long-nosed viper (*Vipera ammodytes*)

At 20 and 21 years:

John's sand-boa (*Eryx johni*)
Madagascar tree-boa (*Sanzinia madagascariensis*)
Madagascar boa (*Acrantophis madagascariensis*)
Indian python (*Python molurus*)
Water moccasin (*Agkistrodon piscivorus*)

It is interesting to note that six of the nine listed species are pythons and boas. This probably proves little because these are, for the most part, large, valuable species that naturally would receive the best of attention.

Major Flower's work, published some time ago (1937), included reptiles kept in captivity anywhere. It is profitable to compare the more recently published (1952) and restricted records (only reptiles kept in the United States) of C. B. Perkins of the Zoological Society of San Diego, California. The five species named below have 20 or more years to their credit:

Anaconda (*Eunectes murinus*)	28 years
Rainbow boa (*Epicrates cenchris*)	27 years
Black-lipped cobra (*Naja melanoleuca*)	23 years
Corn snake (*Elaphe guttata*)	21 years
Reticulate python (*Python reticulatus*)	20 years

The same anaconda appears twice; it lived twenty-eight years in the National Zoological Park of the United States. There is no other duplication of an individual, although one other species, the reticulate python, appears twice. Perkins's entire list includes sixty species that have lived 10 or more years. Other records of interest published here and there do not, as far as I know, alter the conclusion that the potential life span of snakes in general seems to be from 20 to 30 years; they are not even in the same class with the turtles.

When it comes to exaggeration of size, the true rivals of the snakes are the fishes, the only difference being the stimulus to stretch the facts: the person who encounters a snake is subjected to great emotional pressure, and the image sent to the brain is no doubt a false one; the fisherman, on the other hand, merely tries to assert his superior ability. In both cases concrete evidence must be required, and this is seldom forthcoming with snakes of great size. The difficulties of preserving and transporting such giants are insuperable. Added to this is the lack of scientific emphasis on maximum size. It is true that zoos offer large sums for individuals of gigantic proportions, but who will capture and transport such monsters? If it is argued that skinning a snake is relatively easy, here are two answers: a snake hide stretches in a surprising manner even though the skinner makes no conscious effort to stretch it, and, due to the lack of limbs and the generally uniform shape of a skin, many are the fraudulent efforts made to sew two or more together to produce a giant hide; photographs of snake skins are poor evidence because the camera does not reveal well-concealed stitches. It has been shown that the hide of a snake seven feet long may skin out to measure eighteen inches longer and, of course, such a hide could be stretched several more inches. It is patent that a thirty-foot python or anaconda easily *could* be made to yield a hide forty feet long.

Before taking up the vexing problem of the maximum size of the giant snakes, it will be well to dispose of two common fallacies. One of these concerns the so-called "sea serpents," those mythical monsters that make the real sea snakes (Hydrophiidæ) look like midgets. The genuine sea snakes are usually but three or four feet long; nine feet seems to be the greatest length attained by any of them. The other fallacy is that the boa constrictor rates as *the* giant among snakes of the non-mythical type. Actually, the boa constrictor (*Constrictor constrictor*) reaches a maximum length of only 18.5 feet, and must be rated as a giant constrictor of moderate dimensions that rarely grows to be even 15 feet long.

The largest snakes of the different continents (with the exception of Europe, which has no species of unusual proportions) may be listed as follows, with their probable greatest measurements:

Asia: reticulate python (*Python reticulatus*)	32 feet
South America: anaconda (*Eunectes murinus*)	30 feet
Africa: rock python (*Python sebæ*)	25 feet
Australia: amethystine python (*Liasis amethistinus*)	21 feet
North America: boa constrictor (*Constrictor constrictor*)	18.5 feet

One reticulate python 28 feet long weighed 250 pounds, another, but nine inches shorter, only 191 pounds. A 19-foot anaconda tipped the scales at 236 pounds, but she was gravid and gave birth to seventy-two young soon after being weighed; each baby measured about 3 feet 2 inches. It is obvious that a female with eggs or young will weigh an unusual amount, but there is also a marked individual difference due to the general state of health and the amount of food that has been consumed within the previous months.

The king cobra (*Naja hannah*), with a maximum known length of 18 feet 4 inches, is by far the longest venomous snake, whereas the eastern diamond-back rattler (*Crotalus adamanteus*) may be the heaviest. This rattler attains a length of 7 feet 3 inches (without the rattle), a figure that is exceeded by the "black" mamba (*Dendroaspis polylepis*) of Africa (14 feet), the taipan (*Oxyuranus scutellatus*) of eastern Australia (10 to 11 feet), the fer-de-lance (*Trimeresurus atrox*) of tropical America (8 to 9 feet), and the bushmaster (*Lachesis muta*), also of tropical America (11 to 12 feet). I have used the word "may" in referring to the weight of the diamond-back because its close cousin, the western diamond-back (*Crotalus atrox*), attains a maximum length two inches greater, and may equal it in weight, although the western snake seems to be relatively lighter and is, on the average, smaller, the maximum length notwithstanding. Accurate measurements of gigantic taipans, fer-de-lances, and bushmasters are not available, but probably lie within the range indicated; that is, for example, between 120 and 132 inches for the taipan.

Studies of growth in animals have become extremely complicated, so I shall reduce my account to the simplest terms by giving brief answers to such fundamental questions as how fast do snakes grow, does the rate change with age, especially at sexual maturity, how long does it take to reach maturity, and what effect does hibernation have on growth?

Dr. Charles C. Carpenter recently made a valuable study of the growth of the common garter snake (*Thamnophis sirtalis*) under natural conditions in Michigan. Here the snakes do their growing during five months (May through September) and calculations are wisely based on the month as a unit. No significant growth takes place during hibernation, nor for a short time just before and after. In round numbers, the females (the males differ but slightly) are about 6.75 inches at birth and increase their body lengths from 16.2 to 17.6 per cent per month at first; by the time they are 14.5 inches long and approaching sexual maturity, this rate has decreased to 10.6 per cent. When sexual maturity has been reached at from 17 to 18 inches, the rate has decreased one half, and soon after that it is cut in half once more. Snakes 20 inches and longer (the maximum is about 25) are adding only one to two per cent per month to their stature. From all the available data, Dr. Carpenter concluded that females two years old may give birth, and males are able to mate during their second spring, or when less than two years old. The young are born in the summer.

These facts about the common garter snake, which may be considered a typical snake, answer some of those questions well enough: growth is rapid until maturity is reached, when the rate sharply decreases; few years are required for the attainment of sexual maturity; growth ceases for many months of each year in temperate climates. Information on tropical snakes indicates that their growth is not markedly different. The late Felix Kopstein found on Java that three species of snakes belonging to the family in which the garter snakes are placed reach sexual maturity in twenty, thirteen, and eleven months. The common garter snake would be roughly comparable to the first of these, an interesting datum in view of the fact that the tropical species must have a growing-season at least twice as long as that of the Michigan population.

No doubt we must wait some time for data on the growth of the largest snakes living under natural conditions. It is one thing to capture, measure, mark, release, recapture, and remeasure 143 common garter snakes as Dr. Carpenter did, but quite another to do the same with as many pythons, especially those of the largest size groups. Sylvia, an Indian python (*Python molurus*) that I raised from infancy, added three inches to her length every month during much of her first years. This works out to a percentage increase of only half that of the garter snakes; it must be recalled that the latter were living under natural conditions, and the two cases therefore may not be comparable.

HIBERNATION

THE APPROACH of winter puts a snake of a cold country in a predicament for two reasons: food will soon be scarce or entirely lacking, and the temperature will become unbearable. To a warm-blooded animal, the first of these is the more ominous, but to a reptile, with the ability to survive months of fasting, the second is by far the more distressing. A snake has no effective internal heat-producing mechanism as does a mammal or a bird, and therefore must stay in relatively warm surroundings from which to absorb the necessary heat. Nor has the snake ever developed the habit of traveling great distances to warmer regions as has the bird. Countless millenniums of experience have taught it a shorter route to safety: it merely goes a few feet into the ground, which, after all, is easier than crawling hundreds of miles equatorward.

Just how effective is the protection given by those few feet of earth? A bit of concrete information will suffice to answer this question. In southern Montana instruments buried four feet in the ground beneath eight to fifteen inches of snow did not register a temperature lower than 33.8° F., although the air temperature above went down to minus 43° F. These data were taken during a very cold winter. It is obvious that the vast majority of snakes would not have to go deeper than two or three feet to secure ample protection, especially in a region with a heavy snowfall.

During hibernation very little energy is expended, as all the natural processes of living are greatly slowed down. The hibernating snake loses little weight. The duration of the winter sleep depends on the climate; it may last only a few weeks or as long as nine months. With a greatly reduced rate of living and the basic ability to survive at least a year of fasting, the hibernating snake is put to little strain; indeed, one might expect it to "hole up" in its normal state and thus pass the winter like an Eskimo. The reason probably is that an animal with such low intelligence when chilled quickly would be unable to move, and needs an automatic check on its winter activity. A snake is prepared for hibernation by reacting in a complex way to changes in temperature and other external conditions.

The places where snakes spend the winter are varied: animal burrows, cavities beneath boulders or in old stone walls, deep holes in banks or those left by the decay of roots, and various other protected sites. Few snakes live in special "holes" that they construct. Many individuals may enter the same retreat, or the winter may be spent in solitary grandeur. Experiments have shown that some advantage is gained by hibernating together: less moisture is lost by many entwined snakes than by isolated individuals, and in some places the conservation of moisture can be important. Different species often have the same hibernaculum, and such mixtures may even include two kinds of which one ordinarily eats the other.

ENEMIES AND DEFENSE

THERE IS a great deal of talk about the "rule of tooth and claw" and the "struggle for existence" in nature. To the average mind, this word "struggle" always implies physical conflict in the form of fierce battles. Scientific studies are showing more and more that although there is plenty of struggle, it is very often of a much more subtle kind than an open encounter settled by brute force. Among all groups of animals are found masters at the art of bluffing, which is one of the types of subtle encounter. A bluffer that wins a contest is far ahead of an individual that has been forced to use great strength and possibly suffered much physical damage in overcoming an adversary. A truly dangerous animal may be said to "warn" rather than "bluff," a distinction that is not always drawn.

Because some snakes are venomous and most of them bite, these reptiles are commonly thought of as great fighters, but they do more bluffing and fleeing than fighting; the art of bluffing is at least as well developed as is that of fighting. Not a few well able to defend themselves try to avoid a showdown by giving warning. The cobras and rattlesnakes are classic examples of this. The cobra's hood is made by the erection of the ribs, which, in turn, flattens the neck and adjacent parts of the animal. This is a common method that the cobras have developed to its maximum. Many snakes produce a similar alarming effect by inflating as well as flattening the body. Hissing is usually combined with these processes. The bull snakes (*Pituophis*) of North America blow air against a fleshy flap that rises just in front of the opening to the windpipe, and thus make a surprisingly loud sound. This is accompanied by the elevation of the looped front part of the body, a weaving motion of this part, a vibration of the tail, and quick forward jabs with the head. The actual bite is weak; often the snake appears to avoid the seizing of an adversary. Such actions can only be interpreted as bluffing. The "spreading adders" or hog-nosed snakes (*Heterodon*), also of North America, put on the best bluffing performance of almost any snake (Plates 98, 99, and 100, and page 196), and their vicious jabs are nearly always made with the mouth tightly shut.

The expanding or inflating of the body is primarily a way of making a snake appear much larger than it is, and thus enhancing the over-all threatening appearance. A few snakes have a closely related method that merely involves the sudden display of bright colors. This tactic is most impressive when it involves the tail. The snake raises the brightly colored tail, and may even wave it about as other species do the head. The ring-necked snakes (*Diadophis*) of North America resort to this type of bluffing, but its most famous exponent is the red-tailed pipe snake (*Cylindrophis rufus*) of southeastern Asia and the Malay Archipelago (see page 174).

I have gone into the bluffing of snakes with some care because it is so little understood by the layman. Everyone knows how a snake bites by forward thrusts of the anterior part of the looped body. It might be mentioned that the coral snakes (Elapidæ) do not strike, but bite by merely sideswiping the fore part of the body toward the offending object, taking hold, and chewing. The strike of the cobras, also members of the family Elapidæ, does not involve looping of the body; the elevated part of the snake, kept straight, is simply thrust forward and, of necessity, downward (Plates 122, 125, 126, and 127). The result is a relatively inefficient strike, one that can be dodged by many quick animals. This cannot be said about the type of strike that involves a looping of the elevated part of the body (Plate 132).

Oddly enough, the constrictors do not ordinarily resort to constriction in contending with adversaries, reserving this special method for use in overcoming prey.

Various are the tricks used by snakes in attempting to avoid danger rather than bluffing or fighting their way through it. Making a bad odor, hiding the head under the body, rolling into a compact ball, and becoming rigid or motionless (commonly called "freezing" or "playing possum") may be mentioned among them.

Flight and concealment may also be thought of as methods of defense. As explained under locomotion, the flight of snakes is never really fast, but what they lack in this respect is more than compensated for by their art in concealment, especially when enhanced by the type of coloration that matches the surroundings or the kind that "disrupts"—that is, conceals by interrupting the form and thus causes it to blend with the background. Even without aid of special coloration a snake is hard to find. I once released a large pine snake (*Pituophis*) in a field of short grass filled with children, and watched them search in vain for it, although they immediately swarmed over the point of release. This is an experiment that anyone can perform, but preferably with a snake that one wants to release anyway. The snake has an uncanny way of fitting itself into unexpected crannies. For example, a large individual once escaped in a suite of two rooms and a bathroom. Several persons searched diligently and gave up, convinced that a miraculous escape to the outside must have been achieved. The first person to flush the toilet discovered the snake neatly coiled in the bowl itself but just under the overhanging rim, which provided perfect concealment.

The king snake is alleged to be the sworn enemy of the rattlesnake. This dictum is a loose one because there are many kinds of king snakes and even more kinds of rattlesnakes. Nor is a special fondness for rattlers shown by king snakes (*Lampropeltis*): they eat harmless species just as readily. This business of snakes eating snakes is common enough and forces us to rate snakes among the chief enemies of snakes. Such a fact leads some to call snakes cannibals, but a snake that eats a snake is no more a cannibal than is a man when he eats other mammals. A snake must eat a member of its own species to rate as a cannibal in the sense usually given that word. Nothing is more conveniently shaped for a snake to eat than another snake, and no doubt this fact has something to do with the matter. Lizards, worms, and other elongated animals are also frequently devoured.

Mammals must be rated well up among the enemies of snakes. Not only the mongooses eat snakes, but a vast number of other Old World mammals do so as effectively, among them the hedgehogs. These little mammals are so well protected by their spiny coat that they can slowly eat a venomous snake without bothering to kill it first; the victim has no recourse. In the New World numerous widely distributed groups of mammals include snake-eating species. Opossums, armadillos, skunks, badgers, raccoons, cats, dogs, rats, and hogs all take their toll. Man himself is unsurpassed as a snake-killer, and, as he eats them only occasionally, has less excuse than do the other mammals mentioned. The dread that human beings have for snakes is not an instinctive but strictly a learned fear. Such a strong and unreasonable reaction to a harmless snake is indeed unfortunate for the possessor as well as for the subject.

Many birds eat snakes, among them serpent eagles, hawks, road runners, and the secretary birds. The efficiency with which a bird can find and catch snakes was shown by a male serpent eagle that brought to its nest in ten consecutive hours no fewer than six snakes. This observation was made in Germany by Viktor Zebe.

FOOD AND FEEDING

THERE IS nothing about a snake more remarkable than its feeding habits. One would expect the lack of limbs to require special methods in the pursuit, capture, overcoming, and devouring of active prey, but the remarkable aspects of snake feeding do not end there. The ability to swallow large objects (Plate 84), to fast for months with little apparent discomfort, and to subdue formidable prey by constriction, wary prey by venom, are thrown in as additional attributes of a most unusual nature. If snakes had only become herbivorous, they might have avoided the necessity of developing some of these abilities; no plant-eating snake is known, and the eating of carrion is rare. Live, active food is the almost universal bill of fare.

On the face of it, a long, slender body would seem to be ill suited to the taking in of single, large lumps of food, and yet this is just what a snake must do; lacking limbs, it cannot hold the food while tearing it into pieces, and its backward-slanting teeth are wholly unable to chew food objects or do anything but help force them on into the throat. The size of the thing being swallowed is of great importance; if it is too small, the swallowing mechanism fails to get a grip, and the prey, being still active, may simply escape as fast as it is swallowed. If the object is relatively large, the grip is much better and swallowing goes on apace. The upper limit of size is the astonishing thing, but this is the aspect that has been well publicized; everyone has seen pictures of pythons with enormously distended stomachs. Whereas these pictures are by no means faked, they do not represent the typical state of affairs. A snake that devours such big prey is rendered all but incapable of locomotion and concealment, and the human being that discovers it will go to endless pains to take a photograph. A snake twenty-five feet long will readily swallow a mammal weighing seventy-five pounds, or about half as much as the snake. But it is not so much a matter of the weight as it is of the shape of the mammal; the more elongated it is, the better for the snake. As most mammals are not long in proportion to their thickness, the snake has trouble in getting around them. It is easy for a snake to devour another snake of equal weight, because the former does not have to stretch much in any one place. The presence of horns or antlers is a great disadvantage. No doubt the broad shoulders of man account in part for the extreme infrequency of cases of adult human beings falling victim to large snakes; in fact, I am not aware of any well-authenticated case of one actually being swallowed.

A snake is able to swallow relatively large objects without help of limbs chiefly because of the elasticity of the skin, the loosely connected bones of the jaws, and the arrangement and form of the teeth. Once the prey is seized, the backward-sloping teeth sink into it; the more it struggles, the deeper they sink. The snake then begins the so-called "walking movement" of the jaws: to get an advanced grip, each jaw half is shifted forward more or less independently of the three others. The snake literally pulls itself over the object somewhat as a housewife pulls a pillowcase over a pillow. A copious flow of saliva helps, but saliva is never spread over the victim before swallowing is begun, as popular belief has it. The discovery of well-salivated prey that has just been thrown up by an alarmed snake has led to this belief. When the object is very large, the lower jaw halves become widely separated where they meet in front, and are pushed down and away from the rest of the skull along their entire length. Careful examination of a skull will show how this is possible. The throat muscles soon take over and help force the prey along until sidewise bending of body and throat push it as far down as necessary. Digestion begins at the end farther in while the opposite end of a long object is still in the throat. An animal as resistant to death as a frog may remain alive while its feet are being digested away if they were swallowed first.

Two further points should be noted. The tongue (Plate 95) plays no part whatsoever in the process of swallowing; it rests the while in a sheath of the lower jaw. To avoid suffocation while devouring a large animal (hours may be consumed in the process), the snake pauses periodically and pushes its well-reinforced windpipe forward far enough to allow a few deep breaths to be taken. Sylvia, the Indian python that I raised, always took longer to swallow the first than the subsequent rats of one meal. Apparently the swallowing-mechanism is so complex that it needs to be "warmed up."

Under the section on locomotion (page 155) it is stated that snakes are not fast crawlers, and it can be added that their sight is not especially good. How, then, can they find their prey? This they do largely by trailing it. In trailing they use a combination of the tongue and a special organ of smell, Jacobson's Organ. This lies in a cavity located far forward in the roof of the mouth, and has the same origin as the nose organ. The tongue is flicked out along the trail, and particles picked up by it are carried to Jacobson's Organ. Thus the snake follows the scent by means of the tongue, which itself lacks a sense of taste. Here is also an explanation of the constant flicking of the tongue, an action taken as an ominous sign by those who believe that the tongue is a stinger. Large snakes, especially, are commonly thought of as lying in wait for prey, and certainly any animal that thrives on a few meals a month has plenty of time for ambushing. Just how often this method is used no one knows.

Snakes have not entirely passed up the possibilities in lures. The young of a few pit vipers, the copperhead (*Agkistrodon contortrix*) of the United States among them, entice prey by wiggling a brightly colored tail tip. Oddly enough, similar tails in certain other kinds of pit vipers are not wiggled, presumably because the prey is not of the type readily enticed by wormlike tails.

After a snake has approached or been approached by its victim, the problem of capture and overpowering presents itself. Broadly speaking, the snake may be said to employ one of four methods: simple seizure, overpowering by sheer weight, subduing by constriction, overcoming by injection of venom.

The first of these is the most common; supposedly all snakes use it at times; some of them perhaps use no other. Prey that is relatively small, weak, and inactive is simply seized and swallowed alive even by the large constrictors. Overpowering by sheer weight involves use of the entire body, but not in the refined manner of constriction; the victim is seized and held down by the weight of the coils. Great numbers of species of moderate size use only this or the first method.

Photographs of ten or more uniformed zoo keepers stretching out a huge python give an exaggerated idea of its strength; few readers would stop to think that mere length has a lot to do with the necessity for so many men. Coupled with the belief that snakes are powerful is the one that a giant constrictor crushes its victim with tremendous force, breaking its bones and making a "pulp" out of it. Examination of victims and a little thought will serve to dispel this misconception. A mammal or bird seized by a snake is at once thrown into a state of panic, and struggles violently to escape. This makes its body call for a lot of oxygen. The snake merely has to take advantage of this by throwing its coils snugly about the thorax or chest and keeping them that way. Each time the prey expels its breath, the renewed snugness of the coils prevents expansion, and the inevitable result is suffocation. The friction of one of the predator's coils against another makes it all but impossible for even the strongest prey to resist. Thus, the snake, with a minimum of effort, can overcome the most powerful mammal. The problem is to get the coils in position, and this is accomplished with incredible speed that contrasts sharply with the usual movements of the constrictor. Cold-blooded animals are not so readily killed by constriction, but they seem to be quieted by it and sufficiently subdued to allow themselves to be swallowed. Many snakes besides the large constrictors (pythons and boas) have developed the habit and ability to a considerable degree. Among them the king snakes (*Lampropeltis*) of the New World are noteworthy. Constriction must be an ancient serpentine way of getting a meal, as it is used by such primitive snakes as the boas and pythons.

Finally, the snake came to its last stage in this business of getting a meal with the minimum of effort. Making use of what it already had, many teeth and a copious supply of saliva, it developed some of the former into hypodermic needles, some of the latter into venom. No longer was brawn required; the rattlesnake, for example, achieves with one jab (Plate 64) what the boa constrictor accomplishes with risk of injury and with great physical effort. But this did not occur in one step: the teeth first became grooved, the saliva slightly toxic; the grooves deepened until their edges met, and certain salivary glands became specialized for secreting venom.

It has already been stated that snakes eat only animals, and that snakes are perfectly shaped to be eaten by snakes. Lizards can, of course, be added to this assortment of conveniently shaped victims. David Fleay, Director of the Fauna Reserve of West Burleigh, Australia, writes of a captive eight-foot Australian black-headed python (*Aspidites melanocephalus*) that devoured more than a hundred venomous snakes, one of them about equal to it in size; their bites had no effect. Mammals and birds fall victim to a great variety of species, as do fishes, the sea snakes (Hydrophiidæ) subsisting entirely on them, especially eels. Going down in the scale, we find that the invertebrates are also eaten in great numbers, especially the insects. Crustaceans, such as crawfishes, are not avoided; one water snake of the United States (the queen snake, *Natrix septemivittata*) even specializes in a diet of crawfishes.

The vast majority of snakes do not specialize thus, nor do they have jaws or other parts especially constructed for the handling of one particular kind of food. There are, however, interesting exceptions, and two of them warrant brief mention here. The classic example is the egg-eating snake of Africa (*Dasypeltis scaber*) (Plate 84). In this reptile, projections of the backbone may enter the esophagus; they work like teeth in dealing with the birds' eggs on which the snake lives (see page 190).

The other notable example is the subfamily of snail-eating snakes (Dispsadinæ) found in the New as well as in the Old World. Their teeth are long, slender, and extremely delicate, but well suited to pierce the soft mucus-covered bodies of snails and slugs (see page 186). The lower jaw lacks one structural point that, in most snakes, permits stretching; presumably great elasticity of the lower jaw is not a useful attribute in the swallowing of soft, sticky objects. A snail is seized close to the shell and drawn from it by special chewing movements, the act being accomplished in a minute or two; a slug is swallowed forthwith.

REPRODUCTION

DEALING WITH reproduction in snakes is far more difficult than dealing with it in turtles because the snakes do not follow one simple pattern. From courtship through hatching, these limbless reptiles show a surprising amount of variation in behavior, and we shall be forced to skip whole aspects of the subject and treat others sketchily. A great deal has been learned within the last few decades, and new discoveries are being made constantly. The combat "dances" of male snakes can be cited as an example of a startling recent discovery. These have been mistaken for courtship, and their exact significance is as yet undetermined. There may be rivalry over a mate, a form of territorial rivalry, or a combination of the two. One of them is described on page 209, and others are illustrated in Plates 111 and 137.

The reproductive organs in male snakes are remarkable in structure, location, and use (Plate 57). Instead of having a single penis to effect implantation of the sperm in the female, the snake has two similar organs, each of which is usually called a "hemipenis," and both are housed in the tail rather than in the body. A hemipenis, or penis, as I shall call it, at rest is turned outside in like a glove finger that has been drawn into the palm of the glove. A muscle in the tail pulls it into this resting position. When in use, the penis is forced out so that the surface that was inside lies on the outside. This surface is often beset with spines, a condition that makes the turning-inside-out process necessary to avoid injury to the female upon withdrawal. Instead of passing down a tube extending through the organ, the sperm move along a deep groove in its surface, the depth of the groove being great enough to make it serve as a tube. In some snakes, each penis is itself forked, both forks being excessively slender. One organ is inserted at a time, the choice depending on which side of the male's body happens to be brought against the female. The widely used term "hemipenis" probably originated with the belief that the two penes were necessarily used at once, the groove in one forming with that in the other a tube down which the sperm swam.

The penes of snakes have been observed by human beings since time immemorial; they are the "legs" so often forced into view by the cruel country practice of burning the snake. Many a student of science has been fooled by seeing them in an embryo of a snake and taking them for legs; they are drawn into the tail shortly before hatching or birth. In contrast to this familiarity with the structure in the males, next to nothing is known about corresponding conditions in the females. Certainly they must have suitable receptacles for the penes. Students of snake anatomy have shown little interest in the female, although hundreds of penes have been described.

The male snake must arouse the female before mating, a procedure known as courtship. The little known about snake courtship indicates that a few different types of it exist; in some the male may actually seize the female in his jaws. I shall confine my account to one common type of courtship and copulation, that practiced by the common garter snake (*Thamnophis sirtalis*) of North America.

The excited male begins by rubbing his chin along the female's back, usually toward her head, until their bodies are parallel and close together, their anal regions opposite. Often many males gather around one female and jockey for the cherished position, but there is never any fighting among them. As soon as a male has attained the proper position, convulsive waves pass forward along his body at the rate of one every few seconds, or more frequently. After each series of from three to six waves, a short period of rest intervenes. Actual union is accomplished by a quick maneuver that follows five to ten or even many more minutes of courtship. The male pushes his mate's anal region up with a wedge of his own body, and instantaneously inserts the penis of the adjacent side. The waves now cease to pass along his body, and the female crawls about slowly, often dragging her mate, their bodies having lost their extensive contact. The pair usually remains attached fifteen or twenty minutes. A single male has been known to make three fruitful unions in a period of eighty minutes.

In many higher animals the recognition of male by female or vice versa is simple because of a marked difference in form or color. In snakes, the sexes are nearly always so much alike that recognition must be accomplished in some other way. There is general agreement about the sense of smell being used (probably via tongue and Jacobson's Organ), but experimenters differ as to what gives rise to the odor; in some snakes it appears to come from the skin, in others from the secretion of the anal glands. Many male snakes have tiny tubercles on the chin and knobbed ridges near the anus, these apparently helping in courtship and mating. The former serve to arouse the males themselves, the latter assist the males in adjustment of the anal region at the moment of insertion.

Although most snake mating of temperate climates undoubtedly takes place soon after emergence from hibernation in the spring, it is now known that males are able to and do mate some during the other warm months of the year.

Recent studies of snake sperm (male reproductive cells) have shown that they will live in the body of the female for as long as five months, and certainly retain for one month their ability to fertilize an egg. More surprising still is the fact that a female snake (*Leptodeira annulata* of the warmer parts of the New World) laid fertile eggs five years after its last possible mating. Various confirm-

atory reports have come from different parts of the world. Obviously, in snakes, it is wrong to consider the gestation period (time from fertilization to laying or birth) as the time between copulation and laying or birth. Snakes share with turtles and lizards this ability, excessively rare among other higher animals, to delay fertilization or, possibly, development.

Parental care has never developed in snakes beyond the guarding of eggs, the live-bearing species showing no interest in the young. The females of many egg-layers remain coiled about their eggs, and some even defend them vigorously. There is evidence that the Indian and king cobras of Asia (*Naja naja* and *Naja hannah*) pair during the breeding-season and take turns guarding their eggs. This is perhaps the highest development of parental behavior among snakes, although the temperature increase of the incubating python deserves mention. A captive African rock python (*Python sebæ*) was found to have, while incubating its twenty eggs, about six Fahrenheit degrees of temperature. Another study failed to show an increase in temperature of an incubating python of a different species. Again we need more information. In spite of what a few cobras and pythons may do, the snakes as a whole show little concern for the coming generation. A hatchling or newborn snake is well able to care for itself, and will even live as long as a year without any food whatsoever.

When it comes to the actual method of bringing offspring into the world, snakes have been great experimenters: they have tried everything, so to speak. Eggs are laid by the majority of kinds, the rest giving birth to the young. In the United States there are about three egg-layers (Plate 104) to two live-bearers. However, the relative numbers of the two groups vary from one part of the world to the other. Perhaps the oddest thing about the method is that a live-bearer may be very closely related to an egg-layer. So inconsistent is the method of producing offspring that it is little used in the classification of snakes.

It has often been stated that all snakes are essentially egg-laying, those that produce the young directly simply retaining the eggs in the body until they hatch. There is some truth to this because in a few egg-laying kinds the greater part of the embryonic growth normally takes place before the eggs are laid, and a slight delay may cause the eggs to hatch in the body of the female. Recent studies of the live-bearing snakes have shown that some of them are far removed from the egg-layers and are truly viviparous like the mammals. That is, the embryo grows in vital contact with the parent by means of a placenta. Certain snakes of two different families (sea snakes, Hydrophiidæ, and cobras and coral snakes, Elapidæ) have been thoroughly investigated. Just how many of the innumerable remaining live-bearing species will prove to be truly viviparous remains to be seen. There are three adjectives commonly used in describing the ways of bringing forth young: oviparous, ovo-viviparous, and viviparous. Because these terms are confusing, have been used inconsistently, and much remains to be learned about development in snakes, I have avoided them as much as possible. An egg-laying snake that has a long incubation period may be called oviparous; a snake that has been shown to develop a true placental relationship with its embryos may be called viviparous; the remaining snakes may well be tentatively described as ovo-viviparous.

The number of young produced at a time by snakes varies greatly from species to species and, especially among those that produce large numbers, from individual to individual. It is also a rule that the younger females lay fewer eggs. The pythons seem to be the most prolific, some species laying as many as 100 eggs at a time; the Indian python (*Python molurus*) has been known to deposit 107. This species may also lay only a fraction of this number. The correlation between size of the kind of snake and number of young is not very close. The common garter snake of the United States (*Thamnophis sirtalis*) is only about two and a half feet long and yet the number of young in a brood may be in the seventies. The average size of a brood is but 26. There is evidence that a female of this species can give birth for at least sixteen successive years; therefore an individual might well bring forth 500 young during her lifetime. Another big producer is the elephant trunk snake (*Acrochordus javanicus*) that ranges from southeastern Asia to northern Australia; its record number for a birth is 72. Some vipers also rate high in this respect: Russell's viper (*Vipera russelli*) of southeastern Asia has been known to bring forth 63 young at a time. The tiger snake of Australia, *Notechis scutatus*, has a record equaling that of the elephant trunk snake. It is always the greatest numbers that are the most interesting. Probably the average number for snakes in general is 10 or fewer, and some kinds produce no more than 3 or 4.

Snake eggs have certain characteristics in common (Plates 89 and 104). All of them are circular in one cross section, oval in the other. The more slender species may lay eggs with one diameter three to four times as great as the other. All snake eggs are white or nearly so (cream) in color; as they are invariably concealed, they do not need a protectively colored shell like that of many bird eggs. All snake eggs have tough, parchment-like shells formed of layers of minute fibers, the fibers of one layer lying at right angles to those of the next. The fibers are laid down while the egg passes through long tubes (oviducts) in the female. Calcium carbonate is deposited in the outer layers, giving the egg its granular surface. The size of the egg varies roughly with that of the snake and the number produced at a time. The average egg of the Indian python (*Python molurus*) measures 4.75 inches in its greater diameter, which is about twice that of the lesser. A blind snake (Typhlopidæ) with a body diameter of only an eighth of an inch necessarily lays a truly minute (though surprisingly elongated) egg. The eggs of a single clutch that come in contact when laid, stick together; a coating of a secretion from the oviducts dries to form an adherent.

A snake's nest, compared with that of a bird, is scarcely worthy of the name. Or, we might say, where the snakes left off the birds began, the best snake nest being roughly comparable to a primitive bird nest. It is now recognized that the king cobra (*Naja hannah*) does construct a true nest; although it looks like a heap of leaves, it has two compartments: one below for the eggs, the other above and separate for the guarding parent. The vast majority of snakes do no more nest-construction than a simple shaping of a suitable cavity for reception of the eggs, including, in some cases, room for the brooding parent.

The sites chosen differ enough to defy generalization. Common requirements are soft material such as leaf mold or other decaying vegetation; sawdust or other lumberyard debris; decaying logs; manure piles; or just soft earth. Natural cavities such as animal burrows, holes in old walls or buildings, or those left by decaying roots are often used. Some species resort to situations where heat of decomposition will increase the rate of development of the eggs. The ringed or grass snake of Europe and adjacent regions (*Natrix natrix*) is the most familiar example of a snake that apparently recognizes the value of such warmth. This species is also famous for the habit of the gathering of many females to lay at one site. As many as three thousand eggs, probably including some three hundred clutches, have been found together, and there are frequent reports of hundreds of eggs in one place. The ring-necked snake (*Diadophis punctatus*) of the United States and Canada is another species that may group its clusters of eggs, but the aggregates produced by it are on a modest scale compared with the European grass snake, which is very exceptional.

As snake eggs develop, they absorb moisture and swell. The tension thus produced no doubt facilitates in some way escape of the young, but the egg tooth, a purely temporary toothlike structure that projects from the tip of the snout, is the chief means of escape. As the young snake moves about, this cutter makes long slits in the shell. The hatchling does not at once crawl out to freedom, but lingers for hours as if reluctant to enter the world; thus the hatching of an entire clutch may take two or three days. The egg tooth has also been noted in live-bearing snakes; here apparently it no longer serves a purpose, the snakelet escaping from the delicate, transparent birth membrane by means of its struggles alone. The escape may be made at once, or not until hours have elapsed. The newborn or hatchling snake sheds its skin soon after freeing itself from birth membrane or eggshell. Shedding may take place at once, or it may be delayed for as long as two weeks; it usually occurs in about four or five days.

LOCOMOTION

How DOES a snake get about? This is a problem so complex that even experts have until recently disagreed on certain important aspects of it. Agreement has been reached at last, and the crawling of snakes can be reduced to four types of locomotion, which I shall treat in the order of importance to snakes.

The horizontal undulatory, lateral undulatory, or serpentine movement is the usual way a snake has of moving over the ground. In this type of crawl the body is kept in a series of curves just as in swimming. The entire animal seems to flow along, every part of the body following the winding track. If the crawling is done in sand, the track consists largely of curved piles of sand. Here is the key to the method: the body of the snake pushes at the rear of each curve and this push piles up the sand as the snake moves forward. If the surface is perfectly smooth, the snake simply remains "swimming" in its tracks. The same thing would happen in dust too light to give support to the forward thrust. All snakes rely on this method for much of their locomotion. The conventional illustration of a crawling snake, especially those pictures in old books on natural history, attempt to show the snake using this method, but commit the error of making the body curve up and down instead of from side to side. No snake can crawl in such a way; the body must be kept flat against the ground.

The horizontal undulatory crawl can be demonstrated easily. Place a snake on a smooth sheet of glass, preferably one with a lightly oiled surface. After watching it attempt to crawl there, fix a row of pegs across the glass and see how readily it now moves by making use of these pegs.

The caterpillar or rectilinear crawl is used by many heavy-bodied snakes on the prowl and at certain other times. The body is kept straight, and of course the track is just as straight. The belly of most snakes is covered with narrow scales that cross it and are well overlapped. This overlapping permits considerable expansion and contraction in a forward and back direction. In the caterpillar crawl, whole sections of the belly scales are raised slightly and moved forward before being put down again. This goes on along the body in waves like those that seem to flow down the body of a caterpillar as it moves.

The mention of the caterpillar is apt because the innumerable ribs of the snake have often been thought of as concealed legs taking part in this type of crawl just as do the legs of the caterpillar. The snake was described as "walking on the ends of its ribs." This was a reasonable supposition, but it has been shown that the ribs do not take part; the skin, and to some extent the muscles attached to it, move independently of the relatively fixed ribs. There is another even more prevalent misconception about this type of crawl. It is usually said that the free edges of the belly scales take hold; these edges are in fact extremely delicate and are not used separately to catch on roughnesses on the ground. A heavy snake easily crawls caterpillar-fashion over the smoothest surface in spite of the lack of anything for the edges of the scales to catch on; it is merely a matter of friction between the scales and the surface below.

Almost any snake can progress by throwing its body into a series of curves, alternately straightening out the forward part and then bringing up the rear. This, called concertina locomotion, may be thought of as an auxiliary to the others.

The final and truly fascinating type is sidewinding or crotaline crawling. It is used chiefly by desert snakes and enables them to move effectively over loose sand, which yields to the thrusts of horizontal undulatory crawling and thus reduces not only the efficiency of the effort but the speed of progress. A study of this method is recommended for anyone who likes to be confused. The sidewinder (*Crotalus cerastes*), a rattlesnake of our own southwestern deserts and those of adjacent Mexico, is a master at this type. When one of these snakes moves, it seems to flow sidewise or obliquely over the sand. Examination of the track will show that it is a series of almost straight, disconnected, but parallel impressions, proving that the snake is bounding or rolling along with much of the body off the ground a great deal of the time. No piles of sand are produced, and therefore no effort is lost in horizontal thrusts. It may or may not help to know that a length of wire twisted into slightly less than two turns will, when rolled over the sand, leave a similar track.

Other classes of locomotion used by snakes in either fact or fancy are swimming, climbing, and flying. Swimming has already been mentioned, and appears to be a more or less natural ability of snakes, due no doubt to the similarity between the ordinary motions of swimming and those of horizontal undulatory crawling. A snake put on water merely starts crawling in its ordinary way without even assuming a special position. The extended distribution of the weight on the surface helps tremendously. In order to swim, so many other animals must take an unusual position and move the limbs in a special way.

Like the ability to swim, the ability to climb is possessed by snakes in general. A snake in climbing actually uses movements based on the types of ground crawling with the exception of side-winding. The type used is modified to fit the situation. Here again the concept of a snake winding itself around a pole like a ribbon is entirely wrong. To ascend a slender pole (it must not be *too* smooth) the snake uses a modified concertina method, which in this case, is better thought of as progress by a series of alternate hitches and releases; the hind part of the body grips while the forward part reaches up to get its hold.

The ultimate in climbing is attained by snakes—species of rat and chicken snakes (*Elaphe*), for example—that ascend a straight, vertical, limbless trunk of a tree too big to be conquered by the method just described. The trunk must have a rough bark. A climber slowly but surely pushes its body up by a modified lateral undulatory movement (in this case the term horizontal would not seem appropriate). But like the telephone-pole workman with spikes on his legs, the snake that climbs well in this way has specially made belly scales that form an angle extending along either side of the belly. This angle gives each scale two corners that readily catch on the roughnesses of the bark and afford good support to the body. A few species have long, slender bodies light enough to be supported by leaves and small twigs of thick vegetation, especially that of tropical regions. Snakes of this form crawl about at will through any plant growth strong enough to hold them up. It is merely a matter of their distribution of weight balanced against stiffness of leaf and twig.

There is little talk of flying snakes in the New World, whereas in the Asiatic and Malay island regions certain tree-loving species— the golden tree-snake (*Chrysopelea ornata;* Plate 82), for example —are commonly said to "fly." The belief is based on an ability to leap from trees and hold the body more or less parallel to the ground so that the resistance of the air breaks the speed of the fall, allowing the snake to glide or volplane to earth. The snakes that do this have slender bodies that they greatly flatten and even make somewhat concave along the lower or ventral side.

Snakes are commonly thought of as fast travelers, but this is just another false belief based on two facts: the moving snake is usually perceived by a mind under emotional tension, and the places commonly frequented by snakes are prone to produce an illusion of rapid motion. Drive a car down a lane with trees crowding on either side and then drive at the same rate across a bare plain or a desert; you will see that the car on the lane seems to be speeding, whereas in the open country it seems to be barely moving. A snake crawling through grass or bushes is comparable to the car running down the lane.

Careful experiments have shown that the notorious coachwhip (*Masticophis flagellum;* Plate 103), a fast species, moves at a rate of only three miles per hour, and prowls at a much slower one. Allowing for the difficulty of persuading a snake to make its best time during an experiment, we still conclude that the speed of a snake is anything but great. Moreover, a fast-crawling snake quickly tires because of the slow rate of oxygenation of the blood. Snakes ordinarily crawl at what is truly a snail's pace.

I have devoted much space to locomotion because it is so inseparably bound up with the snake's structure and way of life. The snake has lost its limbs and in losing them has developed a mode of life and a form unusual among the higher animals. All signs of front legs and their internal supports have disappeared, and only vestiges, completely useless in locomotion, of hind ones have persisted in a few of the living snakes. The feeding habits of snakes are similarly tied up with this limblessness and odd structure. This subject, considered elsewhere, is mentioned here only to provoke thought while the intimately associated matter of locomotion is in mind.

POPULAR BELIEFS

HAVING TACT and knowing about snakes would not ordinarily be considered as a useful combination of attributes, and yet the two go together very well. Reptile men soon learn that telling the truth about snakes can bring most unpleasant results. Two points are involved in the explanation of such results: nearly all startling accounts of fantastic performances by snakes describe events that took place many years ago, and most persons are more sensitive about reflections on their parents than on themselves. Before making denials, it is well to ask just who saw the performance. In nearly every case the account will involve a parent or even a grandparent. Right here is where the tact comes in; many a narrator will be deeply wounded if not outright insulted by any implication that "Papa" or "Grandma" could tell a falsehood.

Without even going into the matter of what a snake can or cannot do, I shall present strong evidence against the standard snake myths. This evidence is based on two facts: first, as already pointed out, the vast majority of the stories are moldy and consequently cannot be checked; second, they are based on the alleged experience of thousands of observers and therefore *must* be of common occurrence. Only the second fact calls for discussion. If every layman living in the country sooner or later witnesses one of these performances, why do men who spend their lives studying reptiles in natural surroundings, in zoos, or in laboratories fail to do so? Tens of thousands of country people see hoop snakes rolling about like hoops, but these snakes quickly stop rolling and crawl when a herpetologist looms in sight. This would be the only explanation for the complete ignorance of the reptile student on the rolling ability of the renowned hoop snake. Herpetologists are still discovering startling snake habits, but rarely are such habits the kind on which myths are based.

Popular beliefs about snakes are in themselves a fascinating study for the anthropologist, the student of folklore, or even the psychologist, though we must confine ourselves to considering them from the point of view of one who wants to separate the scientific wheat from the chaff; they are all chaff to us. There are so many of them and so many versions or variations of most of them that only a few of the most common ones can be taken up. Even these few could be classified in many ways: those that can be verified and those that cannot; those with a grain of truth and those without; those that are harmful to the believer and those that are merely quaint; those based on the behavior of a single species and those of wide application to snakes in general.

I shall review several of the beliefs chosen at random because of their ubiquity or perhaps because they appeal to me.

Mother-snake-swallowing-young-for-protection myth. This one, even believed by some herpetologists, is probably based on the fact that big snakes do often eat little ones of other species, and on the frequent observation of fully developed though unborn young escaping from a badly mutilated parent. The casual observer is usually too frightened or excited to observe accurately.

There is a kind of snake, the "glass" or "joint" snake, that breaks into pieces like a glass rod when struck, but can reassemble itself and be none the worse for the shattering experience. This is based on legless lizards with tails much longer than the body (see page 244 and Plate 219). Many lizards, those with legs as well as those without, readily lose the tail and soon grow a new though inferior one.

The "hoop" snake takes its tail in its mouth and rolls about like a hoop, usually chasing unwary persons and even killing them with the sting in the end of the tail. This is pure or, rather, impure fiction; no snake is known to roll like a hoop, nor does any have a sting in the end of the tail.

The milk snake milks cows. No snake milks cows: the cow would object vigorously because of the snake's sharp teeth; snakes have no ability to suck; the amount of milk that is supposed to disappear is vastly more than a milk snake could consume. The milk snakes, members of the genus *Lampropeltis*, live in the New World, and are often found about farmyards, where they prey on rats and mice (see page 203).

Snakes sting with the tongue. The most elementary knowledge

of snake anatomy will suffice to dispel this belief and show that snakes bite like other reptiles.

Snakes subdue their prey and, on occasion, human beings by charming them with a steady gaze. Perhaps this belief is based on the fact that snakes appear to stare without blinking because they have no movable eyelids.

A snake, though badly battered, or injured in some other way, will not die until the sun sets; at least, the tail will wiggle until then. This seems to be part of a conviction that certain things will not happen until the sun sets or the thunder roars.

The coachwhip (*Masticophis flagellum*), a species of Mexico and the southern United States, whips human beings; these are often chased, wrapped around, and severely lashed. The coachwhip's scales, especially those of the tail and the rear part of the body, strongly suggest a plaited whip, and hence the name. The species is unable to lash with the tail, even though the tail and part of the body may be flung about wildly when a specimen is seized.

The age in years of a rattlesnake equals the number of its "rattles." There is a confusion of terms here; the entire structure carried by one snake is commonly called the "rattle," as is each part of which the whole is made up. It is better to call the whole the "rattle" and each part a "segment." The age of the snake does not equal the number of segments of the rattle because more than one segment is added each year (one at each shedding of the skin) and the terminal ones almost invariably are lost when the snake is only a few years old. The number of segments in a *complete* rattle is, therefore, much greater than the age of the snake in years, and for the vast majority of individuals more than two or three years old, the rattle is incomplete (see page 217).

Belief in snake myths seems to have little to do with individual truthfulness. In the country, nearly everyone "sees" snakes do remarkable things. The situation is comparable to what I encountered as a boy in a rural part of the southern United States: nearly everyone there had seen ghosts. It is about as hard to corner a hoop snake as it is to corner a ghost. Fear of the snake and fear of the ghost prevent rational thought and behavior. The child is not naturally afraid of snakes (I refuse to go into the matter of fear of ghosts!) and therefore should be taught to handle harmless snakes as an antidote to the fear that certainly will be instilled by thoughtless adults.

SNAKEBITE PREVENTION AND TREATMENT

I COME to this section with fear and trepidation because no other subject in this book is so hard to deal with. The snakes themselves are not the only difficulty; a basic trouble is with the human mind. The fear of snakes, the fear of death, and the reluctance of people to learn about snakes are big problems. A little sound learning will largely eliminate all of these. The fear of snakes can be taken care of in advance by good education. Exact figures on the danger of death are hard to give because of varying conditions, but, broadly speaking, the chances of recovery are always several to one; the victim should never give up hope. A combination of these two fears will render a victim (possibly only scratched by a brier or bitten by a harmless snake) all but helpless, and may even cause death.

I shall give advice valid over all the snake-inhabited world. First and foremost, get over your fear of snakes, or as much of it as possible. Many persons can do this by simply handling harmless species a few times; city dwellers should go to the local zoo and ask to be allowed to hold a snake. Do not go on a holiday or week-end; then the keepers are always very busy (Tuesday, Wednesday, and Thursday are good days). Second, learn something about the snakes of your area or of the region you plan to visit: which species, if any, are venomous, what type of country they live in, and how they may be recognized. Third, before working in or visiting infested areas, study the five bits of advice that follow.

Remember that it is the snake you do not see that will bite you. Because snakes lurk where they are most inconspicuous, in and under cover, you are safest when you can clearly see what immediately surrounds you.

Remember that venomous snakes of the New World will not attack or chase you, and that, with few exceptions, the same is true of dangerous snakes of other parts of the world. If you are at a distance slightly greater than the snake's length, you are perfectly safe (unless it is an individual of one of the few aggressive Old World species).

Wear high, heavy shoes and loose, thick trousers (when the danger is great, which will be seldom). These do not have to be absolutely snakebite-proof; anything that gets in the way greatly reduces the effectiveness of the bite.

Watch where you step, reach, or sit; let the eye precede the foot, hand, or posterior—especially the last, for bites on the trunk cannot be dealt with successfully.

Use extreme caution in handling live venomous snakes or examining "dead" ones. A small living snake (less than two feet in length) can be safely examined by maneuvering it with long sticks or long forceps; the larger ones are best left alone. Snakes that appear to be dead often bite, and reflex action of the proper muscles will sometimes cause a freshly killed one to bite. Many a reader will wonder why this last item is included. My answer is simply that the best way to learn how to recognize the local species is to form the habit of examining the dead ones found along the road or killed by you, assuming that you, like most other persons, will insist on killing the venomous ones.

Now we come to the bite itself. The three tough problems that present themselves will be discussed separately.

First of all is the impossibility of telling how much venom has been injected. This has not been fully appreciated in the past because of the unjustified assumption that a snake discharges its full load whenever it bites. Experiments (results not published) performed by R. Marlin Perkins, Director of the Lincoln Park Zoo, Chicago, Illinois, and me convinced us that this is not the case. Beliefs in many odd "cures" for snakebite probably originated in this difficulty. If an appreciable number of individual snakes withhold much of their venom, and, in certain other cases, fail to get a good enough grip to allow efficient injection, almost any "cure" will seem effective to the casual observer.

Second, snake venom, once mixed with the body fluids, cannot be separated from them by any known process. It is frequently assumed that prompt cutting at the site would allow the "pocket" of venom to be drained. The truth seems to be that the affinity of the flesh and its fluids for the venom is so great that nothing short of drastic mayhem is really helpful. Simple bleeding at the site may do little but waste valuable blood. Fortunately the victim does have time, the threadbare statement that action of the first ten minutes is the deciding factor notwithstanding. In the types of bites that do respond to incision, the cutting can as well be delayed until a little swelling provides something to cut; most bites are in or near the hands and feet, parts of the body that have very thin layers of soft tissues and offer ample opportunity for inadvertent damage to tendons, nerves, and blood vessels.

Third, every treatment for snakebite is so drastic that the victim may suffer more from the treatment than from the venom. When bitten by a small snake, one that is not very dangerous, or by a big one that withheld most of its load, the victim might well ponder the desirability of submitting to treatment. The human body can absorb a certain amount of venom, whereas considerable danger goes with all treatment. The rule is that every pound is able to absorb a given amount of venom: a child of fifty pounds is in three times the danger from a given bite as a man of a hundred and fifty pounds. Pure fat must be largely discounted except as a superficial protection preventing the fangs from reaching the more normal tissues; unluckily, snakes seldom bite areas protected in this way.

Snake venom is modified saliva that helps a snake digest its food as well as capture it; digestion of the victim starts even before it is swallowed. The defensive use of the venom probably is secondary, a probability that gives little consolation to the victim of poisoning. Snake venoms are complex proteins not yet fully analyzed chemically, although much has been learned about their effects on animals and even plants. They may be divided into two types: one causing local congestion, swelling, and bleeding by damaging blood cells and rupturing small blood vessels; the other depressing or stopping either lung or heart action or affecting both of these vital organs. The first type is known as hemotoxic or hemorrhagic, or both; the second as neurotoxic. Unfortunately for experimenters and victims, venoms are not pure and can be classified only as predominantly one or the other type. In general, the cobras and coral snakes

(Elapidæ), as well as the sea snakes (Hydrophiidæ), have venoms chiefly neurotoxic in effect, whereas the true vipers and the pit vipers have venoms that mainly attack the blood and its vessels.

Just as there are two types of venoms, so are there two corresponding mechanisms for their injection, that of the cobras and coral snakes and that of the true and pit vipers (Plates 58, 59, 60, 61, 62, 63, and 64). A third and minor type, that of the rear-fanged snakes, will not be described because of lack of space. The venom apparatus of the vipers, the most highly evolved and by far the most efficient of the two major types, is essentially a pair of hypodermic needles and two venom-filled bulbs. The needles (the fangs) are so long that they must be folded backward and upward against the roof of the mouth or else the lower jaw would be pierced; herein lies the chief difference between this and the type, in which the much shorter fangs are permanently erect. The bulbs (the venom glands) lie on either side of the head and are enormously developed. Our analogy breaks down a little here because the venom glands manufacture the venom as well as store it, whereas the ordinary bulb must be filled. One of the nicest things about the apparatus is the remarkable mechanism that permits the periodic (every few weeks) shedding of fangs to take place without rendering the snake unable to bite. The venom duct does not actually enter the hollow fang but covers its base; the new fang may become fixed in place beside the old one so that its own base is likewise covered by the duct.

I repeat here for emphasis that the tongue or "stinger" of a snake has nothing to do with the injection of venom. The most venomous of snakes with its jaws held shut by adhesive tape is entirely harmless, although it can freely extend the tongue.

When a person has been bitten, the first thing that he must find out is whether the snake is venomous. From what I have written about the pair of fangs and from general hearsay, the victim might think that the bite of a venomous snake leaves only two punctures. The complicating factors here are two: coral snakes and certain of their relatives, especially the kraits (*Bungarus*) of the Malay Archipelago and southern Asia, chew in biting; the viper, in spite of its

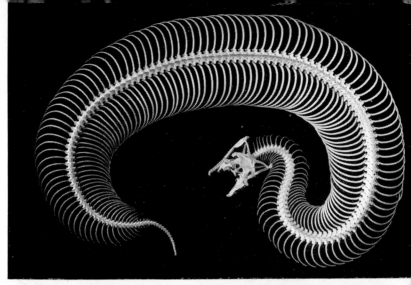

Skeleton of a snake
(Gaboon viper) showing
the numerous ribs and
spines of the back
(vertebræ).

(Courtesy The American
Museum of Natural
History)

Penis of a snake
(banded rattlesnake) in
functional position.
This type is forked and
has spines at the base.
Each rattlesnake
possesses two such
organs.

(Photograph by Howard K.
Gloyd, Chicago Academy of
Sciences)

Skull of a viper
(Gaboon viper) showing
the two fangs (through
which venom is
ejected) and the
ordinary teeth of both
upper (two rows) and
lower (two rows) jaws.
The reserve fangs, which
will later replace the
functional ones, can be
clearly seen.

(Courtesy The American
Museum of Natural
History)

(*Plates 59–64, all high-speed photographs by Walker Van Riper,*
Denver Museum of Natural History)

59.   Prairie rattlesnake (*Crotalus viridis*) biting soft object made to
release flash. A strong bite, not a stab, is indicated here.

60.   Prairie rattlesnake (*Crotalus viridis*) biting soft object made to
release flash. In this case more of a stabbing action is indicated.

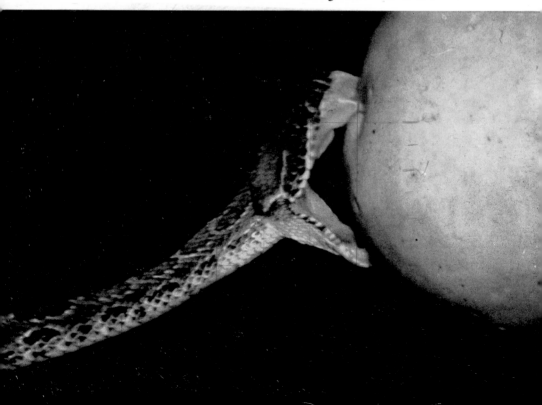

61. Prairie rattlesnake (*Crotalus viridis*) biting soft object made to release flash. The flash was delayed twenty milliseconds after contact, indicating that the action did not terminate in a strong bite.

62. Prairie rattlesnake (*Crotalus viridis*) striking balloon, fragments of which can be seen.

63.   Prairie rattlesnake (*Crotalus viridis*)
withdrawing after striking balloon directly overhead.

64. Measuring the speed of a rattlesnake's strike. This prairie rattler moved at the rate of seven and a quarter feet per second. The target is a warm, soft latex bulb.

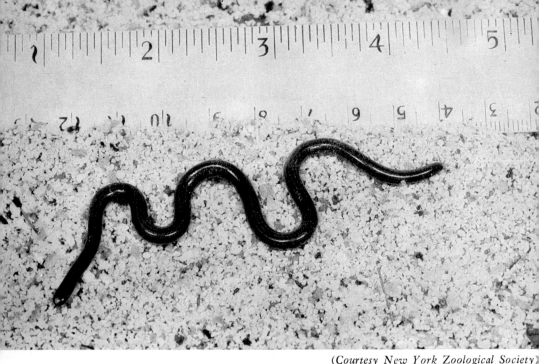

(Courtesy New York Zoological Society)

65. Blind snake (*Leptotyphlops tenella*)
of Brazil, British Guiana, and the island of Trinidad.

66. Loxocemus (*Loxocemus bicolor*). This snake was long considered to be the only python of the New World; now it is recognized as a relative of the sunbeam snake.

(Photograph by Isabelle Hunt Conant)

67. Ball python (*Python regius*).
This African python has an average length of only five feet.

68. Rock python (*Python sebæ*). This, the common African python,
is the largest of the three true pythons found on that continent.

69. Reticulate python (*Python reticulatus*).
This giant is usually considered to be the largest of snakes.

71. Diamond or carpet python (*Morelia argus*).

(*Photograph by Violet Wyld*)

70. Indian python (*Python molurus*). Sylvia and friend Danny.

72. California boa (*Lichanura roseofusca*).
This individual was found near Victorville, California.

73. Boa constrictor (*Constrictor constrictor*).
This is the most familiar of the giant snakes but it is by no means the largest.

74. Anaconda (*Eunectes murinus*).
No other snake of the New World rivals this one in size.

75. Skinning an anaconda (*Eunectes murinus*) twenty-three feet long
on the upper Essequebo River, British Guiana.

(*Courtesy Howard K. Gloyd, Chicago Academy of Science*

76. Cuban boa (*Epicrates angulifer*).
This species eats bats.

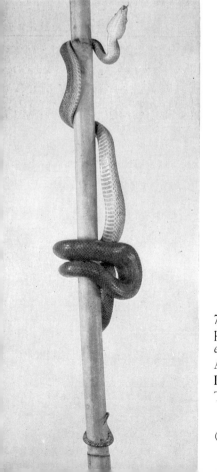

78. Cooke's tree boa climbing a smooth
pole. This is a subspecies (*cooki*) of *Boa
enydris* or *hortulana* and lives in Central
America, northern South America, the
Lesser Antilles, and on the island of
Trinidad.

(*Courtesy New York Zoological Society*)

(*Photograph by Isabelle Hunt Conant*)

77.   Emerald tree boa (*Boa canina*).

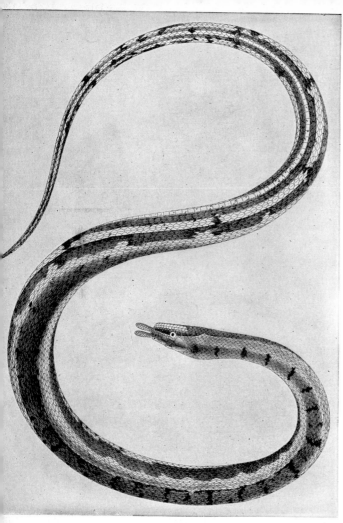

79. Tentacled snake (*Herpeton tentaculatum*). This drawing was made in Italy during the last century as part of an attempt by Jan and Sordelli to illustrate all the snakes of the world. Their monumental, though incomplete, work is now rare and valuable.

80. BELOW: wart or elephant's trunk snake (*Acrochordus javanicus*). The hide of this snake is especially valuable.

(Photograph by Carl F. Kauffeld)

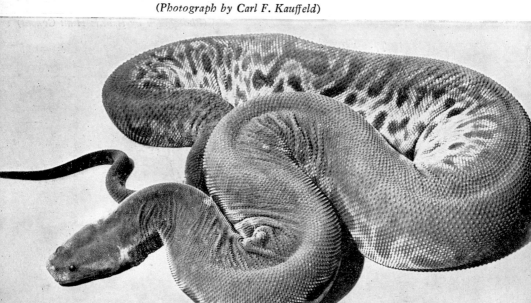

(*Zoological Society of Philadelphia*)

81. Japanese rat snake (*Elaphe climacophora*).

82. Golden tree-snake (*Chrysopelea ornata*). An ability to make long leaps from trees has given this reptile the name "flying snake."

(*Photograph by Isabelle Hunt Conant*)

83. File snake (*Mehelya capensis*).
This species lives in southern Africa.

84. Egg-eating snake (*Dasypeltis scaber*) with egg in throat.

(*Photograph by Isabelle Hunt Conant*)

85.   False cobra (*Cyclagras gigas*). When annoyed, this South
American snake spreads the neck and behaves much like a king cobra.

86.   Vine snake (*Oxybelis æneus* or *acuminatus*). This
arboreal snake, remarkable for its slender form, ranges from
southern Arizona southward to central South America. The
individual shown represents the typical subspecies (*æneus*).

87.   Tropical whip snake (*Masticophis mentovarius*) from El Zamorano,
Honduras. This species ranges from tropical Mexico to extreme northern South
America.

Photographs by Walker Van Riper, Denver Museum of Natural History

88. An immigrant from Ecuador (*Leptophis ahætulla* or *Thalerophis richardi*). It came as a stowaway to the United States with bananas and is bright green in color. Note the threatening attitude with gaping mouth and expanded glottis. 89. BELOW: eggs of the banana stowaway from Ecuador.

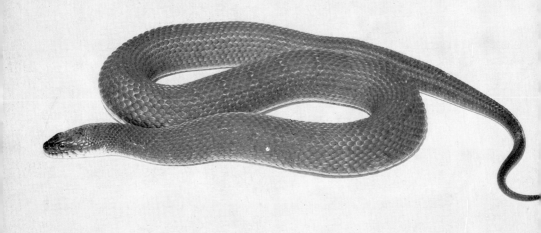

(*Photograph by Isabelle Hunt Conant*)

90.　Plain-bellied water snake (*Natrix erythrogaster*) from the Mississippi-Louisiana region.

91.　Common water snake (*Natrix sipedon*) from Florida.

(Courtesy The American Museum of Natural History; photograph by M. Young)

92. DeKay's snake (*Storeria dekayi*) from the city of New York. One of the most abundant and familiar of our snakes, this small species (average length about ten inches) is exceptionally persistent in cities and their suburbs. It ranges from southeastern Canada southward throughout the eastern United States and on through extreme eastern Mexico.

93. Ribbon snake (*Thamnophis sauritus*). This individual represents the common subspecies of the eastern United States and southeastern Canada.

(Photograph by Isabelle Hunt Conant)

(*Photograph by Isabelle Hunt Conant*)

94. Common garter snake (*Thamnophis sirtalis*) from eastern North America.

95. Western garter snake (*Thamnophis elegans*) from the Great Basin and Rocky Mountain regions of North America. Extended tongue caught with high-speed flash, one twenty-thousandths of a second.

(*Photograph by Walker Van Riper, Denver Museum of Natural History*)

96. Narrow-headed garter snake (*Thamnophis angustirostris*) from Oak Creek Canyon, Arizona. This species is found in Arizona, New Mexico, and northern Mexico.

(*Courtesy The American Museum of Natural History; photograph by H. C. James*)

(*Photograph by Walker Van Riper, Denver Museum of Natural History*)

97. Head of western hog-nosed snake (*Heterodon nasicus*) showing upturned snout and extended tongue, the latter caught with high-speed flash, one twenty-thousandths of a second. This is a species **of** the west-central United States and adjacent Canada and Mexico.

98. Common hog-nosed snake (*Heterodon platyrhinos*) from the eastern United States and adjacent Canada. The head and neck of this individual are spread a little.

(*Photograph by Isabelle Hunt Conant*)

(Photograph by John C. Orth)

99. Common hog-nosed snake (*Heterodon platyrhinos*) with head and neck fully spread

100. Common hog-nosed snake (*Heterodon platyrhinos*).
This one, from Highlands County, Florida, is just starting to play
dead, hence the open mouth and the head blurred by motion.

(Courtesy The American Museum of Natural History; photograph by Charles M. Bogert)

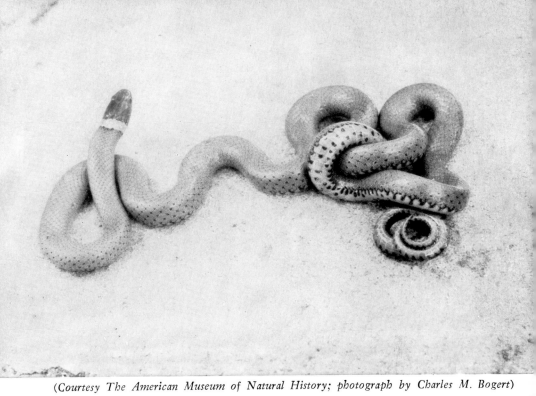

101. Regal ring-necked snake (*Diadophis regalis*) from the Santa Rita Mountains, Arizona.

(Photographs by Isabelle Hunt Conant

102. Racer (*Coluber constrictor*).

103. Coachwhip (*Masticophis flagellum*) from the southeastern United States.

(*Photograph by Howard K. Gloyd, Chicago Academy of Sciences*)

104. Striped whip snake (*Masticophis tæniatus*) from Mimbres, New Mexico, with her eggs. The species ranges from the Rocky Mountain and Great Basin regions southward over much of Mexico.

105. Smooth green snake (*Opheodrys vernalis*).

(*Photograph by Isabelle Hunt Conant*)

(Photograph by Isabelle Hunt Conan

106.   Indigo snake (*Drymarchon corais*)
from the northeastern Mexico-southern Texas region.

107.   Rat snake (*Elaphe obsoleta*) from Brown County, Texas. The species is
widely distributed over the eastern United States and reaches adjacent Ontario.

(Courtesy The American Museum of Natural History; photograph by Howard E. Evans

108. Trans-Pecos rat snake (*Elaphe subocularis*) from the Chisos Mountains, Texas. This species is found only in Trans-Pecos Texas and adjacent New Mexico and Mexico.

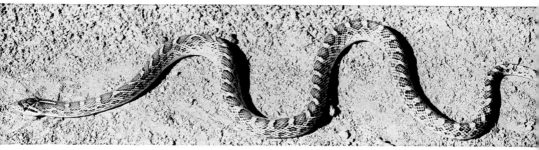

109. Glossy snake (*Arizona elegans*) from seventeen miles west of Saltillo, Coahuila, Mexico. The species is widely distributed in the southwestern United States and northern Mexico.

110. Head of bull snake (*Pituophis catenifer*) showing extended tongue caught with high-speed flash, one twenty-thousandths of a second.

111. Combat "dance" of male pine snakes (*Pituophis melanoleucus*) as photographed in the San Diego Zoo. The battle resembles a wrestling match rather than a punching or biting contest and ends in exhaustion, not injury.

A. The entwining begins.
B. The entwining completed with much tension and hissing.
C. Two pairs of males battle.
D. A throw.

(Courtesy Zoological Society of San Diego; photographs by G. E. Kirkpatrick)

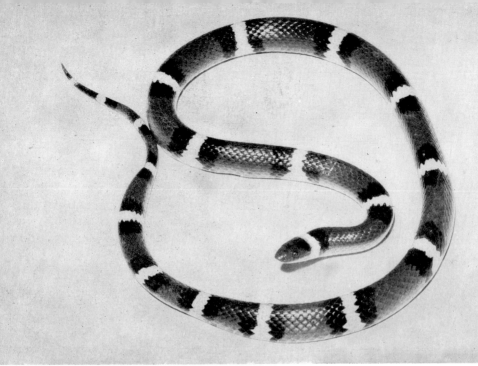

(*Photographs by Isabelle Hunt Conant*)

112. Milk snake (*Lampropeltis doliata*). This species is extremely variable in color from one part of its range to another. The beautiful subspecies shown, the scarlet king snake, lives in the southeastern United States from southeastern Louisiana to southeastern North Carolina. The narrow, black paired bands enclose yellow ones (white in photograph); the wide bands are red.

113. King snake (*Lampropeltis getulus*). This species is extremely variable in color pattern from one part of its range to another. The subspecies shown, the speckled king snake, has a wide range in the south-central part of the United States.

(*Courtesy The American Museum of Natural History*)

14. Long-nosed snake (*Rhinocheilus lecontei*) from the southwestern United States.

15. Ground snake (*Sonora episcopa*) from Brown County, Texas. This species is found in the south-central United States and adjacent Mexico.

(*Courtesy The American Museum of Natural History; photograph by Carl Gans*)

(*Photograph by Isabelle Hunt Conant*

116.   Montpellier snake (*Malpolon monspessulanus*) from the Mediterranean region.

117.   The common coral snake of the United States (*Micrurus fulvius*).

(*Zoological Society of Philadelphia*

118. Central American coral snake (*Micrurus nigrocinctus*) from Honduras. The range of this species extends from Central America into adjacent Mexico and South America. The narrow, light, paired rings are yellow and enclose black ones; the rest of the body is predominantly red.

119. Tiger snake (*Notechis scutatus*). No other land snake has such potent venom.

120. Black snake of Australia (*Pseudechis porphyriacus*).

121. Banded krait (*Bungarus fasciatus*) of southeastern Asia and
the Malay Archipelago. The bands are yellow (or buff) and black.

122. Indian cobra (*Naja naja*) with "hood" spread, showing the "spectacles" pattern.

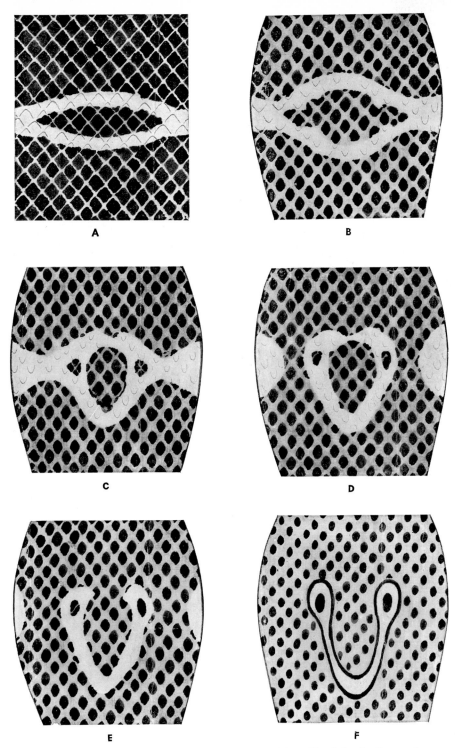

123. Evolution of the "spectacles" on the "hood" of the Indian cobra. Clearly shown are steps in the development of the pattern from a slightly modified body band. The illustration, semi-diagrammatic, is based on a study of cobras from the island of Hainan, China.

(*Drawings by Charles W. Dawson*)

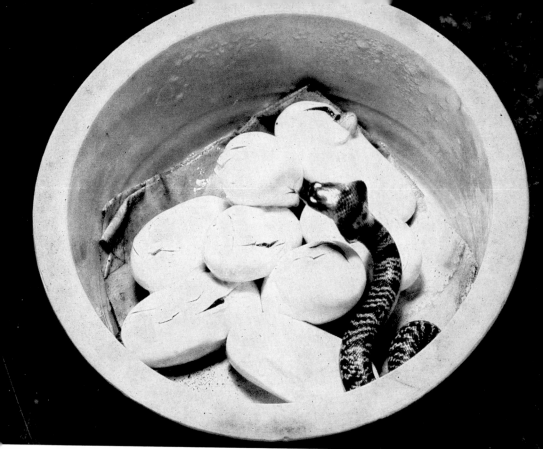

124. ABOVE: hatching eggs of Indian cobra (*Naja naja*) and hatchling. Note slits made in shells by egg teeth of hatchlings. 125. BELOW: hatchling Indian cobra (*Naja naja*) ready and able to defend itself, and egg about to hatch.

(*Zoological Society of Philadelphia*)

126. King cobra (*Naja hannah*).
No other venomous snake attains a length of eighteen feet four inches.

127. Ringhals (*Hemachatus hæmachatus*). This is one of the two
cobras that habitually spits (ejects the venom at an enemy).

(*Photograph by Howard K. Gloyd, Chicago Academy of Sciences*)

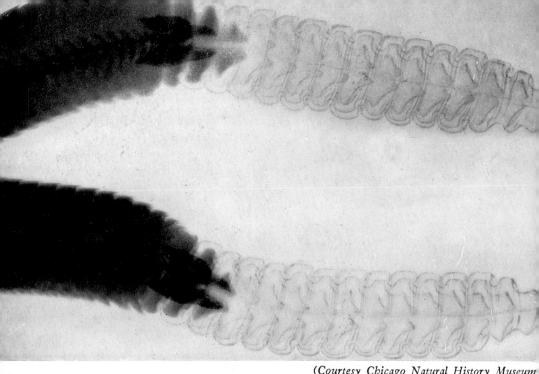

(*Courtesy Chicago Natural History Museum*

128. X-ray of the tail of a rattlesnake (western diamond-back) showing two stages of growth of the same rattle. Distinctly shown is the dark core formed by the coalescence of several bones of the tail. Twelve segments can be seen (more or less clearly).

129. Pigmy rattlesnake (*Sistrurus miliarus*) from Highlands County, Florida. This represents the smaller of our two species of pigmy rattlesnakes.

(*Courtesy The American Museum of Natural History*

(*Photograph by Isabelle Hunt Conant*)

130. Eastern diamond-back rattlesnake (*Crotalus adamanteus*).
Attains a length of seven feet three inches (without the rattle).

(*Courtesy New York Zoological Society*)

131. Western diamond-back rattlesnake and young (*Crotalus atrox*). The picture does not imply parental care.

132. Western diamond-back rattlesnake (*Crotalus atrox*) ready to strike. This individual was found in Pinal County, Arizona.

(*Courtesy The American Museum of Natural History; photograph by Charles M. Bogert*)

(*Photograph by Isabelle Hunt Conant*)

133.   Banded rattlesnake (*Crotalus horridus*).
The color pattern of this species is extremely variable.

134. Tropical rattlesnake or cascabel (*Crotalus durissus*).
This species is perhaps the most dangerous of all rattlesnakes.

135. Sidewinder or horned rattlesnake (*Crotalus cerastes*).
This species is a true denizen of the desert.

136. Shield-headed rattlesnake (*Crotalus scutulatus*).
This species ranges from the highland of central and northern
Mexico northwestwards to southern Nevada and adjacent territory.

A. *The start.*

137. Combat "dance" of male red diamond rattlesnakes (*Crotalus ruber*) as photographed in the San Diego Zoo. The battle resembles a wrestling match rather than a punching or biting contest and ends in exhaustion, not injury.

(Courtesy Zoological Society of San Diego; photographs by G. E. Kirkpatrick)

B. *One male attains superior position.*

c. *Sparring.*

d. *Sparring.*

E. *A throw.*

F. *A throw.*

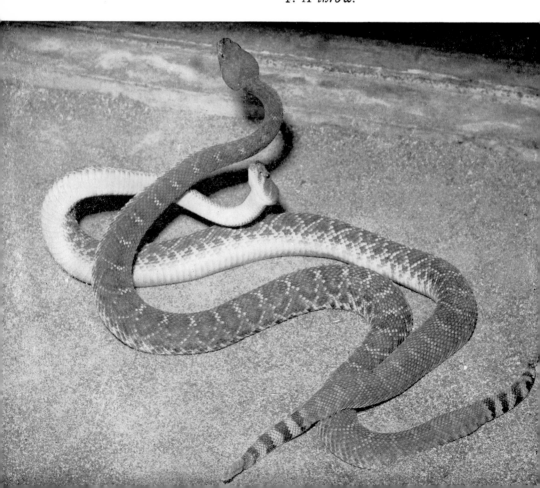

G. *"Dirty" tactics.*

H. *A double fall.*

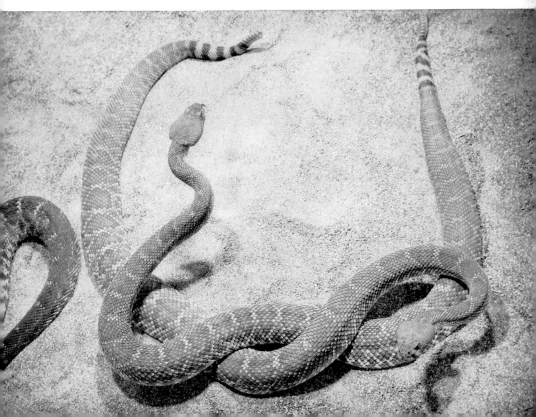

(*Courtesy The American Museum of Natural History*

138. Tiger rattlesnake (*Crotalus tigris*) from the Agua
Caliente Mountains, Arizona. This species ranges from
south-central Arizona southward through the state of Sonora, Mexico.

139. Water moccasin or cottonmouth (*Agkistrodon piscivorus*).

(*Photograph by Isabelle Hunt Conant*

(*Photograph by Isabelle Hunt Conant*)

140.   Copperhead (*Agkistrodon contortrix*).

141.   Chinese viper (*Trimeresurus monticola*) guarding eggs; her nest is in bamboo waste (Fukien Province, China).

(*Photograph by Clifford H. Pope*)

(*Courtesy The American Museum of Natural History*)

142.   Fer-de-lance (*Trimeresurus atrox*) from the state of Hidalgo,
Mexico. This species is the most notorious of tropical American vipers.

143. Bushmaster skin
(*Lachesis muta*) from
Colombia. This male
measured 113 inches.

(*Photograph by Frederick Medem*)

(*Photograph by Isabelle Hunt Conant*)

144.   Neuwied's viper (*Trimeresurus neuwiedi*). This species occurs in eastern and southern Brazil and countries adjacent to southern Brazil.

145.   Two vipers of Central America and adjacent Mexico: hog-nosed viper, *Trimeresurus nasutus*, (also ranges southward in the coastal region to Ecuador), left; Godman's viper, *Trimeresurus godmani*, right.

(*Courtesy The American Museum of Natural History*)

146. Crossed viper (*Trimeresurus alternata*).
This species occurs in southern Brazil and adjacent countries.

147. Jumping viper (*Trimeresurus nummifer*) from
Honduras. This species of Central America and central
and southern Mexico is notorious for its pugnacity and
ability to jump.

148. Arboreal vipers
(*Trimeresurus nigroviridis*).
This predominantly green
species is found in
Central America and
adjacent Mexico.

(*Courtesy The American Museum of Natural History*)

149.　Russell's viper (*Vipera russelli*).
This beautiful but dangerous true viper commonly attains a length of five feet.

(*Courtesy New York Zoological Society*)

(*Photographs by Howard K. Gloyd, Chicago Academy of Sciences*

150. Common European viper (*Vipera berus*). This individual, a male, lived in Germany

151. Sand viper (*Vipera ammodytes*). The range of this species extends from Austria southeastward to Syria.

(Photograph by Hymen Marx)

152. A desert viper (*Cerastes cerastes*) of northern Africa and southwestern Asia has buried itself here in sand, leaving only faint traces on the surface.

153. Puff adder (*Bitis lachesis*).

(Photograph by Howard K. Gloyd, Chicago Academy of Sciences)

(*Photographs by Howard K. Gloyd, Chicago Academy of Sciences*)

154.   Gaboon viper (*Bitis gabonica*). This true viper reaches a length of six feet; it is remarkably docile in spite of a formidable appearance.

155.   Night adder (*Causus rhombeatus*).
This species is widely distributed in Africa south of the Sahara Desert.

long fangs, is apt to pierce the skin with the many ordinary teeth of the upper as well as those of the lower jaw. Most snakes have four rows of teeth in the upper jaw and a pair in the roof of the mouth plus the lateral pair lying just inside the lips; the true and pit vipers lack the lateral pair, which has been replaced by the fangs. Where only two punctures are found, the indication is that the bite is dangerous, but the reverse cannot be concluded when rows of tooth marks are evident. Later swelling is apt to obscure the tooth punctures, but by that time the swelling will have revealed the nature of the bite. If, as already pointed out, the treatments were not so drastic they might be used as a safety measure in doubtful cases.

Coming to the practical matter of treatment, space will allow only generalizations to help evaluate any detailed directions at hand. Not only is there much difference of opinion among authorities, but many specious accounts are in circulation. Perhaps the snakes are at fault. In countries with adequate research laboratories, the death toll is so low that almost no investigators take serious interest in the subject, and progress is slow. If thousands instead of barely a hundred deaths occurred annually in the United States, for instance, the problem would be quickly solved. M. Graham Netting, of Carnegie Museum, Pittsburgh, Pennsylvania, basing his estimate on the conviction that being bitten is a sure "method of getting national coverage," puts the figure as low as twenty-five.

The first consideration is the type of venom involved. If it is neurotoxic or predominantly so, serum treatment is indicated for all severe cases, local cutting and drainage being of doubtful value. In the United States, only the coral snake (*Micrurus fulvius;* see page 207) bite necessitates the serum, and even with its bite the local treatment is often recommended just as a precautionary measure. Serum should be given by a physician or some experienced person who thoroughly understands the dangers involved. A few individuals are killed outright by it, many others get "serum sickness" several days after the injection. This is not dangerous, but very unpleasant. Fortunately, it is subject to control with drugs. Most serums are accompanied by adequate directions, and these include tests for sensitivity to serums. Persons who sneeze when in the vicinity of horses or who are known to be sensitive to horse serum can avoid the use of anti-snakebite serums without bothering to take any tests.

Anti-snakebite serums, known as "antivenins," are available over the world, four being produced for Africa, five for Asia, as many for South America, one each for Australia, Europe, and North America, making a total of seventeen. At least one is available for the most important venomous snakes of each continent, although there is none for our coral snake. The Anti-elapid Antivenin produced in South America should be used for its bite.

If the venom involved is predominantly of the blood- and blood-vessel-damaging type (bites of true and pit vipers), local treatment is effective and should be relied on entirely if the bite is not severe or if the victim is sensitive to antivenin. This treatment is merely an effort to confine the venom and drain it from the body, a tourniquet doing the first, cutting and sucking the second. Both aspects of this effort will be discussed to bring out certain crucial or moot points.

The tourniquet is by all odds the important first-aid measure. Application is simple and proper use involves no pain or danger. Almost any long, flexible thing will do: piece of string, strip of cloth, shoestring, necktie, and so on. Apply it between the wound and the heart but reasonably near the former; adjust it so that only the surface circulation is shut off. A tight tourniquet is not only painful but dangerous, whereas one that does not shut off the pulse in wrist or foot is not painful, and may be left on for hours. It is usually stated that the tourniquet must be loosened at regular intervals, but this is unnecessary if it is not too tight. It must be borne in mind, however, that a constriction about a single bone cuts off the circulation much more effectively than does one about two bones. The upper arm contrasted with the lower is a case in point.

The next thing to do is to get medical help. If this can be done without running, or taking more than an hour, it is best to allow the physician to do the cutting under both aseptic and painless conditions. The bitten person is already under a nervous strain, and subjecting him to painful cutting may not be advisable. I have stated that the first few minutes are not so crucially important as they were formerly thought to be. Pairs of short crossed cuts should be made where swelling is evident, and if it progresses up a limb, these must be continued at the base of the swelling. Bleeding is harmful; the intention is to drain off the lymph mixed with the venom. Mild, even suction should be applied with several suction devices used simultaneously; if suction is too strong, the wounds will be turned inside out, and if the cuts are long, proper suction will be prevented through leakage. This suction, or, rather, slow drainage may have to be continued for many hours, and can be facilitated by sterile hot dressings of epsom salts or boric acid. The tourniquet may have to be shifted from time to time to keep ahead of the swelling. Suction by mouth is not advisable because it cannot be kept up long enough to be effective, and it introduces into the wounds gross bacterial infections.

It might be mentioned here that alcoholic stimulants are in general harmful, and that the wound should never be cauterized or have potassium permanganate crystals rubbed into it.

All ordinary precautions against shock must be taken. Transfusions of whole blood or plasma are necessary whenever acute symptoms develop or the swelling spreads unduly. The physician will have to use his common sense and general knowledge of medicine in deciding what to do after the first few hours.

The chilling method ("L–C Treatment"), recently revived and publicized, has serious drawbacks, as pointed out in detail by Dr. Frederick S. Shannon (see bibliography).

CARE OF SNAKES

IN SPITE of widespread conviction to the contrary, a snake makes an interesting pet and is vastly easier to care for than is a mammal or a bird. It does not, of course, ever become as responsive as does a warm-blooded animal. The first thing to get used to in a snake is its slow or delayed reactions; it may be hungry and yet appear indifferent to food; living for weeks without eating is no strain on the average one. Feeding a snake is perhaps the hardest part of taking care of it, and therefore, in selecting an individual, its readiness to feed should be a major consideration. The fact that it has to be fed only about once a week is one of the reasons why the care of it is so simple. Correlated with this habit of eating at long intervals is that of infrequent defecation and the necessity of cleaning the cage only once in a long while. As a snake is carnivorous, it must live on other animals, and it prefers these alive or freshly killed. This, one must admit, is a difficulty for most owners, and should be pondered well when deciding on the type of pet desired. This difficulty can often be overcome by persuading, usually with expenditure of patience, a pet to take strips of lean raw meat much of the time. Such a diet is not sufficient and should be supplemented with whole animals. A snake in good condition will thrive on regular weekly or biweekly feedings of meat exchanged three or four times a year for a whole-animal meal. A snake kept warm during the winter months will not hibernate but may lose much of its appetite; at such times monthly feedings suffice.

Snakes live well in simple boxes that provide reasonable ventilation and do not have wire netting on which the inmates can rub the snout, a habit all too common in freshly caught specimens. Water for drinking and a flat object, such as a piece of bark or a thin board under which to hide, should be provided, although the latter is not indispensable. The cage or box should be kept dry even though the pet is a water-loving species. The temperature should be maintained between 70° and 80° F., and sunlight must never be allowed to flood the cage completely; snakes like some sunshine and no doubt derive benefit from direct rays, but they absorb heat rapidly, and quickly die if overheated.

All snakes, in spite of apparent lethargy, are natural Houdinis and make the most miraculous escapes. Few persons are wise enough to profit by warning and have to learn the hard way, which is by losing choice pets.

A snake in perfect health is free from sores of the mouth, blemishes of the skin such as blisters, and external parasites such as mites. These are the three defects often found on captives. In addition, the appetite should be good and shedding of the skin should take place every few months. In the best individuals, the skin comes off in one piece; at any rate, all of it should be shed at the same time. For several days before shedding the eyes are bluish or cloudy and the pupil cannot be seen, but the eyes become clear a short time before the actual shedding takes place. A pan of shallow, lukewarm water in which the snake may soak will often help it over this critical time, and some heavy object with a rough surface must be provided for use in getting the skin off.

WHERE SNAKES LIVE

IN GIVING an account of their total distribution we must divide snakes into two very unequal groups just as we did the turtles. The sea snakes, relatively few in number and living in a special environment, are subject to influences differing greatly from those that prevail for the land and fresh-water snakes. The sea snakes range from southern Japan southeastward as far as the Samoan Islands and westward along Asiatic coasts to the Persian Gulf. Only one kind (*Pelamis platurus*) has reached the western coasts of the New World and the eastern coast of Africa. This species is also an exception to the rule of sea-snake distribution in ranging so far south (to the tip of Africa) and so far north (to the northwestern coast of Mexico and, at least formerly, to the Asiatic coast of the U.S.S.R.).

The rest and vast majority of snakes are limited by the necessity of hibernating in the colder parts of the world. This keeps them from entering regions of permanently frozen subsoil. As they are better suited to warmer climates, the number of species increases as the equator is approached. For example, in a relatively uniform tropical forest of South America, as many as seventy-five species may inhabit an area several square miles in extent, whereas a similar area thirty or forty degrees from the equator would scarcely harbor more than a third of that number.

The Arctic and Antarctic are all but devoid of snakes. One species reaches the Arctic Circle in Scandinavia where the Gulf Stream greatly modifies the climate; to the east in Eurasia the extremity of the range lies several degrees farther south. In North America they range as far northward as the latitude of southern Hudson Bay; in the southern hemisphere only the extreme southern part of South

America is without them. The number of species greatly decreases at high altitudes in temperate regions because of the sharp reduction in temperature due to the elevation.

It is a remarkable fact that there are so few marine snakes. The entire Atlantic is free of them, and, in addition to the sea snakes already mentioned, only the two species of the genus *Acrochordus* can be called marine. These two stay close to shore in and near the mouths of rivers; they keep one foot on land, so to speak. The fresh waters of the earth have not been neglected by snakes; water-loving species are found in abundance on all the continents except Australia, with its special development of the family to which our coral snakes belong (Elapidæ).

Few warm land areas are avoided by snakes; open grasslands, rugged mountain terrain, and desert country all have their quota. The hottest deserts come nearest to making an exception, although deserts of a less extreme type are by no means snakeless. Perhaps their greatest development would be found in a warm region of low, rugged mountains interspersed with dissected plains and plateaus. To complete the conditions for a serpentine paradise there should be good rainfall, watercourses of various sizes, and stretches of forest.

Broadly speaking, a terrestrial animal has to live either in the ground, on it, or above it in some type of vegetation. The snakes have made use of all of these possibilities, although species said to burrow usually live near the surface or under flat objects rather than far below the surface. So many snakes habitually conceal themselves when resting that it is hard to draw a sharp line between the true burrowers and those that merely conceal themselves temporarily or spend nearly all of the time just out of sight. Perhaps the best example of a subsurface group is the family of shield-tails (Uropeltidæ) of Ceylon and the Indian peninsula (see page 173).

The vast majority of snakes, including those that often enter fresh water but live very well when kept away from it, dwell on the surface. Arboreal or climbing species may be abundant, especially in some limited areas of dense tropical forests where so many arboreal animals reach their greatest development. Snakes have never developed true flight, although a few kinds volplane to a limited extent. Their ability to do this is considered under the section on locomotion, where the method of climbing is also treated from the point of view of structure of the body and scales (see page 154).

CLASSIFICATION

SNAKES AND lizards are closely related; in fact, they are usually combined to form an order of reptiles, Squamata, whereas the turtles alone constitute an order, as do the crocodilians. When it is recalled that many lizards lack usable limbs and that some primitive snakes have vestigial legs (remnants of hind limbs), this close relationship is more easily understood. Snakes gave up limbs as really useful aids in living, carried an elongate form to an extreme degree, and developed a special type of skull (see pages 129 and 130). "Serpentes" is the technical name of the suborder of snakes.

Snakes themselves are hard to classify because of the lack of limbs, generalized shape of the body, and the circumstance that their skulls do not fossilize well. The student has to depend largely on a comparative study of living types of snakes, some two thirds of which are so much alike that they have to be included in one family, the Colubridæ, treated separately farther on. With some twenty-five hundred species of snakes alive today, the task of arranging them in some logical order is tremendous. Basing figures on the most recent lists and monographs, the dates of which are given, the numbers of species in certain parts of the world follow:

Malay Archipelago (1950):	345
Southeastern Asia (from the Indian Peninsula and adjacent territory eastward to the South China Sea) (1943):	389
Europe (1940):	31
United States and Canada (1953):	114
Mexico (1945):	336

There is, of course, considerable duplication between the first two items as well as between the last two. The number of species in the United States is the same as that given for this country and Canada, the Canadian snake fauna being merely a spillover from the United States.

Snakes

The snakes may be thought of as a flourishing rather than a vanishing group of animals. Because of the deep concern that mankind has for them (chiefly in the form of fear, it must be admitted), almost every person has some conception of the groups of snakes: the vipers, the giant constrictors, the cobras and coral snakes, and so on. These vague concepts roughly correspond to the families of the technical student. Rather than give diagnoses of the families here, I shall take them up one by one and let the reader build on the knowledge he already has.

Account by Families

✴

BLIND SNAKES
(Families Typhlopidæ and Leptotyphlopidæ)
PLATE 65

THERE ARE two families of wormlike, harmless, secretive, burrowing snakes that are widely distributed and usually called blind snakes to distinguish them from various other blunt-tailed snakes known as worm-snakes. In spite of the resemblance of some blind snakes to worms, the former can be recognized at once by the numerous rows of polished scales and the dry skin. The eyes are hidden beneath the head scales. To the layman, the species of the two blind-snake families look just alike, but they differ in various points of structure, the most understandable being a lack of teeth on the upper jaw in the Leptotyphlopidæ, the presence of teeth there in the Typhlopidæ; in the lower jaw of the Typhlopidæ there are no teeth, or merely one on a side, whereas in the other family numerous teeth are found there. Remnants of a pelvis are usually present in species of both families, but they are much less reduced in the Leptotyphlopidæ than in the Typhlopidæ.

A few facts about the Typhlopidæ follow. Nearly 200 species are unequally divided into five genera, four of which are very small and occur only in Central and South America. The fifth, with about 170 species, is world-wide in distribution, being found from the West Indies and Mexico to Argentina in the New World; in Africa, southeastern Europe (one kind), southern Asia, the Malay Archipelago and Philippine Islands, Australia, and some of the Pacific islands. Africa with some 50 species and the Malay Archipelago with 29 are regions well supplied; about 20 are found in the Americas. One Old World kind (*Typhlops braminus*), with an average length of barely five inches, has been widely transported by man. It is now found in Mexico as well as in Honolulu, where it appears to be thriving and threatens to force the inhabitants of the Hawaiian Islands to admit that they "have snakes." Perhaps those isolated Americans will try to convince the world that these blind snakes are only snakelike worms rather than wormlike snakes! Under *any* name this reptile is hardly a threat to human safety.

The species of *Typhlops* are mostly egg-laying, although Dr. Smith found fourteen advanced embryos in an Asiatic species. The usual length is not more than 7 or 8 inches. Larger sizes are reached by many. For example, according to the late Edgar R. Waite, the four species of South Australia have lengths ranging from 18 to 24 inches. Dr. Rose gives the greatest length of *Typhlops dinga* of southern Africa as 30 inches; I know of no larger typhlopid. The question of the greatest length of snakes usually associated with worms has a fascination all its own, especially in Australia, where even earthworms reach gigantic proportions.

The other family, the Leptotyphlopidæ (sometimes known as Glauconiidæ), has a greater claim for our attention because two species are found in the southwestern United States, where their combined ranges cover an approximate quarter of the country. Five species in addition to these same two live in Mexico. The range of the family southward includes nearly all of South America and some of the West Indian islands. In Africa, leptotyphlopids are found throughout the savanna and semi-arid areas, but not in the truly desert region of the northern part. In southwestern Asia the distribution extends to Pakistan.

The species, about 40 in number, are placed in a single genus (*Leptotyphlops*). They are smaller than the snakes of the other family, and consequently more wormlike.

SHIELD–TAILED SNAKES
(Family Uropeltidæ)

THE SHIELD-TAILED snakes have perhaps become more thoroughly adapted to a burrowing, subsurface life than any other family. The bones of the cranium are solidly united, the head small and pointed, and the muscles of the front part of the body strongly developed. This probably gives preserved specimens their characteristic crook in the neck. The colors are often brilliant combinations of red, orange, and yellow; bright colors are seen in many other burrowing snakes. But the most conspicuous and unusual characteristic of this family is the tail. This organ is always short and, in somewhat more than half of the forty-four species, ends abruptly in a flat disc set at an angle to the axis of the body, giving the appearance of a snake that has had its tail cut at a slant. No one knows certainly what use this tail serves. Perhaps it acts as a stopper to the burrow, or possibly the snake obtains with it a purchase as it makes its way underground.

These oddities of reptile life are further peculiar in having an extremely limited distribution: Ceylon and the Indian Peninsula. They live in mountainous or hilly country, preferring forested areas. They do not bite and are so small and have such small heads that their bite could do little harm. Most of them grow to be no longer than fifteen inches, and the maximum size attained is about twenty-nine. The species are diverse enough to be divided into seven genera, one of which (*Uropeltis*, formerly often called *Silybura*) includes half the species. As far as is known, all the kinds bring forth directly from three to eight young at a time. Earthworms seem to be the staple diet.

PIPE SNAKES
(Family Anilidæ)

FOR WANT of a better name, I shall call this little family of but eleven species after the name generally given to its only genus with more than a single species. This genus (*Cylindrophis*) occurs on Ceylon (one species) and from Burma southeastward into the Malay Archipelago, where the rest of its eight species are found. One additional species placed in a genus by itself occurs on Sumatra, and the family is then completed by a snake found in northern South America east of the Andes (*Anilius* or *Ilysia scytale*). Only two species of the entire family have ranges that amount to anything: this single New World member and *Cylindrophis rufus* of southeastern Asia and the Malay Archipelago. The latter is famous for its habit, when alarmed, of flattening the body and showing the brilliant crimson of the under side of the tail by simply raising it or curling it over the body, presumably a sort of bluffing action that is especially effective because of the strong resemblance of the tail to the head.

The pipe snakes have cylindrical bodies, and the scales on the belly are not greatly widened as in most other snakes. The bones of the cranium are solidly united. There are vestiges of hind limbs that show at the vent as a pair of spurs. These snakes are burrowing in habits, and seem to live chiefly on eels and other kinds of snakes. The young are brought forth directly. All pipe snakes are harmless. The family long went under the technical name Ilysiidæ.

SUNBEAM SNAKE
(Family Xenopeltidæ)
PLATE 66

A SINGLE species is usually assigned to this unimportant family, which is included for the sake of completeness. The names "sunbeam" and "iridescent earth snake" are given it because of its highly polished, iridescent scales. The range extends from Burma southeastward into the Malay Archipelago and the Philippines. It grows to be a little more than three feet long, is secretive and nocturnal in habits, and eats birds, small mammals, frogs, and other snakes. When annoyed, the sunbeam snake is conflictingly described as defending itself by biting ferociously or even refusing to bite at all.

There is general agreement that it does vibrate the tail very rapidly to show its displeasure.

As explained on page 176, the Mexican and Central American "python" (*Loxocemus*) is now classified as a xenopeltid.

BOAS AND PYTHONS
(Family Boidæ)

ALTHOUGH THE giant boas and pythons are perhaps the most readily recognized of all snakes, the family to which they belong, the Boidæ, is anything but easy to deal with because of its world-wide distribution and the varied habits and appearance of its members. The boas and pythons can be briefly defined for our purposes as non-venomous, primitive, constricting snakes with both lungs developed and, except in the Round Island species (Bolyerinæ), vestiges of hind limbs visible as small spurs near the base of the tail. (The tendency in snakes has been to lose one lung.) An interesting characteristic of many species is a development of sense organs in the scales of the lips. These "labial pits" serve essentially the same purpose as the pit viper's pits (see page 216), which are much more complex and fewer in number. In many boas and pythons the labial pits are readily discernible, especially those of the upper lips. The fossil history of the Boidæ confirms their age. They were diverse and widely distributed in Eocene times, some fifty million years ago. We might imagine that truly gigantic kinds existed then; but the largest one known (*Gigantophis*) lived in Egypt and probably reached a length of only about fifty feet.

No term applied to snakes is more confusing than the word "constrictor." There is little wonder, for this word has various distinct meanings, two of them technical. If anyone describes a snake as a "constrictor," he is making an ambiguous statement. He might mean that it is a member of the family Boidæ because members of this family are commonly called the "giant constrictors." On the other hand, he might be merely describing the habits of the snake; many species of various families constrict the prey, and can be called both popularly and technically "constrictors." Thus a member of the genus *Constrictor* can justly be thought of as a constrictor in three senses of the word.

About a third of the sixty living members of the Boidæ are set apart as a subfamily, the pythons (Pythoninæ). The pythons differ from nearly all the rest (the boas, Boinæ) in two skull characteristics and the habit of laying eggs instead of bringing forth the young directly. Some students doubt that this time-honored separation is based on true relationship, and would throw nearly all of the sixty species into a single family, the Boidæ. Until the matter has been studied further, it is just as well to keep the two groups apart. Research on the two rare Round Island boas, to be taken up below, indicates that they should be set apart as a third subfamily; hence my use of the word "nearly" above. This is a very recent fly in the ointment.

PYTHONS
(Subfamily Pythoninæ)
PLATES 67, 68, 69, 70, AND 71

A single species that has wandered far from the fold is always disconcerting to the taxonomist. The subfamily Pythoninæ formerly included such a species, *Loxocemus*, the rare little "python" of southern Mexico and Central America. Very recent studies have proved this to be a member of the family Xenopeltidæ. The Pythoninæ now have a reasonable distribution: Africa, southeastern Asia, the Malay, Philippine, and certain Pacific islands, and Australia. Even here the few species are thinly scattered.

I shall divide the pythons into two parts, and the African genus *Calabaria*, with its single species. One of these two parts rests on relationship, the other on geographical occurrence. The first part is the genus *Python*, a happy case in which the popular and technical names are the same. Its seven species we shall call "true pythons." These include the giant snakes so popular with showmen and therefore familiar to the layman. The second part is an assemblage of relatively unknown pythons found in the Malay Archipelago, the Philippine and the Pacific islands, and in Australia. They are so diverse in structure that the ten species usually recognized are assigned to five genera, only one of which has more than two species.

Since two of the seven true pythons exceed a length of twenty feet, a size reached by only two snakes of other genera (see page 133), and the Indian python (*P. molurus*) attains that length, the genus *Python* may justly lay claim to distinction in size of its members. There are also true pythons of small size, the ball python of Africa (*P. regius*), for example, having an average length of only three feet.

Three die-hard beliefs about pythons (and other gigantic snakes) must be dealt with together here, although two of them have already been considered. The first is a conviction that a snake's head is often used as a sort of battering-ram. Kipling's Kaa had a punch equal to that of a heavyweight boxer. Nothing could be further from the truth, as the snout of a snake is extremely delicate and is never purposely used like the human fist. A captive snake often violently strikes a glass cage front simply because of poor vision. The second belief is that a human who encounters a python in the wild may be hugged to death. Oddly enough, a python normally defends itself by striking just as other snakes do. The third, and no doubt the belief with nine lives, enormously exaggerates the general strength and the crushing power of the big snakes. This has already been refuted in considerable detail on page 143.

Three true pythons live in Africa. The rock python (*P. sebæ*) is widely distributed south of the great northern deserts, whereas the others have relatively restricted ranges in the central and western tropical parts of the continent. The relation between man and these snakes is complex. Certain peoples of Africa have long worshipped the python; death by cruel torture was often the punishment for killing one, and even those who accidentally brought about the death of a python were sometimes buried alive. These serpents were both protected and pampered. The python has been symbolized in West Africa as the god of war, worshipped as the god of wisdom and of other virtues, and even credited with making women pregnant. In contrast to this adulation stands the relish of other African peoples for its flesh, and the relentless persecution of the modern hide-hunters who slaughter pythons by the millions instead of by the dozen.

The reticulate python (*P. reticulatus*), usually considered to be the largest of snakes, is found from Thailand (Siam) and adjacent mainland regions southward and eastward through the Malay and Philippine islands. This giant reptile has an astonishing ability to survive and even thrive in proximity to man. In the early part of this century it was common in compounds of the busiest sections of Bangkok, living near the river, where hundreds of persons constantly passed. Dr. Smith caught specimens in his compound situated within one hundred yards of the city's main thoroughfare. In the wilds, it seldom wanders far from water. As many as a hundred eggs are laid at a time and brooded by the female. The hatchlings are two to two and a half feet long.

The common true python of southeastern Asia, the Indian python (*P. molurus*), occurs from West Pakistan, Ceylon, and India eastward into southern China and southward through the Malay Archipelago to Celebes and Sumbawa. Like the reticulate python, it is a good climber and prefers to live in the vicinity of water. Sylvia, the female that I raised, became incredibly tame; small children could pull her around at will; she attempted to bite only once and that was the day I received her. Her growth was at first rapid, about three inches a month.

The blood python (*P. curtus*), a small species of the Malay Peninsula, Sumatra, near-by Bangka, and Borneo, is one of the two true pythons native to the Malay Archipelago (including the adjacent Malay Peninsula), the other occurring only on Flores and Timor. The late Dr. G. K. Noble studied the brooding habits of a captive female blood python five and a half feet long. He failed to detect a rise in the body temperature of the female while she brooded her sixteen eggs. This is surprising in view of the fact that two other species of true pythons are known to increase the body temperature while the eggs are being brooded.

The pythons of the Malay, Philippine, and Pacific islands and Australia are few in number but diverse enough in structure to be assigned to five genera. Three of these have only one species apiece, and limited ranges. The ringed python (*Bothrochilus* or *Nardoana*) lives in New Guinea, the Bismarck Archipelago, Union Islands, and northern Australia. The diamond or carpet python (*Morelia argus*, long known as *Python spilotes*) is found in New Guinea, the Union Islands, and Australia. This, much the largest of the three, rarely exceeds a length of ten feet. The green python (*Chondropython*) is found from New Guinea and adjacent small islands eastward to the Solomon Islands. This beautiful snake, predominantly green in color when adult, is strongly remindful of the emerald-green boa of the New World (see page 182).

Liasis is the only python genus of the Malay, Philippine, Pacific island, and Australian region that has spread itself widely. The collective range of four of its five species extends from Timor and Wetar eastward through New Guinea to the adjacent D'Entrecasteaux Islands, and southeastward into Australia.

The giant of the genus, the amethystine python (*Liasis amethistinus*), not only has a maximum length two and a half times as great as that of any other *Liasis*, but may boast a size surpassed by few snakes (see page 133). The range is extensive: from the Philippine Islands southward through the eastern Malay Archipelago, New Guinea, the Bismarck Archipelago, and into northern Australia. In the part of its range where wallabies live, it feeds largely on them, being well able to tackle an adult wallaby. I know of no other snake that would compete with it for such prey.

Australia has produced but two species of pythons all its own, and they constitute our fifth and last python genus of the Malay, Philippine, Pacific island, and Australian region. One of these two, the black-headed python (*Aspidites melanocephalus*), grows to a length of eight feet. In spite of an insatiable appetite for other kinds of snakes, including such deadly species as Australian tiger and black snakes (see page 144), it is remarkably docile in captivity and can be handled with perfect safety.

One obscure little python, the only species of its genus (*Calabaria*), completes the account of the pythons of Africa. This snake is characteristic of the heavy forests of tropical Africa, and reaches a length of three feet. It has the disconcerting habit of crawling on the forest floor with the head directed downward and the tail held up. As the blunt head and tail are shaped alike, and the latter is often moved to and fro, a crawling individual presents an odd appearance. When greatly annoyed, *Calabaria* rolls itself into a compact ball that is no doubt another way of disconcerting or frustrating an enemy.

BOAS
(Subfamily Boinæ)
PLATES 72, 73, 74, 75, 76, 77, AND 78

The boas, in contrast to the pythons, are well represented in both the New World and the Old World, slightly more than two thirds of the species living in the New. Because of this relatively even division, it is best to treat them on a geographical basis, those of the Americas first. I shall group these rather arbitrarily, considering the two temperate genera, the only boas of the United States, as a unit; the familiar and popular boa constrictor and the anaconda as a second unit; the remaining five genera as a third and highly arbitrary one. No boas live in southern Africa, although the subfamily is well known on Madagascar. The only boas of Africa are a few species of sand boas (*Eryx*).

Only the two small genera of New World boas live in a temperate climate; one of them, the rubber boa (*Charina bottæ*), the more northern in distribution, is confined to the United States and the extreme southwestern corner of Canada; the other genus (*Lichanura*) ranges from southern California and adjacent Arizona into northwestern Mexico. It has two species, the widely distributed one being known as the California boa. Few persons realize that perfectly good boas inhabit the United States (the nine westernmost states) and even reach Canada.

The rubber and California boas, both distinctly blunt-tailed, are among the most inoffensive of snakes, defending themselves by rolling into a tight ball rather than by biting. The rubber boa may actually swing the tail in a motion suggesting the strike of other snakes. The California boa lives in granite-chaparral country, the other in the drier parts of our northwestern coniferous forests. Both species bring forth directly small broods of living young and feed largely on small mammals. The average adult rubber boa is only a foot and a half long, whereas the California boa usually grows to be about six inches longer.

The name "boa constrictor" has been so widely used to designate *the* giant among serpents that it might almost be considered as a general term for any gigantic snake. The difficulty is the perfectly good boa constrictor whose scientific name was for a long time just that, *Boa constrictor*. The more correct technical name is now *Constrictor constrictor*, and it is not such a giant when the whole snake world is taken into consideration; there are several snakes, one of them even venomous, that rival or exceed it in maximum length. The boa constrictor is only the second-largest species of the New World, none but the anaconda exceeding it in length and bulk. (See page 133.)

Another surprising thing about the boa constrictor is the fact that it ranges northward on both coasts of Mexico well into the Mexican states (Sonora and Tamaulipas) that adjoin the United States, and consequently is found not far from our borders. The species has an enormous distribution over tropical America and temperate South America as far as central Argentina. It varies noticeably from one part of the range to another and has been given several valid technical names. The boa constrictor of Trinidad and the Lesser Antilles is sometimes considered as a distinct species. Evidence of the ability of the boa constrictor to live in different types of country is seen in western Mexico, where it thrives under virtual desert conditions; typically it is a reptile of tropical forests. Needless to say, it is a good climber.

The anaconda (*Eunectes murinus*), the great water boa, is widely distributed over tropical South America east of the Andes, including the island of Trinidad. No other snake of the New World compares with it in size. Like the boa constrictor, it varies greatly from one region to another and has therefore received five different technical names. As with the other boas, the young are produced directly. It is a strange fact that little is known about the habits of these two large and familiar snakes.

We have now considered our little boas of western temperate North America as well as the boa constrictor and anaconda. There remains in the New World an assortment of some twenty-seven species assigned to five genera. Many are small, others medium or even large. Most of the kinds will have to be omitted; all the genera, but only the outstanding species, are worth mentioning.

The largest genus (*Epicrates*) has about ten species, whose collective range extends from the Bahamas and West Indies to southern Central America and over South America as far south as Argentina. The rainbow boa (*E. cenchris*), the single mainland member of the genus, ranges from Costa Rica to Argentina. The iridescence of the scales is responsible for the common name. The giant of the genus, the Cuban boa (*E. angulifer*) of Cuba and the Isle of Pines, reaches a length of ten or perhaps eleven feet and has a bad temperament. It is said to feed on bats.

The ground boas (*Tropidophis*) constitute the genus next in size. These unfamiliar snakes, though typical of many of the West Indies, do not occur in the Lesser Antilles. One species reaches the Bahamas. There is a peculiar gap in the total distribution, two of the nine species being found in a remote part of South America (Ecuador, Peru, and southern Brazil).

The little known about ground-boa habits indicates that the common name is essentially applicable even if the ground-living habit has been contradicted by the discovery of a specimen in a bromeliad growing thirty feet above the ground. Frogs, lizards, and birds are definitely known to be included in the diet, and the young seem to be brought forth directly. The boid habit of protection by coiling into a compact ball is well developed, and the astounding defensive trick of bleeding at the mouth has been repeatedly observed in the Cuban species, *T. semicinctus*, which may reach a length of 16.5 inches. About four drops of the nearly odorless, inoffensive blood slowly flow from the mouth of an annoyed individual. At the same time the eyes turn to a ruby-red.

The genus *Boa* has but three species, one of them (*B. canina*) predominantly emerald-green in color. There are few snakes more striking in appearance than this arboreal species of tropical South America, which likes to rest coiled compactly about a limb. A second species ranges from Costa Rica into Colombia; a third is found in the Lesser Antilles, on Trinidad, and in Central America and tropical South America.

Two genera of dwarf boas are astonishing for their size, adults usually measuring eighteen inches or less in length. The genus *Ungaliophis* with three species occurs from extreme southern Mexico to Colombia; the genus *Trachyboa*, with but two, lives in Panama and northern South America. The boas of the latter genus are arboreal, whereas little is known about those of the former.

The boas of the Old World, being much fewer in number of species, are more easily dealt with than are those of the New World. As in the case of the latter, three convenient divisions may be made: the sand boas (*Eryx*), the Pacific boas (*Enygrus*), and those of Madagascar. (The two Round Island boas, being set off as a subfamily by themselves, are, of course, excluded here.)

The seven or eight species of sand boas are by far the most interesting because they have departed so widely from the typical habits of the vast majority of pythons as well as boas. Although these snakes live in dry country, they are not true desert reptiles as their extensive distribution will show. However, the adjective "sandy" is frequently used in describing their habitat. The range extends from central Asia through southeastern Europe into northern and even central Africa (east of the rain forests). One species occurs as far eastward as Ceylon and northeastern India, another as far in this direction (north of Tibet) as northwestern China. The temperaments of the species differ, the Theban sand boa (*E. colubrina*) sometimes delivering several sharp slashing bites in rapid succession, the javelin sand boa (*E. jaculus*) refusing to bite at all. The young are brought forth directly. Adult sand boas are usually less than three feet long.

The Pacific boas (*Enygrus*) are small snakes with angular snouts (when viewed from the side). The range extends from Celebes eastward through the New Guinea region to the Society Islands of the Pacific Ocean. Little is recorded about the habits of the three species. One (*E. australis*) feeds on lizards, and another (*E. asper*) has the unusual habit of jumping. The spurs, or remnants of the hind limbs, of *E. carinatus* show a marked sexual difference in development, those of the male being much more conspicuous than those of the female.

The island of Madagascar alone can boast two handsome boas,

both of which were formerly aligned generically with New World groups but are now assigned to two genera, *Sanzinia* and *Acrantophis*.

ROUND ISLAND BOAS
(Subfamily Bolyerinæ)

Tiny Round Island lying just east of Madagascar and near Mauritius also has its two boas (*Casarea* and *Bolyeria*), rare species recently shown to be links between the boa-python and the cobra-coral snake families, the Boidæ and the Elapidæ. These Round Island species, the only members of the Boidæ that entirely lack all vestiges of the hind limbs and their supports, are now assigned to a subfamily all their own.

COLUBRID SNAKES
(Family Colubridæ)

THE GREAT family Colubridæ, the members of which I shall call just "colubrid snakes," has ever been the nightmare of the classifier of snakes. Most of the living species of snakes have always been thrown together into this unwieldy assortment, and one all-important task of herpetologists has been, first, to see how many groups could reasonably be removed from it and, second, to try to split it up into good subfamilies. The ins and outs of these time-honored processes are far beyond us here, so I shall treat the entire family on a geographic basis, dividing the world into five regions, four of them areas where colubrid snakes abound, and one (Europe) a place where herpetologists abound and interest in the scientific study of reptiles and amphibians prevails. This method of treatment, though somewhat unscientific, will avoid the necessity of a monotonous enumeration of scores of genera, and give the reader some idea of faunal units. The hatchet will have to be used more drastically than anywhere else in this book, as mere lists of genera can be of little interest to the general reader.

This arrangement is not complete, but does recognize the most distinct subfamilies, those over which there is no great controversy.

184

The remainder—that is, all the vast array of genera that do not fit into any of these distinct subfamily groups—will be treated under the term Colubrinæ and, for want of a better name, be called "typical snakes."

A great advantage of this geographic basis is that it allows me to treat as units the three unrivaled and primarily tropical assemblages of the family: the colubrid snakes of southeastern Asia and its adjacent huge archipelago, those of Africa, and those of tropical America. I shall also treat as units the colubrid snakes of temperate North America and those of Europe. The temperate North American unit is large and valid from any point of view; the European one is somewhat arbitrary, as its snake fauna is a part of the fauna of Asia.

It will be noted by those familiar with snake classification that use is not made of the presence or absence of grooved teeth in the rear of the upper jaw ("rear-fanged snakes"). This characteristic, once considered of great importance, is now thought to be of distinctly subordinate value, and can be all but omitted from a work of this nature. I mention the matter here so that those with some knowledge of the older snake literature will not become confused.

COLUBRID SNAKES OF SOUTHEASTERN ASIA, THE MALAY ARCHIPELAGO, AND THE PHILIPPINE ISLANDS
(Family Colubridæ)

BY FAR the greatest diversity of colubrid snakes (Colubridæ) is found in southeastern Asia and the large archipelago lying between Asia and Australia. Two of the five small, sharply distinct subfamilies are confined to this region, and all are well represented here. This superb snake fauna peters out on the one extreme at the southern edge of the Tibetan and adjacent highlands and deserts, on the other in northern Australia. Dr. Smith (1943) gives no fewer than 56 genera and 236 species for southeastern Asia alone; a few species should be added to this number to allow for those that occur in Asia just beyond the limits of his area. A brief account of this vast assortment of largely tropical snakes follows, each subfamily being considered as a unit.

SNAIL-EATING SNAKES
(Subfamily Dipsadinæ)

About sixty species of snail-eating snakes make up an assortment that, being hard to fit into the scheme of classification, has been variously placed. It was long set apart as the family Amblycephalidæ. The prevalent subfamily characteristics are arboreal habits and a peculiar development of the head apparently correlated with the diet of slugs and snails (see page 145). The delicate teeth are long and slender, and the jaws have lost the ability to stretch about a large object. Stretching would be entirely unnecessary in swallowing a soft thing like a slug or the body of a snail, but the long teeth are needed to hold the soft, mucus-covered prey. In most snakes a straight groove extending along the middle of the lower side of the head separates the scales into two equal sections, and facilitates the stretching of the skin of the lower jaw. The snail-eaters typically lack this groove, the scales of one side being dovetailed into those of the other.

Most of these odd, inoffensive snakes live in the New World, where the thirty-two species of one large genus (*Dipsas*) occur from the coastal regions of southern Mexico to northern Argentina. There are two additional genera in the New World, and a total of two in the Old World, one of these (*Pareas* or *Amblycephalus*) with some fifteen, the other with a single species. Certain of these Old World kinds have the quaint habit, when annoyed, of falling to the ground and becoming semi-rigid. This makes the performer look like a dry, twisted twig. Some of the snail-eaters are as well suited to climbing and living in vegetation as are any other snakes.

XENODERMINE SNAKES
(Subfamily Xenoderminæ)

This subfamily is another small collection of nameless oddities. Some nine species are found in the Old World from Japan and central China southward into the Malay Archipelago, and one species (*Nothopsis rugosus*) occurs in the American tropics from Nicaragua to Ecuador. The fact that so few species must be placed in five genera, three of them with a single species apiece, indicates the diversity of structure. There is no single, obvious characteristic of all the species; one (*Xenodermus javanicus*) has peculiarly irregular scales, a very unusual condition among snakes, and in another Old World species some of the snout scales are turned up in a remarkable way. I found that one kind from southern China simply dries up if left exposed to the air, although it is not in the least aquatic.

FRESHWATER SNAKES
(Subfamily Homalopsinæ)

PLATE 79

About thirty species of aquatic snakes with nasal passages that can be tightly closed, nostrils on top of the snout, and eyes directed upward are found from the region of the Indian Peninsula eastward through Asia and southeastward through the Malay and Philippine islands to northern Australia. There is no widely used English name for the subfamily, which Dr. Smith calls simply "freshwater snakes." With few exceptions, they are not aquatic enough to mind leaving their element a little, and often abound in the shallow water of flooded fields. Although they have grooved teeth in the rear of the upper jaw, they are not dangerous. They feed largely on fishes, and bring forth the young directly.

So diverse are these snakes in structure that they are divided into ten genera, most of them with a single species, and only one (*Enhydris*) with more than two. *Enhydris* has some eighteen species that range over the entire region delimited above as distribution of the subfamily. The most remarkable species of the subfamily is the tentacled snake aptly named *Herpeton tentaculatum* of Thailand (Siam), Cambodia, and Cochin China. Two large, scaled appendages project from the snout. They can be moved, and point forward when the snake is at rest in the water, which it never leaves. No one knows what use is made of them.

EGG-EATING SNAKE
(Subfamily Dasypeltinæ)

The Indian egg-eating snake is considered along with the African species (see page 191).

WART SNAKES
(Subfamily Acrochordinæ)
PLATE 80

It is a relief to describe two species that almost anyone would at a glance set off by themselves as a distinct group. "Wart snakes" seems to be the most widely used name, although one of the two has been known as the "elephant's trunk snake." These non-venomous reptiles are covered above and below with vast numbers of tiny scale-like structures, each with three points, the central one the highest. The skin is loose, and much of it shows between the three-pointed structures. The bodies are stout and in adults usually three or four feet long. The wart snakes are found from the western coast of peninsular India eastward and southeastward through coastal Asia and the Malay and Philippine islands to northern Australia and the Solomon Islands. River mouths and adjacent seas are frequented. So aquatic are these snakes that their clumsy progress on land suggests a gigantic worm. They live on fishes, and bring forth the young directly, one of them (*Acrochordus javanicus*) producing from twenty-five to thirty-two at a time, although as many as seventy-two have been recorded. The other (*A. granulatus*) is sometimes set off as a separate genus (*Chersydrus*) because it has a fold of skin along the middle of the belly. The wart snakes are persecuted unmercifully by commercial hunters and the hides are made into an excellent grade of leather.

TYPICAL SNAKES
(Subfamily Colubrinæ)
PLATES 81 AND 82

The typical snakes of southeastern Asia and the Malay and Philippine islands number hundreds of species. These species in turn are grouped into about sixty genera. A few of these genera (*Natrix, Elaphe, Coluber, Opheodrys*) are familiar elements of the snake fauna of the United States, and will be dealt with when that fauna is under consideration. Obviously, it would be futile to attempt to describe this vast array of essentially tropical serpent life. Suffice it to say that all types of life histories are included, and use is made of every kind of environment: the fresh waters, the earth, and the vegetation above it.

COLUBRID SNAKES OF AFRICA
(Family Colubridæ)

TYPICAL SNAKES
(Subfamily Colubrinæ)
PLATE 83

From the point of view of the typical snakes, we may take Africa as a unit comparable to southeastern Asia, the Malay Archipelago, and the Philippine Islands. The few snakes found in the extreme north of Africa are really a part of the European fauna, and should not be counted. This leaves us with an essentially tropical array, to which is appended the moderately rich typical snake fauna of southern Africa. The fact that South Africa lies south of the tropics helps to compensate for the lack of large islands that form so prominent a part of the Asiatic and Malay Archipelago region.

189

Large islands well supplied with mountains and lowlands are excellent areas for the development of species because of the isolation of so many populations.

The hundreds of species of typical snakes found in this African region are in turn divided into a great many genera, which seem to be about the same in number as those of the Asiatic-Malay island region. The two faunas are comparable in having species that invade all parts of the environment, the fresh waters, the earth, and the vegetation. This is the interesting thing to the student of evolution.

From the point of view of classification, one fact should be noted: the elements of the Asiatic-Malay island fauna that give it a slight resemblance to that of the United States are conspicuously weak or entirely lacking in our African fauna.

EGG-EATING SNAKES
(Subfamily Dasypeltinæ)
PLATE 84

If we had to award a prize to a single kind of snake for being an oddity, I should vote for the egg-eating snake of Africa (*Dasypeltis scaber*). This small reptile has two claims to a place in the snakes' Hall of Fame: the habit of living on eggs, and the ability to cope with a hen's egg; and the rare serpentine accomplishment of making a bluffing sound not by expelling air, but by rubbing together certain of the body scales just as the saw-scaled viper does (see page 227). The swallowing of a hen's egg by a slender snake three feet or less in length is an accomplishment that calls for explanation.

Although the egg-eating snake was described by Linnæus in 1754, and some of its major peculiarities were noted by another scientist eighty years later, a full explanation of how it can stretch its jaws over a smooth object more than twice the vertical diameter of the head remained to be presented in 1952 by Dr. Carl Gans. These peculiarities may be briefly summarized. The lining of the mouth adjacent to the lips is capable of great extension and lies in folds when at rest. The teeth are greatly reduced. Many of the vertebræ of the forward part of the backbone are provided with projections that may enter the esophagus, and have tips of hardened bone (not enamel, as often stated). These processes help to crack the egg-shell and, with the help of highly developed body muscles, crush it and force it forward to the mouth, through which it is ejected. The part of the esophagus near the stomach is modified into a special valve that retains the egg fluids while the shell is being pushed forward. Because eggs of wild birds are not available more than twice a year (during the breeding seasons), the egg-eater also has developed a special ability to store fat for use during the lean months.

In East Pakistan and adjacent India there lives an obvious relative of the African egg-eater. The fact that the former has grooved teeth influenced classifiers of the past to place it in a subfamily (Elachistodontinæ) by itself. Now that this "rear-fanged" characteristic is considered of less value than formerly (see page 185), these two snakes are unhesitatingly placed together. Unfortunately, no one has ever made an observation on the habits of the Asiatic member, nor undertaken anything but a cursory study of its structure.

COLUBRID SNAKES OF TROPICAL AMERICA
(Family Colubridæ)

TYPICAL SNAKES
(Subfamily Colubrinæ)
PLATES 85, 86, 87, 88, AND 89

Coming to our third array of typical snakes, we have some interesting facts to note. These inhabitants of the New World tropics live in an area bounded on the north by dry highlands (those of northern Mexico). Our African area is also bounded on the north by an arid region, the Asiatic-Malay island one largely by cold highlands (Tibet) and deserts. The New World area has a southern extension into the temperate region (southern South America) just as Africa has, but differs from both the Old World regions in having an archipelago (the West Indies) as part of its northern extremity. As one might expect, this relatively small, somewhat northern island group has a typical snake fauna in no wise comparable to the vast one of the Malay Archipelago and the Philippine Islands. Some two thirds of the approximately forty-five West Indian species belong to two of the few genera, a fact proving great lack of diversity. One aspect of this poverty is the complete absence of venomous snakes on all the Greater and most of the Lesser Antilles. This statement, out of place here, is made for emphasis and will be appreciated by many inhabitants of the islands in question. The island of Trinidad with its rich animal and plant life, essentially like that of the adjacent mainland, is not faunistically one of the West Indies.

The typical snakes of tropical America number hundreds of species; these in turn are grouped into considerably more genera than are those of Africa or of the Asiatic-Malay island region. The profusion of genera may be taken as a rough indication of the diversity. It is surprising that the Asiatic-Malay island region with its great diversity of terrain, vast east-west extent, and huge islands should not be ahead of the other two. The African one is larger than the tropical American one but does not have a part comparable to southern Mexico and Central America, where a relatively small area is made up of many more or less separate mountainous and low, flat sections ideal for the development of species, such sections being something like islands with their more obvious separation by expanses of water.

The typical snakes of our New World area have, needless to say, taken just as good advantage of all available parts of the environment: the fresh waters, the earth, and the vegetation. Only in this way could so many genera have evolved.

XENODERMINE SNAKE
(Subfamily Xenodermine)

The single New World representative of this subfamily is considered along with its Asiatic relatives (see page 187).

SNAIL-EATING SNAKES
(Subfamily Dipsadinæ)

The snail-eating snakes of tropical America are dealt with on page 186.

COLUBRID SNAKES OF TEMPERATE NORTH AMERICA
(Family Colubridæ)

TYPICAL SNAKES
(Subfamily Colubrinæ)

In his recent "Check List" (see bibliography; 1953) Dr. Schmidt lists ninety-two species of typical snakes (Colubrinæ) as living in the United States and Canada. As Canada has no species of its own, the ninety-two is also the total for the United States alone; many of these same ninety-two occur also in northern Mexico. These species of our country are grouped into thirty-eight genera, twenty-eight of which include only one or two species. Obviously, we cannot consider all these species or even genera; in many cases the two are really synonymous. The picture can be vastly simplified by leaving out the small and otherwise inconspicuous snakes, and considering the remainder by groups or genera.

The ten groups of really important typical snakes of the United States include fifty species, and will be taken up group by group. This will give us an abbreviated view of our entire snake fauna with the exception of the blind-snake, the boa, and the coral-snake families (each with only two species), and the seventeen species of pit vipers (including the fifteen rattlesnakes). All of these are, of course, treated under their own separate family headings.

Snakes

One of the thrilling pastimes of my boyhood was wading up creeks and streams hunting for water snakes. These wary reptiles sun themselves on trunks and branches growing over the water, and catching them calls for considerable skill. Only the experienced ear can tell the difference between the soft splash of a snake and the plop of diving frog or falling turtle. This pastime is perfectly safe in the higher parts of the southern states (north of the range of the water moccasin) and in the northern states (see page 223). Copperheads and rattlesnakes would rarely if ever be encountered in the watercourses. The water snakes abound in swamps, ponds, and lake borders as well as in creeks, streams, and rivers.

The water snakes, with eleven species, constitute our second-largest genus, being barely surpassed in number of species by the garter snakes. In North America, the center of water-snake distribution is the southeastern United States; two of our kinds range into Mexico, and one may even reach Guatemala, but Mexico has only one species all its own. None is known in the Rocky Mountains and territory thence westward. A few reach extreme southeastern Canada. Some species vary from one part of the range to another and have consequently received more than one technical name.

Many of the water snakes are large species with dark bands crossing the body and tail, browns predominating in their colors. They may be vicious in temperament and formidable in appearance; in fact, a large water snake is often more forbidding than a true water moccasin. The bite of the former is, of course, never dangerous although it may cause slight bleeding. Water snakes eat just what one would expect them to eat, small animals that live in and about water. These include fishes, frogs and tadpoles, salamanders, and even crawfishes. Catfishes are devoured in spite of their fin spines, which often pierce the body wall of the snake and drop off, doing no serious harm. Many fishermen believe that the water snake does great damage by destroying game fishes, but this is not true. The slower-moving fishes are usually taken, and, on the whole, the water snake is not an enemy of the fisherman.

All of our water snakes seem to bring forth the young directly, but such is not the case with Old World *Natrix*, many of which lay eggs. The broods in a few of our species may be very large; there are records of some made up of two- to three-score young, and an occasional one even larger.

GARTER SNAKES
(*Thamnophis*)
PLATES 93, 94, 95, AND 96

If any type of snake deserves the name of *The Snake* of this country, it is the garter snake. There are not only more species of *Thamnophis*, but they are more widely distributed, usually the most abundant, and always the most persistent large snakes, making themselves at home where man himself has built his towns and cities. I have a friend who caught more than a thousand garter snakes on vacant lots in one of our large cities. The range of the genus extends from southern Canada to Central America, with more species living in Mexico than anywhere else, several more than the eleven of the United States. Some garter snakes have extensive distributions, and vary so much from one place to another that it has required the most modern statistical studies to determine what is what among the bewildering array of individual differences. This variation is not only from place to place but from specimen to specimen of any one locality.

Most garter snakes have an unmistakable look about them. The predominant elements of the pattern are one to three yellow stripes extending down the back, and more or less distinct checkerboard dark spots, two rows to each side of the back. But there are enough exceptions to make the matter interesting if not puzzling. The diet is largely cold-blooded fare with an occasional small mammal or bird thrown in. Frogs, tadpoles, salamanders, fishes, and earthworms make up a large percentage of the food, but crawfishes, insects, and other items enter in. Dead or even decaying animals are often devoured. The number of aquatic creatures included in the diet indicates a preference for a water environment, and, indeed, garter snakes have a tendency to live in or near water. This tendency is correlated with aridity; in the moist country of the eastern states these snakes are found broadcast over the land, whereas in the dry west they gravitate to water, even becoming confined to its vicinity as conditions approach those of a desert; the name "water snake" is sometimes substituted for "garter snake." Incidentally, one of our slender species (*Thamnophis sauritus*) is commonly called "ribbon snake." The young are brought forth directly, usually in broods of moderate size; a few species rival the water snakes (*Natrix*) in producing two- to three-score young at a time, the maximum number being in the high seventies.

HOG-NOSED SNAKES
(*Heterodon*)
PLATES 97, 98, 99, AND 100

The bull snakes are the big, blustering bluffers of this country, but their tactics are as child's play compared with the protracted, refined bluffing of the hog-nosed snakes. In the first place, the latter have a viperlike mien that puts the bull snakes' commonplace appearance to shame. Then the hog-nosed snakes have a whole repertoire, not merely one big show with no change of technique. A hog-nosed snake starts by flattening itself, an action that brings to sudden view new colors and fills the ordinary person with horror. Next it strikes, hissing sharply while doing so. But right here is evidence of its bluffing; the teeth are rarely brought into play, the strikes being merely harmless butts. If the adversary does not flee, the determined reptile starts on its second round of antics: it appears to be dying, writhing of the body being accompanied by a wide-open mouth and a trailing tongue. The writhing slowly ceases, and the snake, with its mouth full of dirt and sometimes even bloody, comes to rest on its back as though dead. If the adversary is intelligent enough to turn the reptile on its belly, it will at once roll over to rest again on its back!

The combined ranges of the three species of hog-nosed snakes cover nearly all of the United States east of the Rocky Mountains, and a little of adjacent Canada; one of them is found in the northern highland states of Mexico. All of them are fond of eating toads, and reproduction is by means of eggs. These perfectly harmless snakes have always aroused great fear in man and been branded with such awe-inspiring names as "puff adder," "spreading adder," and others just as bad. The tip of the snout is turned up, hence the name used here and by all herpetologists.

RING-NECKED SNAKES
(*Diadophis*)
PLATE 101

In almost every part of this country (except its north-central section) and adjacent southeastern Canada, one may encounter a small, inoffensive snake with a slate-colored back, a black-bordered yellow, red, or orange band just behind the head, and a predominantly orange or yellow belly. Such snakes, aptly known as ring-necked snakes, are usually 15 to 20 inches long when fully grown. They are essentially inhabitants of wooded areas, and frequently live under stones, or in and under decaying logs or rotting wood in other forms. Often individuals are found near together in a single log. Some ring-necked snakes have the odd habit when annoyed of curling the tail so that the brilliant colors of the lower side are brought into view. This is no doubt an attempt to bluff their way out of danger. The diet is surprisingly varied, including worms, insects, frogs, salamanders, lizards, and even other kinds of snakes. Reproduction is by means of eggs.

There are three species, a widely distributed eastern, a far-western, and a third with an intermediate range. This last one usually lacks the bright band behind the head. The two western species also occur in northern Mexico. The Pacific and the eastern species vary enough from one part of the range to another to have been technically christened several times. The intermediate species is the largest, reaching a maximum length of 29.5 inches.

RACERS, WHIP SNAKES, AND COACHWHIP
(*Coluber* and *Masticophis*)
PLATES 102, 103, AND 104

The racers, whip snakes, and coachwhip are long, slender, nervous, and highly active reptiles with a reputation for speed and for skill in climbing in bushes and in trees with low branches. Tape measure and stop watch fail to confirm the alleged ability to crawl at a rapid rate (see page 155), but a little experience amply confirms their general activity. Few other snakes, harmless or venomous, will put up such a fight when cornered; some species have the diabolical method of jerking the head to one side as the jaws take hold, and literally ripping the skin of the victim. Making several vigorous bites in quick succession is another disconcerting habit. The common names applied to our five species are too involved to go into here, although it might be well to state that the only kind (*Coluber constrictor*) found in the northeastern states and (extreme southeastern) Canada is commonly known as the "blacksnake." In the other nine groups considered herein as units, a single technical generic name covers all the species; in the case of the present group, two names are usually applied, as indicated above by the heading. *C. constrictor*, like most of the other species, varies greatly from place to place and consequently has several technical names.

The genus *Coluber*, with its single species in this country, is circumglobal in distribution, being prevalent in Asia, southern Europe, and even reaching northern Africa. The species of the other group (*Masticophis*) are, in contrast, New World snakes found from the southern United States to Venezuela, and attaining their greatest development in the dry, relatively open country of northern Mexico and our southwest. Their *relatively* fast crawling is in keeping with this choice of home. The feeding habits are varied and interesting. Small birds and mammals are often eaten, although cold-blooded animals, such as lizards, other kinds of snakes, and frogs are by no means neglected. Even insects are included in the fare. Reproduction of all New World species, as far as known, is by means of eggs, including the single species of *Coluber*. The coachwhip (*Masticophis flagellum*), widely distributed in Mexico and the southern United States, is notorious for its alleged ability to overtake and severely whip terrified human beings (see page 158).

GREEN SNAKES
(*Opheodrys*)
PLATE 105

Many people think that a green snake must be dangerous, but nothing could be further from the truth in the United States, where two beautiful green species live. Neither of these slender snakes can inflict any appreciable injury, and many individuals will not even defend themselves. Although actually hard to see in grass or other green vegetation, the green snakes are well known because, when once sighted, they attract attention, and one of them, the smooth kind, has a way of turning up in flower gardens. The smooth green snake is the more northern in distribution, being found in southern Canada as well as in the United States. It lives on the ground most of the time, though it will climb into bushes. The food consists of insects and spiders.

The rough or keeled green snake is perhaps our most slender eastern snake; because of this and a habit of climbing skillfully, it is unsurpassed in graceful movement. Each scale of the back has a sharp ridge or keel extending down its midline, and hence the name. The distribution is more southern, the species rarely turning up north of the flat pine lands of southern New Jersey, and ranging as far southward as northeastern Mexico. The food is mainly insects and spiders, although occasionally a frog is eaten.

Both of the green snakes lay eggs. The smooth species is unusual in having a very short incubation period; it may end in a few days and never lasts more than twenty-three. Obviously, the development of the young takes place largely before the eggs are laid.

INDIGO SNAKE
(*Drymarchon*)
PLATE 106

Many persons in looking at an indigo snake (*D. corais*) fail to realize that it is one of the few really tropical snakes to be encountered in the Gulf states east of Texas. Also, there are few other snakes of this country with ranges extending as far as Brazil. It must be admitted that the individuals of our southeastern lowlands differ in appearance from those found far to the south; the indigo snake is a species that varies from one part of its range to another, so much so in fact that it has been given eight different technical names. In the southeastern Gulf states the indigo snake is simply a glossy black color, whereas in Texas the front part of it is brown, the black being present only posterior to the brown.

This is the largest harmless snake of the United States and Canada, and no doubt rivals in length any kind of this area, venomous or harmless; the big rattlers are shorter but much stouter. Dr. Carr saw a skin from southern Florida eleven feet long; if we allow one foot for stretching, the snake itself was still a giant. Because of this great size, the indigo snake is often exhibited in shows of various kinds. It is docile enough to make a good pet. Captives will eat a variety of animals: mammals, birds, frogs (including toads), lizards, and even other kinds of snakes. Strips of raw meat are also taken by some individuals. The prey is not constricted, but merely overpowered by the jaws and the sheer weight of the predator. Reproduction is by means of eggs.

RAT SNAKES AND CHICKEN SNAKES
(*Elaphe*)
PLATES 107 AND 108

The rat snakes and chicken snakes are perhaps our most colorful harmless snakes, taking the meaning of that word in both its senses. The species of this group as a rule have bold patterns of large spots or blotches, and attain sufficient size to make them conspicuous. In temperament, they are not nervous like the whip snakes and racers, but deliberate and slow; in human terms they might be described as dignified rather than impetuous. Individuals of some species may be picked up without becoming greatly alarmed. As handsome pets such docile specimens of a brightly colored species are unsurpassed. The arboreal habits of some kinds are more highly developed than those of any other large, widely distributed snakes found in this country. Climbing up the straight trunk of a large tree is a feat accomplished with ease (see page 154). Other species are at home on prairies, although, in general, the snakes of this genus are typically lovers of rugged if not heavily wooded areas.

The rat and chicken snakes have so many common names that I feel arbitrary in using these two; there are many others just as valid. The scientific names were in an even worse state of confusion until the very recent work of Dr. Herndon G. Dowling, who, in bringing order out of chaos, even reduced the number of species. The difficulty was due to a bewildering amount of variation from one region to another of certain species. Currently, only five are listed for this country, four of these with more than a single technical name. The collective range extends from southern Ontario to Central America, with none known from California, Nevada, and the extreme northwestern states. Mexico has a few species all its own in addition to records for most of our five. The genus as a whole is circumglobal in distribution, with some thirty species in Asia and a good representation in the Malay Archipelago and the Philippine Islands. It is unknown in Africa; Europe has one more than the United States.

The rat and chicken snakes are valued for the great numbers of harmful rodents that they destroy, and persecuted because they also eat young chickens and chicken eggs. The balance for or against the snake depends on the situation; certainly one is not welcome in a chicken coop, whereas in fields far removed from chicken yards it is distinctly an asset. In Arkansas I once bet a farmer that the lump in the specimen caught near his farm was caused by a bird or mammal; the farmer held that it was his missing wooden nest egg. A knife soon proved that the farmer was right. The species of this genus do not confine themselves to a diet of rats and chickens; any small bird or mammal is acceptable, such animals making up the great bulk of the diet. Reproduction is by means of eggs.

BULL SNAKES
(*Pituophis*)
PLATES 110 AND 111

If snakes can have personality, the bull snakes have it; they are the big, blustering characters of our serpent world. When annoyed, a bull snake puts on a show; it coils, throws the neck into loops, hisses loudly, vibrates the tail, and weaves the body. Although it will bite, it does so halfheartedly because primarily it is a bluffer more interested in frightening than in injuring an adversary. The average adult is about five feet long, and such a size combined with conspicuous blotches and the defensive behavior make a sight not easily forgotten. The bull snakes probably have the highest rating as a friend of the farmer. They are typically inhabitants of open, cultivated country, where the rodents they devour in great numbers do the most damage to crops. Although relatively powerful constrictors, these reptiles could not injure a person unless the entire body of a large one were wound about the neck and the ends lost sight of. Reproduction is by means of eggs.

Only two species live in this country: one, often called "pine snake," in the east; the other over the central and western parts, its range including adjacent southern Canada and the northern highland states of Mexico. Both the species vary from one part of the range to the other and therefore have been given several technical names.

KING SNAKES
(*Lampropeltis*)
PLATES 112 AND 113

The king snakes are popularly thought of as the sworn enemies of the rattlesnakes. Although in the interests of good science this statement must be rejected, it does contain an element of truth. King snakes are fond of eating other kinds of snakes whether venomous or harmless, and certainly it is this habit that won them the reputation of taking sides with human beings in the effort to exterminate rattlers. The king snakes are powerful constrictors, and at least some of them enjoy a relative immunity to snake venom. With such attributes it is little wonder that they can readily subdue venomous species. In addition to snakes and lizards, many small mammals and some birds are eaten; insects are included in the diet of smaller forms.

A brief account of such a varied assortment of snakes is most difficult. Seven kinds of king snakes are found in this country and Canada alone, and as many additional species as well as nearly all of these seven occur in Mexico; the range of the genus extends southward to Ecuador. Our seven species, taken as a unit, present a bewildering array of patterns, ranging from black snakes with fine yellow lines more or less evident to brilliantly banded snakes rivaling the venomous coral snakes in beauty. The familiar milk snake (*L. doliata* or *triangulum*) of the eastern United States is really one of the king snakes, although seldom recognized as such. This is the only member of the group that lives in Canada, and it, of course, occurs only in the southeastern portion of that country. One kind of king snake or another lives in almost every part of the United States. The habitats of king snakes are as varied as are their color patterns. Some inhabit our deserts, some the dry canyons and mountains of the west, some the prairies, some the great eastern woodlands and cultivated fields. There are sub-surface king snakes, although most of them live on the ground. No species is truly aquatic, the nearest approach being those that often live near water and do not mind entering it occasionally. All of the king snakes lay eggs.

COLUBRID SNAKES OF EUROPE
(Family Colubridæ)

TYPICAL SNAKES
(Subfamily Colubrinæ)
PLATE 116

Although, from the point of view of reptile distribution, Europe is scarcely a unit, it is a region where the scientific study of amphibians and reptiles began and has continued unabated. This is reason enough for us to devote a little space to its typical snakes. Twenty of all the 31 European snakes belong to this category. These twenty species are assigned to eight genera, four of which (*Natrix, Elaphe, Coluber, Contia*) are more or less circumglobal in distribution; three others are widely distributed in the parts of Africa and Asia adjacent to Europe. Only one genus with its single known species is limited in distribution: it occurs in the southern part of the Spanish Peninsula, near-by islands, and adjacent northern Africa. The simple truth is that Europe has no snake genus all its own. Its total of 31 species shows up weakly against that of the United States: 114. The comparative areas of these two parts of the world are: about 3,000,000 square miles for the United States proper; 3,750,-000 for Europe. Europe is situated somewhat farther north, a disadvantage partly offset by the warm current that bathes its western shores. Perhaps the great deserts of northern Africa and southwestern Asia have cut off access from the tropics; the plateau of Mexico has had a somewhat similar effect on the United States. That the Mediterranean Sea is not the barrier one might expect it to be is shown by this fact: almost a third of the species of typical snakes of Europe, and all but one of its genera, are found in northern Africa as well.

St. Patrick is usually given credit for having driven the snakes from Ireland. The grain of truth in this belief is that he drove out serpent worship rather than serpents. This worship had been brought in by immigrants from the mainland, a fact that explains how a people living on a snakeless island worshipped snakes. Ireland has no snakes because it is a relatively old island which was covered with ice during the last geologic epoch, the Pleistocene. How comparatively recent that was is illustrated by the surprising fact that the last European glaciation ended between 12,000 and 15,000 years ago. Now it is only left to explain why near-by Great Britain does have snakes (three kinds). We must know three things: Ireland was connected with Great Britain; both were a part of the mainland during some of the Pleistocene; Ireland was cut off at a relatively early time, which must have been before the snakes had reached it. It is not certain whether the snakes survived in southern England during the times of European glaciation; if they did not, they had ample opportunity to migrate from the mainland.

COBRAS, CORAL SNAKES, AND THEIR ALLIES
(Family Elapidæ)

THIS LARGE family includes several long, spectacular species and an array of small, brilliantly colored ones, as well as roughly half of the non-marine venomous snakes. The extent of distribution rivals that of any other family, and much romance is attached to many of its members. The over-all distribution may be visualized as a dumb-bell with a long, thick grip. One end, comprising about a third of the species, is the great lot of New World coral snakes, so much alike that virtually all of them (some forty-two species) are placed in the single genus *Micrurus*. The other end is the flowering of the assortment that inhabits the region of New Guinea and Australia, where the species, though not greatly exceeding those of the New World in number, far surpass them in diversity of form, and are necessarily divided into a great many genera, some of which have few species. These two ends are connected by fewer than fifty diverse species, the most conspicuous array of the family, distributed widely over Africa, through southern Asia, the Malay Archipelago, and the Philippines to New Guinea, the eastern extremity being in the Fiji Islands. There is difference of opinion as to how many genera the entire family should be divided into, but the number tentatively may be put at thirty. No elapid is found in Europe now, although some twenty million years ago (Miocene times) a species much like modern cobras lived there.

All members of this family are potentially venomous. However, many of them are not dangerous, three factors contributing to their relative harmlessness: secretive habits, small size, and ineffective method of injecting venom. Only the last of these calls for elaboration. The relatively short and permanently erect fangs are not to be compared with the viper's fangs; in many species they are too small to be very effective. Most species do not strike, and therefore they must be actually trodden on or handled to become dangerous. Those that do strike make mere jabs with the elevated head; such jabs are far more easily avoided than the lightning-like strike of a rattler, for instance.

There is no satisfactory way of dividing the members of this diverse family into assortments convenient for my brief treatment. A purely geographic basis, the easiest for the reader, does not do well because, among other difficulties, many of the Asiatic species are more like New World coral snakes (*Micrurus*) than they are like other Asiatic kinds. A grouping based partly on distribution and partly on relationship in structure or habits will be used in default of a really good one.

CORAL SNAKES OF THE NEW WORLD
PLATES 117 AND 118

The coral snakes of the New World are found from the southern United States to Argentina and Peru (including the island of Trinidad). Some forty-two of them placed in the one genus *Micrurus* are brightly colored snakes, nearly all with conspicuous rings of red, black, and yellow encircling the body. One member of the family, found in southern Arizona, southwestern New Mexico, and adjacent northern Mexico, is a desert species excessively rare and too small (greatest length: eighteen inches) to be dangerous. This, the Arizona coral snake (*Micruroides euryxanthus*), is allocated to a genus by itself on the strength of having a minute tooth behind each fang, a tooth not found in any other New World coral snake. Two extremely slender coral snakes of South America, being largely black in color and therefore lacking the characteristic ringed pattern, are placed alone in another genus, *Leptomicrurus*.

All of these American coral snakes, about thirty of which are found in South America, belong to the secretive, non-striking type already mentioned, and are dangerous at close range only—that is, when stepped on or handled. The venom in general is extremely potent, being neurotoxic in action. The well-known coral snake of the United States, *Micrurus fulvius*, reaches a maximum length of thirty-nine inches, and occurs in the coastal lowlands from eastern North Carolina southward and thence westward as far as eastern Texas and the Mexican states of Coahuila and Tamaulipas; in the Mississippi lowlands, it ranges northward to western Kentucky. When a large specimen does succeed in biting an exposed area (the teeth are too short to penetrate ordinary shoes or heavy clothing), the result may be serious, the percentage of fatalities from the bites being relatively high, the treatment difficult and uncertain (see page 163). Death may occur in from eighteen to twenty-four hours.

Two confusing factors enter into man's relation with this coral snake. The first is the deceptive docility of the species that often leads those admiring its beauty, or wanting to "show off," to handle it carelessly. The second factor is its striking similarity to certain harmless snakes that live within its range. These inoffensive reptiles may be much more abundant than the genuine article, and unduly alarm persons greatly fearing it. Various rules and jingles have been proposed to enable anyone to identify a true coral snake. I suggest the following:

If the snake has bands of red, yellow, and black more or less completely encircling the body, see whether the head as far back as the eyes is black; if so, the snake must be a coral snake.

When the head is hidden, a study of the bands will serve to check the identity. Only the coral snake has wide alternating bands of black and red separated by narrow fillers of yellow; there are as many yellow fillers as red and black bands together. In the so-called mimics, the alternating bands are red and yellow, and together add up to equal the number of black bands. The relative widths of the bands in the mimics will not be described for fear of complicating matters. It might be added that if the bands do not completely encircle the body, the snake is harmless. One harmless species has complete bands like those of the coral snake.

ELAPIDS OF AUSTRALIA AND NEW GUINEA
PLATES 119 AND 120

As already indicated, the greatest development of the family Elapidæ is found in the region of Australia and New Guinea. Australia itself is the culmination; here some sixty species all but reign supreme; the three other families represented make up a mere fraction of the total number of snakes. This, of course, means that the vast majority of Australian snakes are venomous, a fact mitigated by the small size and the consequent comparative inoffensiveness of many species.

Rather than give brief descriptions of many Australian elapids, I shall present general accounts of a few species that stand out from among the rest as being large and dangerous.

Foremost among these is the taipan (*Oxyuranus scutellatus*) of eastern Australia, chiefly the Cape York Peninsula. This snake reaches a length of from ten to eleven feet, carries more than twice as much venom as any other Australian snake, and has fangs almost half an inch long—much longer than those of the tiger snake. None of the few persons known to have been bitten has recovered, and a horse died in five minutes after a bite. It will attack at sight, and its actions when enraged inspire dread. Keeping one or two coils well above the rest, it waves the tail to and fro, flattens the body, and delivers several bites in rapid succession. Fortunately, it is rare.

The tiger snake (*Notechis scutatus*) is usually considered the most dangerous of Australian snakes, not being rare like the taipan. The range embraces most of Australia, especially its southern part, and it occurs on Tasmania. It sometimes reaches a length of six feet, and always shows great activity when annoyed, flattening the head as well as the neck, and raising the front part of its body, which it moves back and forth until the strike is delivered. No other land (in contrast to marine) snake has such potent venom; death in man results from paralysis of the breathing-mechanism. It has been calculated that a tiger snake with venom glands as capacious as those of a diamond-back rattlesnake would carry enough venom to kill at least four hundred men. The capacity of this snake to reproduce is remarkable, as many as seventy-two young being born at once. One hundred and nine young were taken from a gravid female, a record astonishing enough to call for confirmation.

From a strictly scientific point of view, the most interesting thing about the death adder (*Acanthophis antarcticus*) is, as the name implies, its resemblance to a viper in having a thick body and broad head. It may be considered the best example of the diversity in structure of the Australian members of the family under discussion, a diversity already referred to and paralleled in a far more spectacular way among the mammals (marsupials). The venom, though potent enough, is only about one third as toxic as that of the tiger snake, and the maximum length but half as great. It has the nasty habit of holding on when it bites. The range embraces almost the whole of Australia and extends northward into the Malay Archipelago.

The black snake (*Pseudechis porphyriacus*) commonly reaches a length of six feet, and is noteworthy because of the fierce duels engaged in by the males, apparently urged by a territorial instinct that may have a bit of sex mixed with it. These battles, fought in rounds lasting about a minute and strongly suggesting human prize-ring affairs, have been described in detail by David Fleay, Director of the Fauna Reserve at West Burleigh, Queensland, Australia. With arched necks and raised heads, the contestants spar for advantage, each trying to get its head above that of the other. When this is accomplished by one, it violently entwines its body about the adversary until the two look like strands of a rope. Furiously writhing and hissing, the two snakes constrict each other as they roll over and over. As if by signal, the round ends suddenly and preparation for the next begins with the same sparring. The contest continues until complete exhaustion ends it. Battling pairs may even be picked up without separating, so engrossed do they become.

The brown snake (*Demansia textilis*), which reaches a length of six feet seven inches, engages in battles even more violent than those of the black snake.

KRAITS, CORAL SNAKES, AND COBRAS OF AFRICA, ASIA, THE MALAY ARCHIPELAGO, AND THE PHILIPPINE ISLANDS
PLATES 121, 122, 123, 124, 125, 126, AND 127

Many of the snakes about to be considered do not have well-established English names, and a few small genera will not even be mentioned. New Guinea is excluded, it having been treated along with Australia because so many species are common to the two areas. In the region as a whole, there are three predominant types of snakes that completely overshadow the few specialties I omit. These three types are the cobras, large snakes with more or less expansible necks, the so-called "hoods"; the kraits, mostly black and white (or yellow) banded snakes lacking hoods; the coral snakes, hoodless, brightly banded, striped, or spotted snakes often reminding one of the New World coral snakes. The cobras are different enough to be broken up into four or five genera with the greatest diversity in Africa, but a good representation extending through southern Asia and well on into the Malay and Philippine islands. The kraits (*Bungarus*) are southern Asiatic with a small spillover into the Malay Archipelago. The coral snakes (*Callophis*) are also Asiatic with a few species in the Malay Archipelago and the Philippine Islands. In number of species, the three groups are roughly equal, each with not many more or less than eleven.

Even though "cobra" is a non-technical name, it has a usefulness because, first, it is widely understood, and, second, it can be conveniently applied to certain large snakes with more or less expansible necks and similar behavior. The scientific names of these species are difficult, involving as they do four group or generic terms.

The cobras may be simply divided into two lots on a geographic basis. Species found in Africa alone or in Africa and immediately adjacent southwestern Asia:

Egyptian cobra (*Naja haje*)
Black-lipped cobra (*Naja melanoleuca*)
Black-necked cobra (*Naja nigricollis*)
Cape cobra (*Naja nivea*)
Ringhals (*Hemachatus hæmachatus*)
Black cobra (*Pseudohaje nigra*)
Gold's cobra (*Pseudohaje goldi*)
Ringed water cobra (*Boulengerina annulata*)
Christy's water cobra (*Boulengerina christyi*)

Species found in southeastern Asia, the Malay Archipelago, and the Philippine Islands (or only on the islands):

Indian cobra (*Naja naja*)
Celebes cobra (*Naja celebensis*)
King cobra (*Naja hannah*)

The Egyptian cobra, the first listed, is the sole species that ranges into adjacent southwestern Asia. Sometimes known as the asp, it is probably the snake with which Cleopatra committed suicide. However, certain true vipers are also called "asps." The Cape cobra and the ringhals are found only in southern Africa; the black, Gold's, and water cobras are central in distribution, the first two typical of the western rain forests, the water cobras of the Congo and eastern lake regions. The Egyptian, the black-lipped, and black-necked cobras are all widely distributed.

The Indian cobra has an enormous distribution that covers the general region of the Indian Peninsula and extends eastward and southeastward to include the Philippines and most of the Malay Archipelago. Certainly more than one species is involved, but no one has ever studied enough cobras to arrive at a satisfactory conclusion. At present, several names are applied to populations of various regions. The Celebes cobra is found only on Celebes, and nothing is known about its habits. The king cobra differs noticeably from the others; it is often justifiably set off as the sole member of the genus *Ophiophagus*.

It would be easy to fill this entire book with fascinating cobra facts and lore, but I shall have to confine my treatment to a few remarks about snake-charmers, mongooses and cobras, and a brief summary of the study of spitting cobra fangs made by Bogert. As snakes are deaf to sounds carried by the air (see page 130), it is patent that they cannot respond to the music played to them by the snake men. The Indian charmer sways his trunk from side to side, a motion that causes the highly sensitive cobra to perform its "dance," apparently to the rhythm of the music.

Mongooses, like many other mammals, enjoy fighting snakes (see page 140). The mongoose does not hesitate to attack an Indian cobra of any size. The battle that ensues is not particularly exciting, as I was able to determine in southern China, where both mongoose and cobra are common. The relatively slow, downward jabs of the snake are met head-on by the mongoose and the four jaws lock; the amount of rolling over and over that may follow depends on the relative size of the combatants. The mongoose likes to fight at close quarters and thus impose a handicap on the cobra, which cannot well shorten its strikes. By sheer superior agility, the little mammal avoids all but direct mouth-to-mouth contact with the snake, whose fangs are at a disadvantage in competing with the numerous, longer teeth of the mongoose. The battle ends when the head or neck of the exhausted cobra is crushed by the jaws of the adversary. The mongoose, being susceptible to cobra venom, cannot allow itself to be bitten.

Three kinds of cobras have the terrifying habit of "spitting" their venom at an adversary. The venom is actually ejected in two fine streams that soon mingle to form a spray. The spitter aims high, and can send the venom several feet, far enough to reach the eyes of a near-by man. In fact, the aim is always high. The venom is harmless to man unless it enters the eyes, where it causes serious irritation or even blindness if not removed at once.

Bogert's study of the fangs of the spitters showed that they differ from those of the non-spitters; the tip of the fang is modified so that venom emerging under pressure is sent out at an approximate right angle to the axis of the fang. Thus the snake, by raising and tilting the head enough, can send the venom in the desired direction out of the slightly open mouth. In the two inveterate spitters, the ringhals and black-necked cobras, the fang is always modified for spitting, whereas in the Indian cobra it is so modified only in the eastern part of the range, the modification being progressive and most highly developed in the Malay Archipelago. The behavior of the cobras is in general correlated with the shape of the fang, except that in the region of southeastern Asia some of them seem to have a fairly well-developed spitting fang but do not spit. The familiar cobra of the Indian region does not spit.

The habit of spitting can be thought of as very advantageous, or the reverse. Certainly it is wasteful of venom under many circumstances. It would seem to be a defensive act directed against large enemies. Small enemies or little animals suitable for prey would be very hard to hit, and those intended to serve as prey could no doubt escape even if hit. It would be especially interesting to know whether a cobra ever spits at a mongoose. The suggestion has been made that spitting was developed by snakes of open country constantly in danger of being trodden upon by large, hoofed animals. Against these the ordinary snake has poor defense, as a little thought will convince anyone; the spitter might stop them by being able to operate at a distance. Bogert raises the objection that the cobras of the Indian and Malay Archipelago regions are perhaps equally exposed to hoofed animals, and one would expect the spitting ability to be developed in both regions. Theories, though the life-blood of science, may be, like this one, impossible of proof.

MAMBAS (AFRICA)

I am giving the mambas (*Dendroaspis*, often spelled *Dendraspis*) undue space because of the notoriety they enjoy as being among the most dread-inspiring of snakes. This reputation is only partly deserved, for some of the mambas are not ferocious, and none of them lives up to its reputation. Certain attributes combine to make the aggressive ones dangerous: agility, size, arboreal habits, and the practice of raising the forepart high when attacking. The last three of these contribute to an ability to deliver bites in the head and trunk, such bites being far more dangerous than the usual ones on or near the hands and feet. There is a story of the virtual extinction of an entire family by a mamba, and others equally bloodcurdling, but the fact is that the mambas have no occult method of dealing with human beings; they are merely large, agile, more or less aggressive, arboreal snakes that must be respected like any others with such attributes. The following brief account summarizes the important facts about the five species, and should help straighten out the vast confusion over the so-called "green" and "black" mambas, which are now thought to be distinct species, not just color varieties of one species.

The "black" mamba (*D. polylepis*). This is the big, aggressive, highly dangerous snake that has given the mambas their bad reputation. It has been hopelessly confused with the green mamba (*D. angusticeps*) because of a general similarity, and the fact that both are green when young. The adult black mamba is dark brown to almost black. It is less arboreal than the green mamba, prefers more open country, and always gapes the mouth when startled. It has a wide distribution south of the Sahara Desert, and reaches a length of fourteen feet.

The "green" mamba (*D. angusticeps*). This, a much smaller species, retains its green coloration throughout life, and is not aggressive. It inhabits more thickly forested or bush-covered areas than does the black mamba, and, in keeping with this preference, is relatively arboreal. The mouth is never gaped. The distribution is extensive though less western than that of *D. polylepis*.

Jameson's mamba (*D. jamesoni*). This species, also smaller than the black mamba, occurs in the lake region and rain forests of central Africa. The coloration is variable, with green predominant, and more or less black and brown evident; the tail is either black or black and green.

West African mamba (*D. viridis*). A species of moderate size; green with dark-edged scales.

Transvaal mamba (*D. mamba*). An unimportant species of the Transvaal.

SEA SNAKES
(Family Hydrophiidæ)

THE SEA snakes should be thought of as cobra-coral snake relatives that have taken up a marine life. The aquatic habits of these elapid-like snakes have not changed the teeth, but have brought about marked differences in shape and structure of body. The tail is greatly flattened from side to side, the body more or less so; the nostrils are usually located on the upper surface of the snout, the nasal passages provided with valves, and the large scales of the belly are lacking in many of the groups or genera. Without these belly scales, the so-called ventral plates, movement of a snake on land is slow and awkward. All sea snakes are excellent swimmers and feel so much at home in the water that they have developed the habit of basking on its surface. They frequent inshore waters, the open oceans being a barrier to their distribution. This dislike of the deep seas has undoubtedly kept them from spreading throughout the warm waters of the world (see page 167). One Philippine species (*Hydrophis semperi*) has even become land-locked in Lake Taal, Luzon, a fresh-water lake.

Two interesting facts have already been brought out: the sea snakes did not give rise to the sea-serpent myth (see page 133), and they live entirely on fishes, chiefly eels (page 144). Many of these are spiny, a fact that does not deter the snake; the spines are eliminated through the body wall of the snake after the eels have been swallowed.

The sea snakes bring forth the young directly, with the known exception of a few species of the genus *Laticauda* that go ashore to lay eggs. It is probable that other species of this and related genera do likewise. Species of *Laticauda* and two other genera still have ventral plates, and can make good progress on land. They are, in short, the sea snakes as yet partly suited to life on land. Dr. Smith, monographer of the sea snakes (see bibliography), puts the thirteen species of these three genera aside as a subfamily, which includes about a fourth of the known sea snakes and may be looked on as a party of conservatives with one foot still planted firmly on land.

This startling statement can be made about the sea snakes: they are at once the most venomous and the most harmless of poisonous snakes. Laboratory tests prove that the venom of one species (*Enhydrina schistosa*), for example, is much more toxic than that of the Indian cobra, and yet sea snakes almost never molest bathers, and fishermen often disentangle them from nets with the bare hands. The biting-apparatus is inefficient compared with that of vipers and the disposition extraordinarily good.

One habit of at least some sea snakes still calls for explanation and that is aggregation in vast numbers, even millions. The individuals of such an assemblage lose their usual shyness, refusing to dive out of sight at the approach of a ship, for instance. Dr. Smith quotes an obscure account describing "a solid mass of sea-snakes, twisted thickly together" extending for some sixty miles at a width of ten feet. The species was *Astrotia stokesi*, large adults of which are about five feet long.

VIPERS
(Family Viperidæ)

THE VIPERS have developed the most efficient venom-injecting apparatus of any reptiles, living or fossil, and this is what sets them off from the other snakes. The fangs are so long that, when not in use, they must be folded backward and upward to rest against the roof of the mouth. In order to accomplish this, the bone carrying the fangs had to be shortened to permit rotation, and this shortening process eliminated the other teeth that the bone carried. The development of the injecting-apparatus of course necessitated many additional drastic changes in the skull and teeth.

The family is readily divided into two assortments or subfamilies, one having a facial pit (Crotalinæ), the other without it (Viperinæ). Members of the first subfamily are the pit vipers, those of the other the true vipers. This facial pit is so large that it has affected the shape of the bone bearing the fangs, giving it a deep cavity into which the pit fits. (Each of these two subfamilies is often, and with some justification, treated as a family.)

To the casual observer, the pit appears as a hole on the side of the head between eye and nostril but lower down than both. Actually, it is a complex sense organ consisting of two cavities separated by a thin membrane something like an eardrum. Many speculations as to its use have been made. Recent experiments indicate that it is primarily a sense organ for temperature discrimination;

the pit viper is able to detect the presence of warm-blooded prey, and bite it effectively.

The true and pit vipers will be dealt with separately. The former occur only in the Old World, the latter in both hemispheres. Australia and New Guinea have neither, a deficiency made up for by the great development there of the (venomous) cobra-coral snake family (Elapidæ).

PIT VIPERS
(Subfamily Crotalinæ)

THE PIT VIPERS have an extensive distribution in the New as well as in the Old World, but are lacking in Australia and New Guinea. They are found from the mouth of the Volga in extreme eastern Europe eastward and southeastward across Asia to Japan and well into the Malay Archipelago. There is none in Africa or extreme southwestern Asia. In the New World, they range from extreme southern Canada southward over the rest of North America and nearly all of South America. In the West Indies, they occur only on Martinique and islands directly south of it.

With almost a hundred species, or half again as many as those of the true viper subfamily, the pit vipers, divided into only five (as against ten) genera, certainly do not show proportionately as great diversity in habits and choice of environment. They do have certain unusual and interesting attributes, abound in the Americas, and include some of our most familiar and, perhaps, most notorious reptiles. I shall take them up by groups that correspond almost exactly to the genera of science, beginning with the rattlesnakes.

RATTLESNAKES
(*Crotalus* and *Sistrurus*)
PLATES 128, 129, 130, 131, 132, 133, 134, 135, 136, 137, AND 138

Perhaps no snake is more easily recognized than a rattlesnake, because every one has a rattle; even at birth the "button," easily recognized as the beginning of a rattle, is present. The rattle is unique not only among snakes, but in the animal kingdom as well. It is a sound-producing apparatus with its own special method of growth. Several of the bones of the tail have come together to form the core of the rattle. Apparently the sound of the rattle serves as a warning that enables the snake to avoid conflicts. It might be compared to the snarl of a wolf or the growl of a tiger, and it promotes conservation of venom. Someone has suggested that the rattle developed in a country where snakes were often trodden on by large, hoofed animals against which the venom had little effect. (See the discussion of spitting cobras, page 213.) The uselessness of the rattle in telling the age of its bearer has been dealt with on page 158.

Twenty-eight species of rattlers are known, and they are divided scientifically into two genera. A large one (*Crotalus*) is made up of species of various sizes and includes all but three of the species. The other genus, the pigmy rattlers (*Sistrurus*), has only small species, as the name implies. For our purposes the two genera may be considered as a single group, the differences being of a rather technical nature.

If we consider the total distribution of rattlesnakes, extending as it does from southern Canada through the rest of North America and over South America (east of the Andes) as far as northern Argentina, we may jump to the false conclusion that the species are uniformly spread over this wide area. Nothing is further from the truth. Rattlesnakes are typically reptiles of the highlands of northern Mexico and the adjacent similar though lower country of the extreme southwestern United States. A point in animal geography is involved here: conditions of climate as we go northward from the equator remain the same only as lower levels are reached. Therefore, the rattlesnake that lives at a relatively low level in our southwest experiences climatic conditions similar to those experienced by the rattler living much higher in Mexico. In southern Arizona alone about one third of all known species of rattlesnakes may be found.

In spite of the fact that rattlesnakes are most at home in the dry southwestern part of North America, several species have wandered far afield to live under conditions that are anything but dry. Some have become dwellers of forests and even swamps. None has become truly aquatic or arboreal, although some enter water occasionally and even climb a little. I shall give an account of six important kinds, the infamous tropical rattler and five species of the United States.

The diamond-back rattlers, the most formidable venomous reptiles of this country, are the giants among rattlesnakes (see page 134). Although similar in appearance, these two species live in quite different types of country, their ranges not even overlapping. The eastern diamond-back (*Crotalus adamanteus*) is a denizen of low, coastal lands from Pamlico Sound, North Carolina, to and throughout Florida; thence westward possibly to extreme eastern Louisiana. It is never found more than a hundred miles from the coast. Palmetto flatwoods are its favorite haunt, but any low, brushy country is inhabited as well. It does not like swamps, but will live adjacent to them.

The western diamond-back (*Crotalus atrox*) is a reptile of dry country and deserts. The distribution is several times as great as that of its eastern cousin, and largely because of this it may be considered much more of a menace. Its disposition, if anything, is worse. The range embraces the extensive territory beginning in central Missouri and eastern (but not far eastern) Texas, and extending westward to extreme southeastern California and through the Mexican state of Sonora. In eastern Mexico the range extends as far south as the state of San Luis Potosí.

Over the eastern half of the United States the banded rattlesnake (*Crotalus horridus*) reigns supreme except, perhaps, in the narrow coastal area of the southeast, where it lives with the eastern diamond-back. The former is not found in peninsular Florida, and therefore the two species live together over a limited area. The only other rattlers that occur east of the Mississippi River are pigmy rattlesnakes (*Sistrurus*) too small to be a threat to human life. Fortunately, it is the smaller of the two pigmy species that lives in the southeastern states where the danger is greater because more people walk around poorly shod and the snake season is longer.

The banded rattlesnake is adaptable, being as much at home in the forests of the Appalachian highlands as in the canebrake of the coastal plain. This accounts for its other names: "timber" and "canebrake" rattler. It is large, ranking third in size among the rattlesnakes of the United States; the greatest length is six feet, a figure that far exceeds the average. It barely reaches southwestern Maine (a state all but devoid of venomous snakes), and ranges thence westward to the region of Niagara Falls, and southwestward to northern Florida. It is not found in the western Great Lakes area, but does occur from the Baraboo Hills of southern Wisconsin southward through eastern Texas and the western Gulf states. Only in the western extremity of its distribution does it overlap other large western rattlers.

Our next species, the prairie rattlesnake (*Crotalus viridis* or *confluentus*), covers the western half of the United States about as completely as the banded rattler covers the eastern, the two ranges approximating along the 98th parallel in the southern half of the country; farther north there is a wide gap between them. One or the other of these snakes is found over some nine tenths of the country; the areas from which they are absent are scattered and not easily outlined, with the exception of all of Michigan and virtually all of Maine and Minnesota. The prairie rattlesnake is the only venomous reptile of the entire northwestern quarter of the United States, a fact that should not be forgotten by people who live in that part.

This species differs greatly in appearance from one part of its range to another, and has consequently received no fewer than seven subspecific names. I mention this by way of warning that such names as the Great Basin rattlesnake, the Pacific rattlesnake, the Grand Canyon rattlesnake, the midget faded rattlesnake, and even others will be found in books about our western reptiles; all of these are varieties no two of which will be found in any one area. The prairie rattler is quick to strike, and attains a large size, the average one being about three feet long, the longest five; some of the varieties are much smaller.

The tropical rattlesnake (*Crotalus durissus*), or cascabel, as it is called in Spanish, has several claims to glory. As the name implies, it lives in the tropics; the range, beginning in southern Mexico, covers all of tropical America except that part of South America lying west of the Andes. Of course it does not live in the Andes themselves, high country that can hardly be considered tropical. This distribution is unmatched in total extent by any other rattler, and, indeed, no other kind of rattlesnake is found in the tropics except in extremely limited peripheral areas. The cascabel is partial to the more arid regions, and therefore the over-all range is deceptive; it is not found in the rain forests or wet coastal plains.

The tropical rattler is perhaps the most dangerous of rattlesnakes. It is one of the largest, being definitely surpassed in size only by the two diamond-backs, and its disposition is especially bad. The venom is very potent, having a high percentage of the neurotoxic or nerve-damaging element. It has a special effect on the neck muscles; the victim cannot hold the head up. This is the basis of the popular belief that this snake "breaks the neck" when it bites.

I have given in detail the ranges of certain big, important rattlers that live for the most part beyond the limits of what might be called the rattlesnake belt, the far southwestern section of this country and adjacent Mexico. Outside the limits of this belt, so few of these formidable species live in any one place that learning the ones that do is simple enough. Within the belt, matters are entirely different in two important respects: the number of species occurring in one place is so great that recognition becomes a problem, and, the country being desert or relatively hot and dry, the snakes are largely nocturnal, the combined heat of the soil and the sun during the day being too much for them. This last fact should be kept in mind by those traveling through the southwest.

The last of the rattlers to be considered, the sidewinder or horned rattlesnake (*Crotalus cerastes*), is perhaps the most interesting species from a scientific point of view because it has best adapted itself to life in the extreme desert conditions of the heart of the rattlesnake belt; in this respect one might think of it as a kind of perfectionist. It is the only rattlesnake with the "horn," a soft process that really is a greatly developed scale, the large one to be seen just above the eye in most snakes. This probably protects the eye from glare of the sun and drifting sand. The horned vipers of the Old World immediately come to mind. In addition, the side-winder has the habit of sinking itself in the sand by means of special movements of the body, and crawling in a manner that avoids loss of effort through the shifting nature of the sand (see page 153). In spite of these means of coping with desert conditions, this rattler succumbs in about nine minutes to the heat of direct noonday sun on open sand.

PIT VIPERS WITHOUT RATTLES

(*Agkistrodon, Trimeresurus,* and *Lachesis*)

PLATES 139, 140, 141, 142, 143, 144, 145, 146, 147, AND 148

The next genus of pit vipers, *Agkistrodon* or *Ancistrodon,* makes up in variety of structure and habits what it lacks in number of species (eleven or twelve). In size, the species vary from the little hump-nosed viper of Ceylon (*A. nepa*) to our own water moccasin (*A. piscivorus*), the former reaching a length of only 15, the latter of 72 inches. The second-largest, *A. acutus,* occurs in southern China and Tongking; the maximum length is five feet. In choice of a home, the species show a remarkable diversity, the extremes of which may be illustrated by the following facts. Three of the Asiatic species are high-mountain forms living at altitudes of about ten thousand feet in the Himalaya Mountains and adjacent highlands; one, the Himalayan viper (*A. himalayanus*), has been recorded from sixteen thousand feet, which is a level considerably above any mountaintop in the United States proper. On the other extreme are our water moccasin of aquatic habits, and the Mexican moccasin (*A. bilineatus*) of Mexican and Central American (tropical) lowlands. As already implied, the range of this remarkable genus is extensive; in fact, the distribution of the whole group of pit vipers given on page 217 delimits the Old World range; in the New World, there are but three species: the two just mentioned and the copperhead. The range of one (the Mexican moccasin) has been indicated, and the other two will be dealt with in some detail below. A certain degree of reproductive versatility is shown, some species of the genus laying eggs, others bringing forth the young directly.

The water moccasin or cottonmouth (*A. piscivorus*) is the center of the greatest confusion to be found among our snakes. Unfortunately, there is a widely distributed group (the water snakes, genus *Natrix;* see page 194) with somewhat similar habits and, often, a more "ugly" appearance than the true moccasin. All over the eastern United States these harmless snakes are mistaken for moccasins, and slaughtered mercilessly. They do not have the pit in the side of the head (see page 216) nor movable fangs in the front of the upper jaw. It will help to remember that the cottonmouth lives only in the southeastern and Mississippi lowlands. The range begins in extreme southeastern Virginia and embraces the coastal plain and the edge of the Piedmont Plateau southward throughout Florida and on westward to include approximately the southeastern half of Texas. In the Mississippi River lowlands, it ascends as far as north central Missouri, avoiding the Ozark Plateau, and reaching Monroe County of southwestern Illinois. Beyond the limits of this range all "water moccasins" are harmless snakes, no matter who says they are dangerous.

The moccasin lives in or near water. Its appetite is broad; cold-blooded animals, including fishes, other reptiles, and frogs, are preferred, but mammals and birds are also eaten. From four to fifteen young are born at a time. The bite is occasionally fatal to man. Gangrene is a common secondary result of the bite.

The English name of the copperhead has for decades actually served a better purpose than has the technical name. The genus is, of course, *Agkistrodon* (or *Ancistrodon*), the species *mokeson* or *contortrix*, depending on the date of the book or article consulted. The copperhead may be thought of as the little villain among venomous snakes of this country; it snoops around and bites persons when they least expect it. A friend of mine lived for years in one of the wildest regions of our southeastern states, where his children were never harmed by snakes; he moved to a city of the coastal plain, and there one of his children was promptly bitten by a copperhead in the back yard within the city's limits. A large rattler is conspicuous and usually gives warning; the water moccasin is large and lives in or near water; the copperhead, in contrast, abounds in almost every type of country, and persists near human habitations.

Fortunately, the bite of the copperhead is not normally fatal to adult human beings.

The copperhead ranges widely over the southeastern states with the exception of Florida, where it is almost unknown. Its northern limits are indicated by a line starting at the northeastern tip of Massachusetts, extending to Pittsburgh and thence to the southeastern corner of Nebraska; its western by extending the line on to the Great Bend of the Rio Grande River. This pit viper differs in coloration from one part of its range to another, and has therefore been christened four times for scientific purposes. The average adult is barely three feet in length, the largest a few inches more than four. The catholic appetite is satisfied by small warm-blooded animals as well as small cold-blooded ones that even include insects. The average number of young born at a time is five.

The final assortment of pit vipers, a few more than fifty species, is found in both the New World and the Old. These snakes have long been divided into two groups, *Trimeresurus* of the Old World, and *Bothrops* of the Americas. As no one has ever shown any but a geographical basis for this division, the whole assortment should probably be placed in the one genus, *Trimeresurus*. These snakes are essentially tropical reptiles, found in the New World from the low, hot coasts of Mexico southward through South America, including the Lesser Antilles, to Argentina; in the Old World from the Indian Peninsula and adjacent territory, including Ceylon, eastward and southeastward through Asia, including southern China, and the Malay and Philippine islands. There are some twenty-two species in the Old World.

The habits vary considerably from species to species; many are arboreal, whereas others live on the ground; both live-bearing and egg-laying methods of reproduction are met with. I found females of one kind (*Trimeresurus monticola*) in southern China guarding eggs laid in nests roughly rounded in shape, and made in piles of shredded bamboo waste.

The many species of the New World together form an important part of the South American snake fauna. By far the most familiar kind is the notorious fer-de-lance (*Trimeresurus* or *Bothrops atrox*). This, the giant of the genus (see page 134), sometimes called "barba amarilla," ranges from the hot tropical coasts of Mexico (the state of San Luis Potosí on the east, Oaxaca on the west) southward over tropical South America to northern Argentina. Islands of the Lesser Antilles are also inhabited. It is ubiquitous, being as much at home in forests as in open country, or even cultivated fields.

The last, but by no means least, of the species to be considered is the bushmaster, the giant among pit vipers (see page 134), a snake so different from its relatives that it is set off in a genus by itself and known as *Lachesis muta*. The range begins in coastal Costa Rica, ends on the Brazilian coasts in the state of Bahia, and includes the island of Trinidad. It lives in humid forests, especially in the vicinity of rivers. The young hatch from eggs, whereas all other New World pit vipers bring forth their young directly.

TRUE VIPERS
(Subfamily Viperinæ)
PLATES 149, 150, 151, 152, 153, 154, AND 155

THE TRUE VIPERS comprise an assortment of snakes that have tried everything; though few in number of species, they have become so diversified in structure and habits that about all left for them is adaptation to water. Their diversity is the more astonishing in view of their continuous range, which is confined to the Old World, and covers Africa and all of the European and Asiatic mainland suitable for snakes (see page 167). They have not reached Ireland or Japan. In the Malay Archipelago they are but poorly represented by one species (Russell's viper, *Vipera russelli*) on Java and two small islands.

When closely related animals differ so much over an apparently continuous area, we look for an explanation; something must have served to separate groups and allow them to evolve in various directions. Great expanses of water are the most obvious barriers, but none exists in the area where the true vipers are found. The Mediterranean Sea is not the barrier one might expect it to be; many European species live in the northern coastal region of Africa, but do not pass the desert lying to the south. A glance at the proper type of map will show, however, that barriers do exist in the form of mountains and cold highlands as well as hot deserts. A continuous barrier made up of these elements stretches right across the land mass of Africa and Eurasia from Tibet through northern Africa.

Taking a broad view of our true vipers, and omitting unimportant details as well as technical names, we can bring out some salient facts and correlations. One lot of species made use of the temperate area from Europe across central Asia to its eastern coast. Another lot of about the same number of species took to the desert part of the barrier just delimited and became able to live under conditions of dryness. You might say that these optimists turned stumbling-blocks into steppingstones; certainly they made use of an area not perfectly suited for serpent life. A third lot, which far surpasses the other two in diversity and number of species, appropriated the forests and savannas of Africa, where they found ideal conditions. The little overlapping involved in this broad view of the true vipers does not spoil the main picture, and will be pointed out below.

This highly simplified view needs amplification that will emphasize interesting facts about the well-known genera and species. Snakes of the European and central Asiatic lot belong to one genus (*Vipera*), with seven of its ten species found in Europe. There is a slight spillover of the genus into extreme northern Africa. Only one species, Russell's viper already mentioned, is a part of the true-viper fauna of tropical Asia; the others live in southwestern and central Asia. The outstanding member of the genus is the common European viper (*Vipera berus*), a reptile that has one of the most extensive of ranges; it is found from the British Isles straight across Eurasia (north of the central barriers just discussed). The species of this temperate lot are relatively normal in appearance and habits; the wandering off of Russell's viper into the tropics is the most radical thing any of them did.

The desert optimists, a lot with scarcely as many species as *Vipera*, have been divided into four small genera, so diverse are they in structure. Most of them can be recognized at once by the peculiar lateral rows of scales set at an angle to those of the other rows. Although as a rule the species have limited ranges within the desert region common to Africa and Asia, one kind, the famous saw-scaled viper (*Echis carinatus*), has burst the desert boundary and extended its range into dry country from Ceylon through peninsular India westward to the region of the equator in Africa. This vicious reptile is protectively colored and has the unusual habit of making a noise like violently boiling water. When annoyed, it inflates the body, throws it into a figure-eight, and rubs the oblique lateral scales against each other. The inflation of the body and the saw-toothed keels extending down the middle of the scales are responsible for the vibration and friction that produce the sound. A pot of boiling vipers would not be the kind of brew to tamper with. Kipling wrote of this snake in his story of Rikki-tikki-tavi, the mongoose, mistakenly calling it a "Karait" (krait).

In southwestern Arabia and the desert of northern Africa the third and big lot, the African true vipers, slightly overlaps the desert lot, but the vast majority of the species of this third lot are by no means desert animals. The notorious puff adder (*Bitis lachesis* or *arietans*) is the one that ranges so widely over Africa and adjacent Arabia, showing a remarkable ability to adapt itself to different conditions; rain forests are about the only environment it shuns. This and a few other species of the genus are the big, chunky vipers so familiar to the traveler in Africa. The giant among them, the Gaboon viper (*Bitis gabonica*), reaches a length of six feet and a weight of at least eighteen pounds. The fangs may be nearly two inches long. In contrast to its formidable appearance, the species is remarkably docile, some individuals allowing themselves to be carried about freely without biting.

The three remaining genera of our third and African lot well illustrate the diversity already referred to. The night adders, members of the small genus *Causus*, look like ordinary harmless snakes, are nocturnal, and, in contrast to most true vipers, lay eggs and subsist largely on cold-blooded prey. The enormously developed venom gland extends far back from the head into the body. The burrowing vipers constitute the single large genus (twelve species) of true vipers, *Atractaspis*, and match the night adders in being unviperlike, an appearance belied by huge fangs; in fact, no snakes have proportionately larger ones. The two groups are also similar in the method of reproducing by means of eggs. When the burrowing vipers took to subterranean habits, they departed from the normal viperine way of life, to put it mildly; I know of no other group of burrowers among the vipers, either true or with pits. The last African genus of true vipers, *Atheris*, is a small one of arboreal species of the rain forests. They are typically viperine in appearance, and predominantly green in color, so that they match the foliage. These tree vipers cinch the claim that in Africa the true vipers have invaded all non-aquatic environments: trees and bushes, the surface of the ground, and the sub-surface.

South Africa, in spite of its latitude, has an abundance of true vipers; among the typically African genera, only the tree vipers, which are snakes of the tropics, do not occur.

For the sake of completeness, I shall mention the stray unviper-like true viper *Azemiops feæ*, of Upper Burma, southern China, and adjacent regions. Little is known about this primitive rarity.

Bibliography

✿

Allen, E. Ross and David Swindell: "Cottonmouth Moccasin of Florida." *Herpetologica*, Vol. 4 (1948), pp. 1–16.

Anthony, J. and J. Guibé: "Les Affinités Anatomiques de *Bolyeria* et de *Casarea* (Boidés)." *Mémoires Institut Scientifique Madagascar*, Series A, Vol. 7 (1952), pp. 189–201.

Barrett, Charles: *Reptiles of Australia.* Toronto: Cassell & Company; 1950.

Benedict, Francis G.: *The Physiology of Large Reptiles with Special Reference to the Heat Production of Snakes, Tortoises, Lizards and Alligators.* Washington: Carnegie Institution of Washington; 1932.

Blanchard, Frank N.: "The Ring-Neck Snakes, Genus *Diadophis*." *Bulletin, Chicago Academy Sciences*, Vol. 7 (1942), pp. 1–144.

—— and Frieda C.: "Mating of the Garter Snake *Thamnophis sirtalis sirtalis* (Linnæus)." *Papers, Michigan Academy Science Arts Letters*, Vol. 27 (1942), pp. 215–34.

Bogert, Charles M.: "Dentitional Phenomena in Cobras and Other Elapids with Notes on Adaptive Modifications of Fangs." *Bulletin, American Museum Natural History*, Vol. 81 (1943), pp. 285–360.

——: "Rectilinear Locomotion in Snakes." *Copeia* No. 4 (1947), pp. 253–4.

Burger, W. Leslie and Philip W. Smith: "The Coloration of the Tail Tip of Young Fer-de-Lances: Sexual Dimorphism rather than Adaptive Coloration." *Science*, Vol. 112 (1950), pp. 431–3.

Carpenter, Charles C.: "Growth and Maturity of the Three Species of *Thamnophis* in Michigan." *Copeia* No. 4 (1952), pp. 237–43.

Carr, Archie: "A Contribution to the Herpetology of Florida." *University Florida Publication Biological Science Series*, Vol. 3 (1940), pp. 1–118.

Conant, Roger: *The Reptiles of Ohio.* Notre Dame, Indiana: University of Notre Dame Press; 1951.

—— and William Bridges: *What Snake Is That? A Field Guide to the Snakes of the United States East of the Rocky Mountains.* New York: D. Appleton-Century Company; 1939.

Davis, D. Dwight: "Courtship and Mating Behavior in Snakes." *Field Museum Zoological Series*, Vol. 20 (1936), pp. 257–90.

Dunn, Emmett Reid: "Los Géneros de Anfibios y Reptiles de Colombia, III." *Caldasia*, Vol. 3 (1944), pp. 155–224.

Edgren, Richard A.: "Copulatory Adjustment in Snakes and Its Evolutionary Implications." *Copeia* No. 3 (1953), pp. 162–4.

Fleay, David: "The Scaled Wrestlers of the Australian Bush." *Animal Kingdom*, Vol. 54 (1951), pp. 84–8.

229

——: "This Australian Python Eats Other Snakes." *Animal Kingdom*, Vol. 55 (1952), pp. 157–9.

——: "Adventures with a Taipan." *Animal Kingdom*, Vol. 56 (1953), pp. 56–9.

Flower, Stanley S.: "Notes on the Recent Reptiles and Amphibians of Egypt, with a List of the Species Recorded from That Kingdom." *Proceedings, Zoological Society London*, Part 3 (1933), pp. 735–851.

——: "Further Notes on the Duration of Life in Animals.—3. Reptiles." *Proceedings, Zoological Society London*, Series A, Part 1 (1937), pp. 1–39.

Gans, Carl: "The Functional Morphology of the Egg-Eating Adaptations in the Snake Genus *Dasypeltis*." *Zoologica*, Vol. 37 (1952), pp. 209–44.

Gloyd, Howard K.: "The Rattlesnakes, Genera *Sistrurus* and *Crotalus*." *Chicago Academy Sciences*, Special Publication 4 (1940), pp. 1–266.

Gray, J.: "The Mechanism of Locomotion in Snakes." *Journal Experimental Biology*, Vol. 23 (1946), pp. 101–20.

Haas, C. P. J. de: "Checklist of the Snakes of the Indo-Australian Archipelago." *Treubia*, Vol. 20 (1950), pp. 511–625.

Haines, T. P.: "Delayed Fertilization in *Leptodeira annulata polysticta*." *Copeia* No. 2 (1940), pp. 116–18.

Hambly, Wilfrid D.: "Serpent Worship in Africa." *Field Museum Anthropological Series*, Vol. 21 (1931), pp. 1–85.

Hoffstetter, Robert: "Contribution à l'Étude des Elapidae Actuels et Fossiles et de l'Ostéologie des Ophidiens." *Arch. Mus. Hist. Nat. Lyon*, Vol. 15 (1939), pp. 1–82.

Kasturirangan, L. R.: "Placentation in the Sea-Snake, *Enhydrina schistosa* (Daudin)." *Proceedings, Indian Academy Sciences*, Vol. 34 (1951), pp. 1–32.

——: "The Allantoplacenta of the Sea Snake *Hydrophis cyanocinctus* Daudin." *Journal, Zoological Society India*, Vol. 3 (1952), pp. 277–90.

Keegan, Hugh L.: "Defensive Behavior of the Rubber Snake." *Copeia* No. 2 (1943), p. 129.

Klauber, Laurence M.: "A Key to the Rattlesnakes with Summary of Characteristics." *Transactions, San Diego Society Natural History*, Vol. 8 (1936), pp. 185–276.

Kopstein, Felix: "Ein Beitrag zur Eierkunde und zur Fortpflanzung der Malaiischen Reptilien." *Bulletin, Raffles Museum*, No. 14 (1938), pp. 81–167.

Loveridge, Arthur: *Reptiles of the Pacific World*. New York: The Macmillan Company; 1945.

——: "The Green and Black Mambas of East Africa." *Journal, East Africa Natural History Society*, Vol. 19 (1947–8), p. 251.

Mertens, Robert: "On Snail-Eating Snakes." *Copeia* No. 4 (1952), p. 279.

—— and Lorenz Müller: "Die Amphibien und Reptilien Europas." *Abhandlungen d. Senckenbergischen Naturforschenden Gesellschaft*, No. 451 (1940), pp. 1–56.

Mosauer, Walter: "On the Locomotion of Snakes." *Science*, Vol. 76 (1932), pp. 583–5.

Noble, G. K.: "The Brooding Habit of the Blood Python and of Other Snakes." *Copeia* No. 1 (1935), pp. 1–3.

——: "The Sense Organs Involved in the Courtship of *Storeria, Thamnophis* and other Snakes." *Bulletin, American Museum Natural History*, Vol. 73 (1937), pp. 673–725.

—— and A. Schmidt: "The Structure and Function of the Facial and Labial Pits of Snakes." *Proceedings, American Philosophical Society*, Vol. 77 (1937), pp. 263–88.

Oliver, James A.: "The Prevention and Treatment of Snakebite." *Animal Kingdom*, Vol. 55 (1952), pp. 66–83.

—— and Leonard J. Goss: "Antivenin Available for the Treatment of Snakebite." *Copeia* No. 4 (1952), pp. 270–2.

—— and Charles E. Shaw: "The Amphibians and Reptiles of the Hawaiian Islands." *Zoologica*, Vol. 38 (1953), pp. 65–95.

Ortenburger, Arthur I.: *The Whip Snakes and Racers: Genera Masticophis and Coluber*. Ann Arbor: University of Michigan; 1928.

Perkins, C. B.: "Longevity of Snakes in Captivity in the United States." *Copeia* No. 4 (1952), pp. 280–1.

Pitman, Charles R. S.: *A Guide to the Snakes of Uganda*. Kampala, Uganda: Uganda Society; 1938.

Pope, Clifford H.: "The Reptiles of China." *Natural History Central Asia*, Vol. 10 (1935), pp. 1–604. New York: The American Museum of Natural History.

——: *Snakes Alive and How They Live*. New York: The Viking Press; 1937.

——: "Copulatory Adjustment in Snakes." *Field Museum Zoological Series*, Vol. 24 (1941), pp. 249–52.

——: *The Poisonous Snakes of the New World*. New York: New York Zoological Society; 1944.

——: "Reptiles." In *The Care and Breeding of Laboratory Animals*, edited by Edmond J. Farris. New York: John Wiley & Sons; 1950.

Rahn, Hermann: "Sperm Viability in the Uterus of the Garter Snake, *Thamnophis*." *Copeia* No. 2 (1940), pp. 109–15.

Rooij, Nelly de: *The Reptiles of the Indo-Australian Archipelago. II. Ophidia*. Leiden: E. J. Brill; 1917.

Rose, Walter: *The Reptiles and Amphibians of Southern Africa*. Cape Town: Maskew Miller; 1950.

Schmidt, Karl P.: "Contributions to the Herpetology of the Belgian Congo Based on the Collection of The American Museum Congo Expedition, 1909–1915." *Bulletin, American Museum Natural History*, Vol. 49 (1923), Part II.–Snakes, pp. 1–146.

—— and D. Dwight Davis: *Field Book of Snakes of the United States and Canada*. New York: G. P. Putnam's Sons; 1941.

Shannon, Frederick A.: "Comments on the Treatment of Reptile Poisoning in the Southwest." *Southwestern Medicine*, Vol. 34 (1953), pp. 367–73.

Shaw, Charles E.: "The Male Combat 'Dance' of Some Crotalid Snakes." *Herpetologica*, Vol. 4 (1948), pp. 137–45.

Smith, Hobart M. and Edward H. Taylor: "An Annotated Checklist and Key to the Snakes of Mexico." *United States National Museum*, Bulletin 187 (1945), pp. 1–239.

Smith, Malcolm A.: *Monograph of the Sea-Snakes (Hydrophiidae)*. London: The British Museum; 1926.

——: *The Fauna of British India, Ceylon and Burma, Including the Whole of the Indo-Chinese Sub-Region. Reptilia and Amphibia*. Vol. 3.–*Serpentes*. London: Taylor and Francis; 1943.

——: *The British Amphibians & Reptiles*. The New Naturalist. London: Collins; 1951.

Stickel, William H.: "Venomous Snakes of the United States and Treatment of Their Bites." *United States Department Interior*, Wildlife Leaflet 339 (1952), pp. 1–29.

—— and Lucille F.: "Sexual Dimorphism in the Pelvic Spurs of *Enygrus*." *Copeia* No. 1 (1946), pp. 10–12.

Stull, Olive G.: "A Check List of the Family Boidae." *Proceedings, Boston Society Natural History*, Vol. 40 (1935), pp. 387–408.

Tihen, J. A.: "Notes on the Osteology of Typhlopid Snakes." *Copeia* No. 4 (1945), pp. 204–10.

Trapido, Harold: "Mating Time and Sperm Viability in *Storeria*." *Copeia* No. 2 (1940), pp. 107–9.

Waite, Edgar R.: *The Reptiles and Amphibians of South Australia*. Adelaide: Harrison Weir; 1929.

Wall, Frank: *The Snakes of Ceylon*. Colombo: Colombo Museum; 1921.

Weekes, H. Claire: "A Review of Placentation among Reptiles with Particular Regard to the Function and Evolution of the Placenta." *Proceedings, Zoological Society London* (1935), pp. 625–45.

Zimmermann, Arnold A. and Clifford H. Pope: "Development and Growth of the Rattle of Rattlesnakes." *Fieldiana: Zoology*, Vol. 32 (1948), pp. 355–413.

Lizards

(Suborder Sauria)

General Account

✲

ORIGIN AND STRUCTURE

ALTHOUGH THE lizards can be traced back to their origin some hundred and fifty million years ago in the Jurassic Period, they are not ancient as reptiles go. The dinosaurs, for example, had already reached a high state of development in Jurassic times. In the following period, the Cretaceous, both lizard and dinosaur made great progress, the former in the water, the latter on land. This early development of lizards reached a climax in the marine mosasaurs, world-wide in distribution and often gigantic in proportions, averaging in length from fifteen to twenty feet. This tendency of the lizards to become aquatic ended abruptly, mosasaur and dinosaur fading out rapidly at the end of the Cretaceous. The monitors of today are more like those ancient mosasaurs than are any other living lizards, and, oddly enough, the snakes seem to have sprung from monitor stock. The love of water and its vicinity, developed so early in lizards, is scarcely discernible today, and all the other groups of reptiles show stronger aquatic tendencies than do the lizards. In fact, the modern lizard is an especially conspicuous part of the desert's fauna.

The lizards as a whole did not, however, fade out of the picture along with the mosasaurs and other water-loving types of the good old days; they continued to evolve, throwing off distinctly new branches such as the aberrant worm lizards (Amphisbænidæ) and the astonishingly different and virile suborder, the snakes. The main line of descent showed plenty of vitality by developing into families, many of which are today still showing tendencies to acquire new attributes and produce an abundance of species, or to "speci-ate," as modern terminology expresses it.

Before taking up the more interesting aspects of lizard struc-ture, I shall draw a few comparisons between snake and lizard. The snake seems to be a bundle of specializations, the salient aspects of its structure being inseparably bound with function; this reptile has committed itself to a particular way of life. In the discussion of snake structure on page 129, I have brought out the close associa-tion between the snake's method of locomotion and its lack of limbs, its slender form, its great number of ribs and of vertebræ; be-tween feeding habits and the shape of its teeth, structure of its skull, and its lack of limbs. Such a close bond between form and function cannot be shown for the lizard, which has never been willing to commit itself to a one-track way of life. To the lizard, unequaled among other reptiles in variation of structure, variety of form and function is the spice of life.

The most obvious as well as the most astounding lack of stabil-ity in lizard anatomy is the incredible variation in degree of limb development, which runs the whole scale from a type with four large, powerful ones down to many with limbs too degenerate to function well, some without any at all, and a few in which even the internal supports, the girdles, have become vestigial; the shoulder girdle may even disappear altogether. In writing about lizards this subject cannot be avoided, and I hope that the reader will be indul-gent with me if I bring it up too frequently.

Instead of always having a glassy stare like that of snakes, the lizard may look out between well-developed lids, the lower one movable; it may peek through a transparent disc in the more or less fixed lower lid; it may stare like a snake through a permanent trans-parent covering of the entire eye; or, as a burrower, it may peer through scales covering the eye and probably all but shutting out the rays of light. The histories of these different types of eye cov-erings are complex; some of them have developed over and over again, first in this group and then in that, and the evolution of a given type has not necessarily taken place in the same way. The type that gives the glassy stare has repeatedly come about in the fol-lowing manner. First, the lower lid acquires a window, and this grows larger and larger until finally the lid becomes fixed to the reduced upper, and the window replaces both lids as an immovable convex cap. Evolution has taken the opposite direction among the few geckos (*Eublepharis*) with movable lids. These apparently developed from a peripheral rim of tissue that surrounded the fixed, transparent disc of nearly all geckos. The rim first grew inward and then became folded into an upper and lower lid. Just what happened to the transparent cap or disc is not evident.

The ear of lizards varies greatly in structure, though its variations can scarcely be comparable to those of limbs and eyes. Superficial examination of many species of lizards will reveal one of the four following conditions in each: a large tympanum or eardrum; a cavity leading to a drum; a shallow depression that dissection will prove to be a tympanum covered with scales; or no ear whatsoever. Internal conditions roughly parallel the external; at one extreme, the ear is well developed and functional in its usual way; at the other, the loss of the tympanum is accompanied by a corresponding filling in of the cavity of the middle ear, and the disappearance or rearrangement of certain important structures. The lizard ear at this extreme is comparable to that of snakes, and certainly cannot function as an apparatus for the transmission of sound waves of the air.

Certain differences between lizard and snake should be pointed out. Putting aside real technicalities, we have difficulty in drawing a sharp line between saurian and serpentine structure. Nevertheless, we can name a useful combination of characteristics of these two suborders:

The vast majority of lizards have relatively short bodies and four limbs. No snakes have front limbs, though vestiges of hind limbs in the form of spurs are evident in some.

By far the greater number of lizards have movable eyelids, structures never possessed by snakes.

Few lizards have a long, deeply forked tongue that is drawn back into a sheath. This is a characteristic of snakes.

Nearly all lizards have some sign of an external ear, whereas no snake has any sign of such.

The two halves of the bony part of the lizard lower jaw are

firmly united where they meet in front; these halves in snakes are joined by a ligament that allows them to be stretched widely apart during the swallowing of large objects, a feat that lizards cannot perform.

AGE, SIZE, GROWTH

MAJOR FLOWER'S extensive studies of the age of animals have already received much attention (see page 131) and will therefore be briefly dealt with here. Only two lizards appear in his list of fifty-five reptiles definitely known to have survived 20 or more years of captivity. One of these is the slow-worm of Europe, a legless anguid technically known as *Anguis fragilis;* the other is Cunningham's skink (*Egernia cunninghami;* Plate 197) of Australia. The first lived 32, the second 20 years. The list of fifty-five is, as might be expected, largely made up of turtles, the Methuselahs of reptiles, although ten snakes manage to make the grade. Elsewhere there are additional, though scattered, records of lizard longevity, but these do not alter the picture. For instance, the San Diego Zoo kept two European glass snakes alive for 25 and 24 years, thus establishing a record. Just why these limbless anguids do so well in confinement is hard to say. It is also impossible to come to a satisfactory conclusion as to the relative life spans of snakes and lizards: it is possible that snakes hold more records because of the greater attention that they receive.

The true chameleons (Chamæleonidæ) make irresistible pets; some have been kept in captivity by scientists during a period of more than a century. For example, during the years 1870–1907 four hundred and ten individuals were received at the London Zoological Gardens. In the Giza Zoological Gardens of Egypt, these reptiles have been kept under conditions almost exactly matching those of their native haunts. Notwithstanding all this, the captive true chameleon rarely lives two years, almost never as long as three. Only four of the horde kept at the London Zoological Gardens passed the two-year mark, and but one of these survived for three. The logical conclusion is that these lizards simply have a short span of life. If this is true, we have the turtles at one extreme of reptile longevity, the true chameleons at the opposite, there being little evidence of such an excessively short span of life in any other reptiles.

In the United States, at least, scarcely anybody gets excited over the size of lizards. One patent reason is that few people live in the parts of this country where lizards abound, and vice versa. I refer, of course, to the great numbers of lizards in the sparsely settled southwestern states and the huge human population of the East, where lizards are less abundant and much less conspicuous. The hopeless confusion of lizards with the innumerable salamanders of our eastern woodlands adds greatly to the lack of clear thinking about lizards. No doubt in many parts of the world where large lizards are common, there is great concern over their size. I doubt that this ever compares with the interest in snake dimensions, because the lizards are almost never dangerous as the snakes so often are. A bright side of this picture is the greater possibility of getting accurate information on lizard size, the human imagination playing fewer tricks with this than with snake lengths and girths. The expression "as big around as my arm" or "leg" is not inevitably applied to the lizard just encountered.

The lizards have their giants just as do the snakes, and these are the monitors (Varanidæ). The largest of these is the Komodo dragon with its great bulk and 10 feet of length (Plate 214). In spite of this, it is not a dangerous animal. The greatest range in size is also found in this family, which includes species only 8 or 10 inches long. The largest of monitors may be fifteen times as long and weigh thirty-seven hundred times as much as the smallest.

Chiefly on the basis of maximum size of the largest species, we may arrange the lizard families in an evenly graded series. After the monitors come the iguanids, headed by the common iguana of the American tropics, a creature that reaches a length of 6 feet 7 inches and, to its sorrow, has meat with a delicate flavor; many other iguanids reach a good size. Next we may name the agamids, saurians of the Old World. They are close rivals of the iguanids; although no agamid approaches the common iguana in length, several of them are in the 3-to-4-feet class. The teiids, a New World family, also include species of this size rank and must be listed next in order, though definitely below the agamids. The teiids have many very small species affectionately known to specialists as "micro-teiids," some of them attaining a length of only 3 or 4 inches. Here we might draw a line and put all the major groups mentioned so far in a classification informally designated as large.

It now becomes increasingly difficult to line the families up on this basis of maximum size of species. The anguids (glass snakes and relatives) as well as the Gila-monster family (only three species) must be credited with a yard of length, and the prehensile-tailed skink of the Solomon Islands approaches such a dimension. The rich skink family, like the teiids, can boast of an array of midgets. To conclude our second informal size classification, which I shall call lizards of medium dimensions, we must name five families, all of them including species about 2 feet long: the chameleons, the gerrhosaurids, the lacertids, the worm lizards, and the snake-lizards.

A single major family remains to be considered, the geckos, a varied assortment with a world-wide distribution; a few species, relatively gigantic to other geckos, attain a length of about a foot. This family shares with the true chameleons the distinction of having the smallest of lizards, each including one not exceeding 1.3 inches in total length. The remaining families belong to this maximum-size-more-or-less-one-foot classification. Only one of these, the girdle-tailed lizards of Africa, comprises more than a dozen species.

In the United States the longest lizards by far are the glass snakes, with a usual length of somewhat less than 3 feet (42.6 inches is the record). These slender reptiles are not as impressive as the chunky and shorter Gila monster (Plate 215) and the chuckwalla (Plate 179), the former with a maximum length of about 2 feet, the latter several inches shorter. None of these compares with the common iguana, the giant of the New World, which, as stated, grows to be more than 6 feet long. Compared with the snakes, even these relatively gigantic lizards are mere midgets: a snake that does not attain the length of our largest lizards is classed as a small species. I cannot resist pointing out the fact, probably a mere coincidence, that the longest of our native lizards are legless species.

Although the growth of snakes has been investigated much

more often than has that of lizards, some good studies of the latter living under natural conditions can be cited to show that they, too, waste little time in becoming mature and reaching a good size. The western skink (*Eumeces skiltonianus;* Plate 199) of North America, for example, is about an inch long (head and body) at hatching and doubles its length in a year. Most of the growth takes place during the first three months of life; by the time it is two years old it measures only two and nine-sixteenths inches and the next year's growth amounts to little. Some individuals may breed when two years of age, though most of them do not do so until three. After maturity is reached, the normal period of survival is probably five or six years and the greatest about nine. These periods must not be confused with potential longevity, which no doubt is much greater. Data for our prairie skink (*Eumeces septentrionalis*) are surprisingly similar.

Our Pacific fence lizards (*Sceloporus occidentalis*) hatch at a head-body length of one and three-sixteenths inches and a weight of less than a gram; most of the growth takes place between the first and second hibernations, August being the height of the hatching season. At the end of the second hibernation they are sexually mature, and many of them can scarcely be distinguished in size from the adults.

As a sample of growth under specialized climatic conditions, a chapter from the life history of the yucca night lizard (*Xantusia vigilis*) is suitable. In the Mojave Desert, southern California, Malcolm R. Miller studied a population of these nocturnal reptiles. The head-body length is seven eighths of an inch at birth in September and October, and growth is slow during the first year. The most rapid growth takes place in the spring, when food is more abundant. At the end of the first year, the length has increased to only one and one-eighth inches, to one and three-eighths at the end of the second, when males are sexually mature; females do not become so for another year.

Growth of the American chameleon (living in the vicinity of New Orleans, Louisiana) has been studied with considerable care, and its rate determined as one that no doubt approaches the maximum for lizards. The hatchling's head-body measurement is fifteen

sixteenths of an inch, and the rapid growth increases this nine sixteenths of an inch by winter, at least in those that do not hatch late.
The extended breeding season causes considerable variation in the
amount of growth before hibernation. The average female becomes mature when about a year old and one and thirteen-six-
teenths inches long; the males require another year to reach maturity, and are then relatively large (two and three-eighths inches
from tip of snout to anus).

The geckos, remarkable lizards in so many ways, give us a
growth-rate record that probably is not surpassed by any other lizard. Dr. Fred R. Cagle studied on Tinian Island, of the Marianas
group, *Hemidactylus garnoti*, a species (head-body length about
two and a half inches) distributed from Asia into the islands of the
Pacific Ocean. Individuals released and recaptured showed, when
young, the average ability to increase the head-body length at the
rate of three fourths of an inch per month. Although this was not
kept up for long, calculations also taking into consideration subsequent rates indicate that sexual maturity is reached from thirty to
forty days after hatching.

As practical methods of age determination in reptiles are few, it
is worth mentioning here the possibility of discerning the age of lizards having osteoderms (bony plates in the skin; see page 243). Dr.
Oliver studied the changes these plates of a skink undergo with
growth, and concluded that the changes may be correlated with
age.

ENEMIES AND DEFENSE

FROM A broad point of view there is much resemblance between
lizards and snakes in methods of dealing with enemies: both are
great bluffers that, in attempting to inspire fear, use tactics involving changes in shape, movements of various parts of the body, and
emission of simple sounds such as hisses. Lizards, as well as snakes,
are also masters at the art of flight and concealment. I shall not repeat here any of the generalities given in the section on snakes or
the details of aggressive behavior that may be found throughout the
discussions of the various lizard families. I shall, however, point out

some of the ways in which these two major reptile groups stand in sharp contrast to each other.

First, in regard to the enemies, most carnivorous animals fond of snakes like lizards equally well. The point of interest rests in the predator-prey relationship between the lizards and snakes themselves, and right here lies the rub for the poor lizards: because of the serpentine specialization in large, long meals, lizards are ideal items on the snake menu, whereas the snake is not especially well shaped to satisfy the appetite of the hungry lizard. My study of feeding habits of the seventy-six species of the snakes of China showed that no fewer than twenty-five were then (1935) known to eat lizards. More detailed study will no doubt greatly increase this number.

Next, many snakes have their venom for protection, and, in this regard, have left nearly all the lizards far behind; only the Gila monster and the Mexican beaded lizard, members of the same small family, are definitely known to be venomous. To make up for this, as it were, numerous lizards have their osteoderms, small bones, imbedded in the skin. When all the scales are underlain by osteoderms, a veritable armor is formed, as with the skinks and anguids. In greater or less numbers and various degrees of development, these bony plates occur sporadically among about half of the remaining families of lizards. The skin of the snake is not reinforced by bones, although some burrowing species have a relatively hard, polished skin that might seem to be. This, an attribute of subsurface life, is shared by burrowing lizards with or without osteoderms.

Finally, among the major groups of backboned animals, the lizards stand out as having made great use of the tail in defensive tactics; it may even be that no other group, except perhaps the crocodilians, can come up to them in this respect. The snakes have concentrated on the head end, developing the art of biting to an extreme degree in their various types of strikes and their complex ways of injecting venom. The bites of lizards are anything but complex.

Let us see what the lizards have been able to do with the caudal appendage. First for originality, usefulness, and extent of application comes tail-dropping. This method, unique among living reptiles, is so interesting that I easily could take up much more than the available space discussing it. When seized by an enemy, a lizard with a fragile tail simply comes in two, an act that is most disconcerting to the predator. The confusion is greatly enhanced by the severed tail's lively contortions; it makes little difference whether the animal itself or the tail has been seized. In the former case, sight of the twisting and sometimes brightly colored tail tempts the aggressor to release the body and go for the tail; if the tail is seized, the body will likely escape before detection of the error.

Tail-dropping is used most effectively and generally by the skinks, the geckos, and the anguids (the glass snakes come here), although various other families also resort to this trick. It is extremely hard to capture whole a lively lizard with an especially loose tail. At times it even seems that the tail is actually thrown off, so little is the resistance required to spring the mechanism. When the tail is from two to three times as long as the body, the creature appears to break itself in two rather than merely drop the tail. The glass snakes of the United States are the classic examples of long-tailed lizards with loose tails; some of the snake-lizards of the Australian region doubtless would be close competitors for honors.

This loss of a whole part of an animal obviously calls for special adaptations in bone and muscle. It might be reasonably assumed that two vertebræ of a tail simply separate at their joint, but such is not the case, for a vertebra itself comes apart at a predetermined place where a partial split is always present. This split may be either at the middle of the vertebra, or near one end. The muscles also separate neatly, leaving, on the stump, a series of cone-shaped depressions that do not bleed profusely. Cells at the point of fracture have the ability to grow, and thus a new, though imperfect, tail is formed.

At the other extreme from relinquishing the tail is the development of it into an effective weapon, a spiny appendage that would severely damage an unprotected human hand and lacerate the mouth of other enemies. Formidable tails have been developed in the girdle-tailed lizards of Africa, the agamids, and the iguanids.

Any of the numerous species with a spiny tail will use it at close quarters by vigorously switching it about; a few of these well-armed saurians go further than this, as described on pages 286 and 321. The monitors (*Varanus*) are popularly believed to lash severely with the tail, and it is easy to see how the lively tail-waving of these gigantic lizards has inspired fear. Such movements are actually part of an elaborate bluffing procedure; an ordinary pair of trousers is sufficient protection for even the most timid person being "lashed" by an angry monitor. Numerous other species of lizards move the tail in various ways as part of their bluffing antics.

Before leaving this subject I must mention the fascinating, though somewhat technical, paper by Dr. Robert Mertens of the Senckenbergische Naturforschende Gesellschaft, Frankfurt am Main, on the warning and threatening antics of reptiles. This work is listed in the bibliography.

FOOD AND FEEDING

THE FEEDING habits of lizards are not nearly so interesting as are those of snakes. The reason for this is obvious: lizards seize, overpower, and devour food after the fashion of many other higher animals. Neither highly specialized teeth such as hollow fangs, nor the ability to constrict and swallow relatively large prey is possessed by lizards. In some groups of lizards the teeth of one species may vary in shape to about the same degree as those of human teeth, but this is not to be compared with the differences found among snake teeth. Even the venomous Gila monster and Mexican beaded lizard have only simple, grooved teeth.

The tongue of the lizard partly makes up for this comparative lack of specialization. Whereas the vast majority of snakes have excessively slender, forked tongues, the tongues of lizards range in form from deeply forked slender ones, comparable to that of a snake, to short stumpy structures barely nicked, or even with the nick, at the tip. So great and constant is this variety from an- tongue is often used in distinguishing one lizard those of snakes in other. Some saurian tongues are also super-

the possession of a sense of taste as well as of touch, and, if thick and strong, in being useful for the manipulation of food as well as for drinking. Lizards also make use of Jacobson's Organ much as do snakes (see page 142).

As there are plant- as well as animal-eaters among lizards, two types of approach to food exist. In an animal that consumes only the tender, readily severed parts, walking up to plants and eating them calls for no special method. The carnivorous lizard, on the other hand, must have a method, especially if the prey is active. Aside from the use of the tongue in trailing, the method is simply one of overtaking and seizing with the jaws. The great agility of most lizards makes this method successful enough. Only the true chameleons have gone to the opposite extreme to develop the gentle art of very cautious stalking. Correlated with this stalking is the one great specialization in lizard feeding, the chameleon's popgun tongue (Plates 191 and 192). This unique apparatus, described on page 288, would be the horror of the African and Madagascan jungle if chameleons reached the dimensions of the larger crocodilians. Imagine walking through the forest only to find yourself instantaneously transported to the open jaws of a perfectly camouflaged monster lurking some forty feet away.

Lacking the ability to constrict powerful prey or to kill it by means of the injection of venom (with the two exceptions noted above), the carnivorous lizard must be satisfied with relatively small victims that can be swallowed whole or chopped up with the strong jaws. True or persistent chewing is not employed, although the chopping process may resemble it. The upper as well as the lower jaw moves freely. A long-necked lizard such as a monitor will make a rat pass down the neck in much the same way that a snake does, and, indeed, the monitors are more snakelike than other lizards. It is in them that the true serpentine tongues are seen.

The numerous lizards with herbivorous tendencies and the very few that subsist on little else but plant matter rarely show specializations, eating what is available. The notable exception is the marine iguana that eats seaweed exposed at low tide on the Galápagos Islands (animals that are 273). In general the carnivorous lizards devour the animals that are readily secured, namely insects, spiders, and other invertebrates of suitable size. A few cases of specialization are pointed out in the treatments of the families. It should suffice to mention here two interesting cases, one extreme, the other less so. The extreme case is that of the caiman lizard of South America (Plate 207) with its snail and mussel diet and special crushing teeth (see page 305); the other, the mountain stream lizard of China (page 318), which includes fishes as well as tadpoles in its unusual diet. The fondness for ants shown by horned toads may be cited as an example of a diet that, from the human point of view, is revolting. The remains of as many as fifty-two ants have been found in a single horned-toad stomach, and a popular pastime in our southwest is placing one of these lizards on an anthill to watch it snap up the inmates as they emerge.

There are various rare feeding specializations or, at least, specializations rarely detected. One of these is seasonal differences in diet, such as that of the crested lizard mentioned on page 276, and there must of necessity be diets correlated with ages of predators. Some common lizards succeed in keeping their feeding habits hidden. Only in very recent years have reptile men begun to detect the true diet of the Gila monster in spite of the fact that it was exhibited in a zoo more than seventy years ago and has since been popular with zoo men. It is now becoming evident that this sluggish lizard, which has long been known to thrive on a diet of raw eggs and meat, specializes in the eggs and hatchlings of birds and the helpless young of mammals. Evidently it has learned to find in the desert nourishment not only delicate, juicy, and palatable, but with little or no ability to escape even the most sluggish of predators.

REPRODUCTION

THERE ARE striking similarities between the way snakes and lizards reproduce, and this is what we should expect to find in such closely related animals. The reproductive organs of lizards, the penes, are, like those of snakes, paired and housed in the base of the tail. In structure they show no basic difference, and are much less diverse, never attaining the extreme peculiarities so often seen in snakes.

The sexing of lizards by the swelling in the tail caused by the penes is relatively difficult in some types because the bony plates (osteoderms) of the skin keep the penes from making an enlargement. Further discussion of lizard penes would merely repeat what is explained in detail for the snakes on page 145.

Our next aspect of reproduction is the one in which snakes and lizards have really grown widely apart—that is, differences between the sexes. As we are accustomed to such dimorphism, to use a technical term, in birds and mammals, it is not hard for us to appreciate its significance. Human beings apparently are not satisfied with the differences given us by birth, but make every effort to augment them with clothing and other kinds of adornments: it is most unusual for one adult to fail to recognize at a glance the sex of another. Lizards stand between us and snakes; in the latter, the differences between male and female are so inconspicuous that, except in rare cases, a male could not tell a female by merely looking at her. Sexual dimorphism in lizards is diverse in nature, and of widespread, though by no means universal, occurrence. In some, striking differences in structure are obvious; in others, the male can make his sex apparent at will by the display of a throat fan or dewlap (Plate 159). For extreme examples of the permanent type, the diverse head shapes of the male true chameleon (Plate 194) and the exaggerated crests of male basilisks (Plate 174) must suffice.

Color disparities between male and female are so numerous and complex that I scarcely dare bring them up. They are of three types: permanent, seasonal, and momentary. The first is a common type well known in the United States—for instance, the bright belly and throat colors of male spiny lizards (*Sceloporus*). The momentary type is also of wide occurrence, especially in iguanids and agamids. Striking examples are seen in the agamid genus *Calotes*, which occurs from southeastern Asia through the Malay and Philippine islands. In a matter of moments the foreparts of the excited males will turn bright red. Seasonal or nuptial colors, apparently rarely developed, are evident in the leopard lizard of our western states, and this time it is the pregnant female that develops them; her belly, sides, and much of her tail become a beautiful crimson color. The male collared lizard becomes adorned with striking colors during the breeding season. This species also lives in our western states.

Having dealt chiefly with the physical aspect of male and female lizard, we now come to the dynamics of its sex life, a far more interesting aspect. We shall consider the special relation to space, the meaning of differences in form and color, the types of courtship and mating. It is pointed out elsewhere that lizards failed to develop parental care, a kind of behavior so advanced in birds. Such cannot be said about space concept; its elaborate development in birds has a strong forerunner in lizards. By this I mean that during the breeding season many species of lizards and birds are keenly aware of territory, and such awareness technically is known as "territoriality." Of course animals in general are restricted in their movements and do not wander aimlessly, but this relation to space differs markedly from sexual territoriality. In this, at the approach of the breeding season, a male stakes out, so to speak, a definite area and defends it against intruders of the same sex, attacking them violently at sight, and desisting when they have been driven beyond bounds. Defense of territory has been observed in lizards of various families. It has been closely studied in our spiny lizards (*Sceloporus*) as well as in our chameleon (*Anolis carolinensis*).

The next aspect of lizard sex life, and by far the hardest one to deal with, is the dynamics of sexual differences and adornment. Plainly it is important for one sex to recognize the other, but the subject goes far beyond mere recognition: just what is the purpose of exaggerated distinctions such as the gaudy plumages of some birds and the numerous adornments of many lizards? Certainly these greatly exceed the necessities of simple identification. Controversy over this has raged since the days of Darwin, who proposed that the superattractions of the male were developed only to attract the female. Observation of and elaborate experiments with lizards have shown that the adornments are used to frighten other males as well as to attract females. Sexually excited male lizards go through stereotyped movements that make their special colors and shapes conspicuous, and such actions are directed toward other individuals regardless of their sex. If the individual happens to be a male, it returns the display or else retreats; if a female, it shows receptivity, allowing itself to be approached. (Under laboratory conditions too confined to permit a return of display, the aggressive male may try to copulate with a quiescent one.) When the second male puts on a vigorous show of its own, a contest is on, which is more or less of a sham affair, as lizards, like snakes, are great bluffers and each male, putting on its best act, may try by intimidation to avoid a battle. Thus a sexual display is an attempt to attract; it also is an effort to intimidate and frighten individuals of the same sex. It is said that in certain human societies a corresponding purpose of adornment exists: the female dresses not solely for the male but also to outdo other females.

Courtship is the logical step to follow sexual contests between males, and the sequence, as a rule, is close, even though the bluffing and fighting are also concerned with the holding or acquisition of territory. These two types of behavior are stereotyped. In fact, copulation patterns seem to have changed but slowly throughout the ages, and each family has its type, which may or may not be similar to those of the others. So fixed are these patterns that they show relationships just as truly as do similarities in structure.

Courtship and copulation have been observed in many lizards, and, in view of their importance as evidence of relationship, make an important and fascinating study. The male ordinarily takes a grip on his mate, more to sustain himself than to restrain her, for, as pointed out above, she is relatively passive. There are two widely used grips, one on her neck, the other on her groin, the latter being considered, from the point of view of phylogeny or evolution, as successor to the former. Once his jaws have made themselves secure, he bends his body and brings the base of his tail beneath and across that of his mate, an act that allows him to insert the penis of the side making contact with her cloaca.

I shall conclude our section on the dynamics of the relationship between the sexes by briefly outlining the behavior of the banded gecko (*Coleonyx variegatus*), one of our two species of the family. This nocturnal reptile was studied in a laboratory by Dr. Bernard Greenberg of Roosevelt College, Chicago. Work with it proved to be especially interesting because Dr. Greenberg was able to make the most reasonable suggestion to date of the use of the spurs, structures seen only in geckos, and of the row or rows of wax cones found in front of the cloaca and, at times, on the adjacent part of the thighs in many male lizards. Each cone is secreted by a gland just beneath it. See Plate 156.

The aggressive male rises high on his legs, arches the back, and puffs up the throat, but keeps the head low. He stalks around his opponent, nudging it on neck, side, or tail. The fight usually ends when the aggressor puts the other to flight by biting him. The duration of this sham affair depends on the response of the opponent; the two may stand side by side for a short time, actually touching each other. Also compare Plates 159, 160, 161, and 163.

In courting, the male, with body low, tail waving, and nose to the ground (Plate 157), pokes the female with his snout, or licks her. Next he bites her anywhere from tail to neck, moving jerkily forward to mount after securing a firm grip on her neck or shoulder. He then rubs his cloacal region across the base of her tail, his wax cones apparently stimulating her to elevate the tail so that he can get his hind region under hers (Plate 158). Now one of the spurs comes into play: the male convulsively moves the adjacent spur across the loose skin behind her cloaca until it takes hold in this skin and draws back the lower lip of the cloaca, allowing the suddenly everted penis to open the cloaca enough to allow insertion. Co-operation of the female is necessary, although her role is comparatively passive. Also compare Plate 162.

Having concluded the dynamic aspects of sex, I shall return to the more prosaic ones, beginning with fertilization. Recent (1953) observations by Dr. Sarah R. Atsatt of the University of California, Los Angeles, indicates that lizards must now join the ranks of the animals able to store sperm and therefore produce successive lots of young after a single mating. As turtles and snakes are well known to have this ability (see pages 72 and 147), the evidence of it in lizards is not too surprising. The reptile in question is a true chameleon of southern Africa (*Microsaura pumila*). The true chameleons thus are shown to be interesting not only because of their grotesque form and queer antics.

In regard to that important aspect of reproduction, the way of getting the offspring into the world, the lizards cannot claim the use of any method not found among the snakes. As in the snakes, both live-bearing and egg-laying habits are widespread and not always uniform even for a genus. Then there is the famous case of the viviparous lizard of Europe and Asia that brings forth the young directly in one part of its range, but lays eggs in another (see page 302). Egg-laying is the prevalent lizard method, and, in fact, it is only in one of the large families, the skinks, that live-bearing may be called predominant. The species of the other big families are nearly all egg-layers; the smaller families are divided, the majority being egg-laying assortments. It is only reasonable that the skinks, with their tendency to adopt the more advanced method, should carry the matter furthest and, in some cases, develop a primitive placenta (see pages 148 and 294).

Among reptiles, lizards produce the smallest broods of young and clutches of eggs. Geckos ordinarily lay two eggs at a time; single layings or births are reported for geckos, skinks, and iguanids. Probably the majority of clutches or broods are comprised of from five to fifteen units, although such a statement is little more than a guess. The monitors often lay at a time as many as thirty or even thirty-five eggs and, among other lizards, the horned toads of North America can approach or even slightly surpass such figures. Compare these data with the hundred and more eggs of turtles and snakes.

Snake and lizard eggs are alike in lacking striking coloration or color pattern. They are white or nearly so when laid, but may become stained and thus lose their pure whiteness. The lizard being less elongated than the snake, the lizard egg is not as elongate and may even be spherical. The most remarkable shape of any is the egg of the agamid *Calotes jubatus*, a species distributed from the Nicobar to the Philippine islands, and often common. This unique egg tapers at either end and is usually described as "spindle-shaped." The shell of gecko eggs is brittle, that of other lizards flexible like parchment. As incubation proceeds, the egg with a flexible shell swells by absorption of moisture and, if it is an elongate type, becomes less and less so. The largest lizard eggs, those of monitors, may be four and a half inches long, or smaller than the largest python eggs. Little imagination is required to picture the approximate size of eggs of very small species, those, for instance, with a total length of only two or three inches.

Lizards, being in some ways more socialized than snakes, might be expected to show advances in nesting habits. Such does not seem to be the case; lizards in general lay their eggs in the simplest of "nests," with locations determined by the habitats of the layers. The actual sites differ enough to defy generalization; any kind of soft material or loose earth will do if it provides a degree of uniformity in temperature and humidity. Some surprising laying habits are worthy of notice. The true chameleons, though arboreal, descend to lay in the ground. The geckos, on the other hand, for a great part arboreal, are well adapted to nesting aloft. When first laid, the typical gecko egg is covered with a substance that becomes sticky upon drying and glues the egg to whatever makes contact with it. Consequently the egg can be placed in vertical cracks of bark and similar situations. Although geckos lay not more than two eggs at a time, great numbers may be found together because of the strong tendency of different females to lay in the same place (see page 270). The habit of laying eggs in termite nests has been developed in various parts of the world by lizards of more than one family (see pages 305 and 312). Thus the lizard causes the industrious termites unwittingly to build its nest, an accomplishment perhaps more clever than building its own.

Parental care of the young is not known among lizards, the nearest approach to it being the brooding of eggs, a habit developed by species of at least four families. Brooding is widespread in anguids of the genus *Ophisaurus* (glass snakes; Plates 164 and 165) and in skinks of the genus *Eumeces*. Both of these genera are found in the eastern as well as the western hemispheres, and therefore brooding lizards can be observed in many parts of the world. Noble and Mason experimented extensively with females of our five-lined and greater five-lined skinks (*Eumeces*) as well as with those of one of our glass snakes (*Ophisaurus*).

These experiments are so interesting that I shall summarize their more striking results here, with emphasis on the behavior of the skinks. Considerable interest is taken by the parent skink in her eggs, and she will spend hours bringing them back together if she finds them scattered. This is accomplished by wending in and out over and under them, pushing them with the snout, and even taking them in the jaws. The female frequently returns to her nest and can find her eggs if they have been placed in a new site. Even a blindfolded parent can do this, for she identifies the eggs with the tip of her tongue. The eggs are frequently turned, the snout or even the tongue being used in this process. One of these species of skinks will brood the eggs of the other but not those of the glass snake or paraffin models of eggs. Shellacking genuine eggs usually caused them to go unattended. The chief value of brooding seems to be protection from enemies, which, if not too formidable, are driven away. The glass snake, however, would not defend its clutch. Some aid to incubation results from heat transmitted to the eggs by the female when she returns after basking in the sun.

I want to make a few final remarks and then give an account of birth in one species. As egg-laying is the rule, I should dwell on this, but, being a mammal myself, I am prejudiced in favor of live-bearing and shall emphasize it regardless of all criticism. In lizards of temperate climates, spring is the usual time for mating, late spring or early summer for laying, midsummer through early autumn for birth or hatching. Tropical species would of course follow different schedules. The rule is a single birth or clutch a year, though we are finding more and more exceptions; one very close to home is given on page 275, and Dr. Atsatt reports embryos of different sizes in a single oviduct of more than one kind of true chameleon. An egg tooth, a temporary structure present in many species at hatching, may be double (geckos). The egg tooth, also found in many snakes, is discussed in greater detail on page 151, the remarks made there applying in the main to the lizard egg tooth.

Dr. Raymond B. Cowles of the University of California, Los Angeles, has given an excellent account of birth in the yucca night lizard (*Xantusia*), a reptile of western North America. He observed eleven cases. Before giving birth, the female becomes restive, making many backward movements and licking the mouth as well as the eyes. A more reliable sign of actual birth is the elevation to a nearly vertical position of the hind limbs, a movement that may be repeated and probably is associated with the stretching of the pelvic and other muscles. Just before expulsion begins, the legs are lowered to hold the body well above the ground. At this time the body is bent so that the snout almost touches the anus. When the fetal membrane appears, the mother rips it open with her teeth. Violent struggles of feet and tail of the young now release it, and it is extruded tail foremost and back down. If the young pauses, the mother usually arouses it by nipping, and, when free, it runs to a distance of two or three inches. The parent now grasps the protruding membrane, pulls it out, and swallows it. The birth is completed when the mother licks up any drops of liquid that may have fallen on the ground. The process from appearance of the membrane to the removal of all traces of it requires only about two minutes. It should be remarked that this habit of swallowing the membrane is not a general one among lizards. The development of the young yucca night lizard within the female is estimated to require about four months.

LOCOMOTION

WHEN IT comes to ways of getting about, lizards are in a class by themselves. This versatility is closely correlated with the casual way in which these reptiles have dispensed with limbs, and, coincidentally, changed body form. As a limbless creature cannot move about like one with legs, it will suffice to point out that about half of the families of lizards include species either lacking legs or with these appendages too small to be of use in locomotion. It is clear that we are about to take up a subject having ramifications, and I might add that most of these have not been investigated in the scientific manner.

The broadest view we can take of this subject is to review the success that the lizards of today have in penetrating the major types of environment offered by the warmer parts of the earth. In contrast to certain snakes, lizards are never truly adapted to a marine life, although the sea is entered regularly by the marine iguana of the Galápagos and occasionally by monitors. Lizards also enter fresh waters much less frequently than do snakes, a fact that will become evident from my accounts by families. This is not surprising because snakes swim without half trying, their most usual type of locomotion admirably suiting them to this activity. Lizards may swim well enough, but often press the limbs to the side, using a snakelike motion not so natural to them. Both lizards and snakes make feeble efforts to enter the air, and the former are vastly more successful, the flying dragons of Asia and the Malay and Philippine islands being accomplished volplaners (see page 284).

The three additional milieus, the trees and other types of vegetation, the surface of the earth, and its sub-surface, are made good use of by both lizards and snakes. There is a striking contrast that should be pointed out here: limbless lizards are never adept climbers, a fact proving that, with them, the loss of limbs is correlated with a tendency to go downward into the ground rather than upward into vegetation. Snakes, of course, do not have limbs useful in locomotion and have developed more than one type of limbless climbing. Limbless lizard locomotion is yet to be investigated carefully, and certainly it is simple compared with the complexities of snake locomotion. Probably these legless saurians use largely the horizontal undulatory type described on page 152. The worm lizards (Amphisbænidæ) form an exception. It is not surprising that these most aberrant of lizards have their own wormlike method of getting about. They are inveterate burrowers so powerful that only with great difficulty is a large one held still (Plate 211).

The students of animal structure have not passed up the fascinating study of what happens inside an animal that is losing its limbs. The bones that support the front legs are known as the pectoral or shoulder girdle, those that do the same for the rear limbs as the pelvic or hip girdle. When the limbs become weak and useless, the girdles no longer have a proper function and tend to disappear. The shoulder girdle is somewhat the less stable of the two: it is entirely lost in all snakes and a very few lizards. If we except the aberrant worm lizards in which it is rudimentary or lacking, its complete absence in any lizard is even open to question until a more thorough study of the elusive Mexican skink relative *Anelytropsis papillosus* has been made (see page 298). Absence of the girdle in this rarity calls for confirmation. The hip girdle is always present in lizards, although it is in a rudimentary state in the worm lizards.

One might argue that it is unfair ever to speak of the "loss" of limbs and girdles. Is it not possible that some lizards are acquiring rather than losing them? Suffice it to say that studies of lines of limbed vertebrate descent reveal only evidence of the degeneracy of limbs and girdles.

Before dropping our limbless saurians altogether, I shall briefly discuss two interesting aspects of the relation between possession and lack of limbs. It is hard for us mammals to adjust our thoughts to the idea of dispensing with so necessary an appendage as a limb. Where can we find a mammal or a bird without limbs? Yet, among the lizards we can see two species of a single genus, one with strong legs, the other with useless ones. Further, we may even find differences in numbers of toes between normal individuals of a single species. What a problem these sudden and drastic changes in methods of locomotion necessarily present!

With so many contemporary stages in limb loss, many species must be at an in-between stage: they have legs but scarcely know what to do with them. How hard it must be to decide when to use them and when to tuck them away and resort to horizontal undulatory crawling. An example of this is the little teiid lizard of South America described on page 306. This midget may move along leisurely, after the manner of a quadruped. If excited, it will change over to serpentine undulating, the legs uselessly fanning the air. The height of ridiculousness is reached in the sand skink of Florida: the sides of this degenerate creature actually have grooves into which the minute and useless front legs fit (see page 297).

Most lizard limbs not undergoing the process of degeneration are merely five-toed appendages with a simple claw at the end of each toe. It is not necessary to explain how such a mechanism works. The geckos are the only lizards that have developed a radically different type of foot, and the geckos have carried this departure to an extreme. This new development, as explained on page 268, is a toe with a pad as well as a claw, although the latter is often lacking. A simple type of pad is also seen in a few other families such as the skinks and the iguanids, but those saurians scarcely got to first base with the invention.

In this connection a widely spread and interesting specialization often seen in sand-inhabiting lizards deserves mention: the possession along the sides of the toes of scales forming a fringe that, in offering resistance to the sand, facilitates movement over that unstable medium. The fringe-toed lizard of our own southwest and adjacent Mexico is an excellent example (see page 278). However, it must be admitted that not all fringed-toed lizards live in sand. For example, the gigantic agamid *Lophura amboinensis* of the Malay and Philippine islands is arboreal and frequently enters water. Some of the sand lizards, I might add, when pursued disappear as if through magic by diving into and swimming for a short distance under the sand.

The gait of lizards has been analyzed to a limited degree, and the basic patterns determined. A walking lizard has at least two legs on the ground at one time, the legs belonging to different sides. The weight of the body shifts from one diagonal to the other. The movements of these opposite legs are not always simultaneous; the hind leg may be advanced either somewhat before or after the front one. Comparing the gait with that of a mammal brings out the important difference in the strong tendency of the lizard to swing the legs far out to the side rather than straight forward, as the majority of mammals do. This difference is present in running as well as in walking gaits. If a comparison must be drawn, a running basilisk can be likened, though not closely, to a trotting horse; the hind leg of the former, in contrast to that of the latter, strikes the ground far in advance of the track left by the opposite front limb.

Walking and running on the hind legs, technically known as bipedal locomotion, is an old stunt for reptiles. Nearly two hundred million years ago in Triassic times the more advanced thecodont reptiles developed the bipedal method and passed it on to the dinosaurs, the majority of which clung to it to the end. In view of this, it is not surprising to find lizards running about on two legs. The surprising thing is that no lizard has become truly bipedal, as did so many of the early reptiles; with lizards, bipedalism is resorted to occasionally or only when great speed is required. The habit has been noted in species belonging to some sixteen genera of four families (Iguanidæ, Agamidæ, Teiidæ, and Varanidæ), and future observations are bound to increase this list greatly.

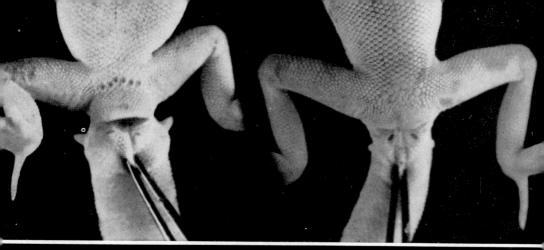

156. TOP: male and female banded geckos (*Coleonyx variegatus*) seen from below. Clearly shown in the male (left) are the six wax cones just in front of the cloaca and a spur to either side of it. Openings to the two postanal sacs are less evident. In the female the openings to the postanal sacs are clear, the spurs reduced in size, and the wax cones absent. 157. ABOVE: with snout down and tail up, this aroused male is apparently giving his mate the eye. In reality the banded gecko, being nocturnal, must court in the dark. 158. RIGHT: the male banded gecko grips the skin of his mate's neck while mating.

urtesy Bernard Greenberg, Roosevelt College, Chicago)

159. How tough can he [?]
An excited male
American chameleon
(*Anolis carolinensis*)
displays his
crimson throat fan.

160. Two male Ameri[can]
chameleons square off.

161. Two other male
American chameleons
about to fight.
The one on the left
has flattened itself
from side to side,
raised the crests,
gorged the throat,
and displayed the
black spot
behind the eye.

162. The courting
American chameleon
(left) is in his strut,
his mate giving her
submissive bow.

163. Male collared lizard (*Crotaphytus collaris*) prepares for battle.

A. He sights his rival.

B. He bobs so vigorously that his right foot leaves the ground.

C. He charges.

...tesy Bernard Greenberg,
...velt College, Chicago)

(Photographs taken on August 17, 1926, by Clifford H. Pope)

164.   Female glass snake (*Ophisaurus harti*) brooding her eggs in Fukien Province, China. The nest is in bamboo waste.

165.   Close view of the same glass snake.

6. Gait of lizard (American basilisk) running on hind limbs.

The left hind leg, raised high, moves forward as the right one completes its backward thrust.

Top speed is attained with tail high and both hind feet off the ground.

The widespread legs in this position suggest a waddling gait, which indeed it is.

(Courtesy
Leonard C. Snyder.
Mobilite photographs
by A. A. Allen)

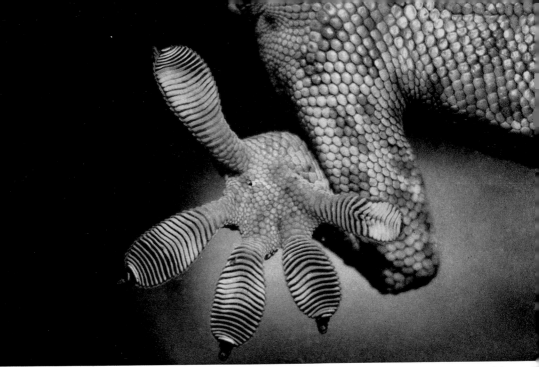

167. Gecko foot (*Gekko gecko*) viewed from below as it rests on a sheet of glass. The ridges that cross the greatly expanded toes are beset with innumerable tiny hooks much too small to be seen with the naked eye. The tiny claw at the tip of each of the four large toes cannot be made out, although the phalange which supports the claw is plainly visible at the end of each expansion.

168. Tokay (*Gekko gecko*), one of the largest and noisiest of geckos.

(Photographs by Isabelle Hunt Conant)

169. The Turkish gecko (*Hemidactylus turcicus*) has been transported by man from its home (southwestern Asia and the Mediterranean region) to the tropics of the New World.

170. Moorish gecko (*Tarentola mauretanica*), a species with a rough (tuberculate) skin and greatly expanded toes. It lives in the Mediterranean region.

171. This smooth gecko (*Thecadactylus rapicaudus*)
of tropical America has greatly widened toes and retractile claws.

172. The ashy gecko (*Sphærodactylus cinereus*) has been introduced to Key
West and Key Largo, Florida, from the Greater Antilles. It has only tiny discs
at the tips of the toes, and attains a total length of about three inches.

173. *Physignathus cocincinus*, agamid of tropical Asia, may be a yard long.

174. A basilisk of Central America (*Basiliscus plumbifrons*).
The dorsal adornments of this male extend from head to tail.

(*Courtesy Frederick Medem*)

175. This female basilisk was killed in Colombia beside the Rio Palenque and on the mangrove root where Dr. Medem photographed it. It measured sixteen and a half inches in total length. Like other females of the genus *Basiliscus*, it lacks the adornments that are so conspicuous in the male.

176. Head of *Læmanctus serratus* from the state of San Luis Potosí, Mexico. This species belongs to a small Mexican and Central American group of iguanids.

(*Courtesy The American Museum of Natural History; photograph by Charles M. Bogert*)

177. False iguana (*Ctenosaura similis*). The false iguanas (genus *Ctenosaura*) include very large species (total length up to four feet) with formidable tails armed with whorls of sharp spines. The range of the genus extends from Panama northward throughout Mexico.

178. This species, *Anolis equestris*, is unsurpassed in size by any other anole; it reaches a total length of half a yard and lives on Cuba and the Isle of Pines.

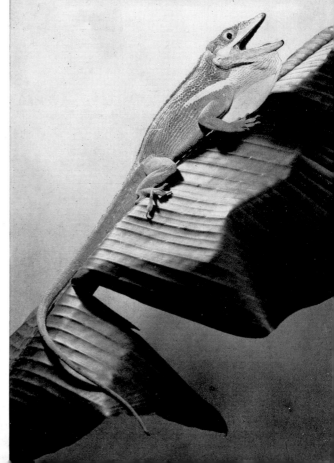

(Both courtesy New York Zoological Society)

179. The chuckwalla (*Sauromalus obsesus*) has more bulk than any other lizard of the United States except the Gila monster.

(Both courtesy The American Museum of Natural History)

180. The fringe-toed lizard (*Uma notata*) is a true desert sprite.

(Above and center courtesy The American Museum of Natural History)

181. Collared lizards (*Crotaphytus collaris*) from California.

Leopard lizards
aphytus wislizeni).

. BELOW: the
scaly lizard
*eloperus
nsetti*) is found
m southern
w Mexico to
tral Texas,
nce southward
l into northern
xico. It is a large
cies, reaching a
al length of
ut twelve
hes.

otograph by Isabelle Hunt Conant)

(Courtesy The American Museum of Natural History; photograph by Charles M. Bogert

184. A Texas horned toad (*Phrynosoma cornutum*) from Samalayuca, northern Chihuahua, Mexico. This, the most familiar of the horned toads, is found from Kansas, southeastern Colorado, and extreme southwestern Missouri southward well into northern Mexico. Not occurring in the forests of extreme eastern Texas, it gets as far west as the southeastern corner of Arizona.

185. Eggs and hatchlings of the crowned horned toad (*Phrynosoma coronatum*). This species ranges from the northern Sacramento valley of California southward (west of the Sierra Nevadas) well into Baja California, Mexico. The eggs are immaculate when laid.

(Courtesy Zoological Society of San Diego

186.   This agama, *Agama bibroni*, is at home in rugged, arid country of extreme northern Africa (Morocco and Algeria).

187.   This, the Egyptian spiny-tailed lizard (*Uromastix ægyptius*), reaches a length of twenty-six inches and occurs in Egypt (east of the Nile), Sinai, and northern Arabia.

188. This water dragon (*Physignathus lesueuri*) reaches a length of four feet. It has been taken in New Guinea, though its real home is Australia.

(*Zoological Society of Philadelphia*)

(*Courtesy New York Zoological Society*)

189. European chameleon (*Chamæleo chamæleon*), a species of Mediterranean countries.

190. This chameleon with a sagacious look and a curled tail represents a species (*Chamæleo dilepis*) with a range (equatorial and southern Africa) rivaling in extent that of any other African chameleon.

(*Courtesy New York Zoological Society*)

The basilisks have long been famous for their bipedal running and they can even make short dashes across the surface of water, an ability that calls for further investigation. The two-legged running itself, however, has been studied by Dr. Richard C. Snyder of the University of Washington. Strobilite photographs of the American basilisk (*Basiliscus basiliscus;* Plate 156) of Central America and Colombia reveal certain interesting facts, the most important of which I shall briefly summarize. First, the front legs are not indispensable for the elevation of the body; when these were taped down, the experimental individual was able to rise and run on the hind legs. Even from a squatting position while at rest, it could get up on the back limbs. Second, the long tail, in contrast to the legs, is necessary; a basilisk with as little as a third of the tail missing experienced great distress in trying to run on the hind limbs. The tail seems to play a double or even a triple role, its chief one being that of a counterbalance. Third, the lizard gait is a twisting or waddling one, due to the outward extension of the thighs. Fourth, the alterations in position of the center of gravity, compensated for in man by swinging of the arms, are taken care of in the lizard by a slight upward and downward motion of the trunk as well as by the weight and position of the tail. Incidentally, the basilisk moving at top speed entirely loses contact with the ground for brief moments.

RELATIONS TO MAN

THE HUMAN imagination has never run as wild with lizards as it has with snakes; the familiar English expression "snake story" does not have its counterpart for lizards. Perhaps the one world-wide false belief about lizards is that they are venomous, and this belief is much harder to explain than the corresponding one about snakes. How could the presence of two poisonous lizards in sparsely inhabited parts of North America give rise to an inter-hemispherical belief that all lizards are dangerous? As a boy living in Georgia, I was taught to fear the little skinks (*Eumeces*) with their brilliant azure tails. The ominous name "scorpion" is applied to them there, to the confusion of many who know the scorpion as an invertebrate with a jointed, stinging tail. In tropical America, Africa, and Asia a general fear of lizards is often prevalent, and it is based on the conviction that all are deadly.

Less absurd beliefs are in the class with the "glass snake" story, a lizard myth that is really a "snake story"; only herpetologists and naturalists know that glass snakes are legless lizards (see page 157). It is possible that the conception of the dragon in China is based on a lizard, for the similarity of a monitor to dragon pictures is striking; the difficulty is that this lizard occurs only in southern China, far from the cradle of Chinese culture. The alligator is a more probable prototype of the dragon.

In the Rhodesian region of Africa, Lucy P. Cullen (see bibliography) studied a widespread fear of the true chameleons and heard from a local chief the following explanation. Back at the beginning He Whose Name Is Not Spoken decided to put men on earth. This He did, but, being displeased with the result, determined to call all men together to make them not only better but different, giving to each group its own special virtues. It was necessary to call a meeting at which the good news could be announced. As the animals always acted as messengers, He sent them out, the leopard to one group, the lion to another, and so on down to the chameleon. Now, in those days chameleons were not the slowpokes that they are today, so there was no harm in using one as a bearer of the good tidings. However, the particular one chosen dawdled and delayed so much that the black man, to whom it had been sent, arrived only in time to receive the poorest of all the gifts. In his anger, this wretched victim put a curse upon the chameleon: forevermore its kind would move no more rapidly than did that messenger while on its errand. The abject dread of the chameleon shown today by the black man is the result of his age-long fear that the frustrated chameleon will someday avenge itself, and there is no telling how horrible his vengeance may be. The chameleon is still called "Go-slowly" by the believers of this legend.

The economic value of lizards is fourfold: their flesh and eggs are eaten, their skins are made into leather, they devour harmful insects, and a limited number are kept as pets. Ever since lizard and man were thrown together, he must have eaten the larger species. It is stated elsewhere that the chuckwalla was relished by certain American Indians; also that the common and gigantic iguana of tropical America is constantly seen in markets. Various other large species of the New World appear in these same markets. This enumeration could be indefinitely extended by mentioning the fondness that the Arabians and other peoples have for the flesh of the spiny-tailed lizards (*Uromastix*), the widespread appetite for monitor meat in the Old World, and so on. The eggs of the latter are especially relished.

The modern market for lizard hides is merely an outgrowth of various older uses to which the saurian skin has been put. It will suffice to mention the monitor-hide drumheads to be seen in many parts of the Old World. In all tropical countries the commercial collecting of the larger kinds of lizards has reached such large proportions that millions of victims are involved, and conservation of the rapidly diminishing supply is greatly needed. A single figure taken from Dr. Smith will have to do for illustration: in 1932 more than six hundred thousand reptile hides were shipped from Calcutta alone; most of these were from lizards, with monitor skins prevailing. A tanned lizard skin is a high-grade leather with excellent wearing qualities and fine grain. The variety of patterns to be found on the skins of the various species enhance the value. Many kinds of articles are made, including expensive shoes.

The good that lizards do as destroyers of noxious insects cannot be easily estimated, though certainly it is great. Dr. G. F. Knowlton has made extensive studies of lizard food habits in the United States and has shown that in Utah these reptiles help keep the beet leafhopper under control. Moreover, he proved that most of the insects found in stomachs of Utah lizards were injurious or of unknown economic importance, only a few of them beneficial. Many additional examples could be cited. Before leaving the subject, I must mention one novel usefulness of a lizard. On Ceylon a monitor (*Varanus salvator*) is protected because it eats crabs that in turn destroy the banks of rice fields. The usual value of monitors as predators lies in their love of rats.

The natural distributions of reptiles have been rarely disturbed by man because these animals have relatively little economic value.

Think of the numbers of insects and other invertebrates, birds, mammals, and even fishes that have been moved about over the globe. Among reptiles, the geckos have been transported most frequently because of their climbing habits and ability to thrive in the proximity of man. To be transplanted successfully animals must not only get aboard ship but take root at the port of destination. Many snakes, for example, are loaded along with bananas but lack the ability to survive at the port of unloading. Seven lizards are listed as having been accidentally added to the fauna of the United States; four of these are geckos, and it is only species of this family that have been brought from beyond the adjacent Caribbean shores. *Hemidactylus frenatus*, a gecko, is now found more or less throughout the tropical regions of the world; other nearly comparable examples could be cited.

The only lizard commonly kept in the United States as a pet is the American chameleon (*Anolis*), and it usually lives in a state of misery, surviving only about as long as it can fast.

VENOM AND BITE

IT IS a startling fact that, in sharp contrast to the snakes, lizards have made so little use of venom as a means of getting a dinner and of defending themselves. The venom and bite of lizards warrant a separate heading merely for the sake of emphasis; countless millions of people throughout the world believe that lizards are venomous, and the sooner this foolish belief is eradicated the better for both man and lizard. The ability and willingness of many large lizards to bite has no relation to injection of venom, because hollow or grooved teeth and venom glands are not present. The sole firmly established exceptions are the two closely related species of the genus *Heloderma*, one found in northwestern Mexico and the southwestern United States, the other only in Mexico (see page 313). The suspicion that the rare and related *Lanthanotus* of Borneo is likewise venomous does not appreciably alter the picture, because that reptile will never constitute a threat to more than a handful of human beings. The mere sight of one of these alive and kicking would be the fulfillment of a dream no student of herpetology has ever realized.

WHERE LIZARDS LIVE

BOTH THE snakes and the turtles are divided into two unequal lots, a large terrestrial one and a small marine one. Although in Cretaceous times, some millions of years ago, the lizards developed successful marine groups such as the mosasaurs, today no truly marine lizard exists. The reason for this is not clear; we can only state that lizards have become the most land-minded of all reptiles. The marine iguana (*Amblyrhynchus*), a large species of the Galápagos Islands, has, we might quip, its toes in the ocean; it lives on the shore and gets its food in the sea. Then there are monitors that may enter salt water. It is even hard to find a genuine fresh-water saurian, even though a limited number do exist. Here is a paradox: lizards, with their lack of ability to cope with the seas, are the reptiles most frequently carried fortuitously across them by man.

The distribution of lizards is controlled by the same major factor that operates for non-marine snakes: the necessity of hibernating in the colder regions, something that cannot be accomplished where the sub-soil is permanently frozen. This and related factors of distribution have been discussed for the snakes on page 167. In spite of the similarity of controlling factors, there are notable differences between the world-wide extent of lizard distribution and that of non-marine snakes. First, the lizards have been far more successful in reaching the islands of the southern Pacific; they occur in the Hawaiian Islands and others to the south, some of them about halfway across the ocean. The snakes are found only on islands lying not nearly so far to the east and in the latitude of northern Australia. Second, the lizards, though ranging nearly as far to the north in Eurasia (the Arctic Circle is not reached), fall far short of the snake limit in North America. This scarcity of lizards is especially evident in the east, northern New England being devoid of them, whereas snakes range even to the region of Hudson Bay. Among the few lizards that reach Canada, none has an extensive range in that country.

Like the snakes, lizards have successfully invaded all types of land areas with temperate or tropical climates; flat, open grasslands, mountainous regions, and deserts have their share. The lizards do better than the snakes in the drier areas, especially the true desert. The possession of legs may account for their better ability to cope with extremes of temperature. Desert lizards use tricks such as raising their bodies off the hot sands or tilting them so as to either avoid or absorb the sun's rays. Snakes cannot do this, although they can bury themselves (Plate 152) as readily as can the lizards; getting into the sand is another way of controlling temperature. Dr. Hobart M. Smith's 1946 map of the United States indicating the number of species found in each state graphically illustrates this love of dry, hot regions. His figures for the extreme southwestern states, taken individually, about double to quadruple the numbers of those of the extreme southeastern ones. The almost total absence in the southwest of lizard-shaped salamanders is an interesting, if somewhat irrelevant, fact.

Coming to the more intimate relation of lizards to their surroundings, we find that they, like snakes, do well in spite of having passed up the oceans and scarcely attained the air. The snakes made use of the oceans, but their volplaning is not in the class of that of the flying dragons (*Draco*). Lizards perhaps take exceptional advantage of the environment afforded by vegetation, whole families such as the geckos being largely arboreal; numerous members of various other families live in tree or bush. A few even make use of a truly specialized spot: high grass (see page 301). The strictly arboreal habitat is connected by them with the terrestrial one in this way: a great many lizards haunt vertical niches, using that word literally as well as figuratively. These they find among rocks, in faces of cliffs, human dwellings, fallen trees, and so on.

It would be hard to maintain that lizards have been more versatile than snakes in taking advantage of terrestrial habitats, although I do not hesitate to maintain that as true burrowers they have surpassed the snakes, especially if we include the worm lizards (Amphisbænidæ). Loss of limbs in lizards usually went with a tendency to go underground or at least live in the sub-surface. This no doubt was because the lizards never did develop a greatly elongated body, all their excessive length being in the tail, and the specialized methods of crawling and climbing made so much of by the snakes depend on the possession of a long body. The worm lizards constitute an exception to this short-body rule.

CLASSIFICATION

WITH FEW exceptions, the species of living lizards, approximately twenty-seven hundred in number, are readily divided into related assortments of families, and in this way they contrast sharply with the snakes (see page 169). The major difficulty in classifying lizards on a large scale lies in separating the agamids from the iguanids, the lacertids from the teiids. The first pair constitutes a case of parallel development, the agamids being Old World lizards, the iguanids chiefly of the New World; this geographical distinction is obviously of enormous practical service. The lacertids and teiids make up a similar and even more striking case: the former are entirely of the eastern, the latter of the western hemisphere. With a little practice, even the beginner can make a good guess at identification if not forced to distinguish between agamid and iguanid, lacertid and teiid. The novice will soon become accustomed to regarding the degree of development of limbs, or even their absence, as of no great significance; as I have frequently pointed out, the lizard reduces or loses a limb more readily than any other higher animal. Once lost in the course of evolution, the lizard limb is never regained.

The close relationship of lizard to snake is dealt with on page 169. Lizards are usually called Sauria, although they were long known as Lacertilia.

The present classification of lizards should stand without major changes, if we make allowance for the removal of the aberrant worm lizards (Amphisbænidæ), burrowing reptiles that are limbless or nearly so and all but confined to tropical regions. A convincing family allocation of a few rare or otherwise baffling species remains to be determined, but work on some of these puzzles is now in progress.

For comparison with the numbers of species of snakes as seen on page 169, a corresponding listing of lizards is given below:

Malay Archipelago (1915): 267
Southeastern Asia (from the Indian Peninsula and adjacent territory eastward to the South China Sea) (1935): 297
Europe (1940): 60
United States and Canada (1953): 79
Mexico (1950): 271

Just as for the snakes, considerable duplication exists between the first two items, and also between the last two. The number of species in the United States and Canada is the same as in the United States alone, Canada having no species all its own.

Account by Families

✿

GECKOS
(Family Gekkonidæ)
PLATES 156, 157, 158, 167, 168, 169, 170, 171, AND 172

GECKOS ARE perhaps the most appealing of all lizards, an appeal that lies chiefly in the following characteristics: inoffensiveness, moderate size, ability to live in close proximity to man, useful habits (devourers of insects, spiders, and the like), and a soft, loose skin that is pleasing to the touch. Availability might also be mentioned, as geckos are surpassed in extent of distribution only by the skinks. Unfortunately, geckos are anything but abundant in temperate North America, where only two kinds are native to the extreme southwestern United States and a few to Mexico. They are very abundant in Africa and the region extending from tropical Asia to Australia. Geckos are the only lizards whose natural distribution has been greatly deranged by man. There is reason to believe that three or four of the eight groups or genera now found in Mexico were carried there by ships of modern times, and no fewer than four species have been introduced to the United States (Florida and Keys). Many kinds of geckos make most attractive pets, and it only remains for some enterprising person to introduce them to the home, where someday they may be as popular as young turtles now are. The gecko can readily adapt itself to life in captivity, whereas the infant turtle cannot.

In technical books, geckos are treated first and described as primitive. Without doubt they are an ancient group, and, oddly enough, one without a fossil record. Their skulls, on the other

267

hand, with reduced and thinned parts, are anything but primitive. The geckos as a whole are a vigorous lot that, in contrast to the snakes, have taken a constructive point of view toward limbs and their usefulness. The student of reptiles can scarcely think of a gecko without thinking of feet; the classification of the approximately seventy genera is based largely on these appendages. Various families of lizards have, like the snakes, taken a dim view of limbs, and tended to lose them or reduce them; the chief differences found in lizard limbs in general is in degree of degeneracy or loss. But not in those of the geckos. The toe of a gecko (Plate 167) varies in structure from a simple fingerlike one with a claw on the end to a complex toe having a greatly expanded pad and a concealed claw suggesting that of a cat; when the pad is in use, the claw can be either extended or kept concealed. All degrees of toe development between these extremes are to be found. There is a close relation between the habits and the type of toe, the species that live on the ground having the simple toes, those that climb the most and live in bushes and trees having the complex ones. Geckos have not been backward in making use of all types of country from deserts to jungle, although they are never abundant in the latter. Not a few kinds are at home in rocky, dry terrain.

There is something fascinating about the idea of a sucking disc or pad in nature. Almost any smooth part of an animal that commonly comes in contact with whatever the creature happens to live on will sooner or later be called a suction apparatus. With the exception of leaves, there are few things in nature having surfaces smooth enough to allow a suction apparatus to take a grip. The toe pad of the gecko has been described as a suction disc, and indeed it feels like rubber. Microscopic examination and experiments have shown that in reality it is composed of thousands of tiny hooks too small to be seen with the naked eye. These hooks grip surfaces that appear to be smooth but, like the pad, are only relatively smooth and do have minute projections. Although a limited amount of friction does play its part, the pads hold in basically the same way that the plainly visible claw on the end of the toe grips. Plainly, the gecko with a good pad has triple insurance against a fall. One of these acrobats climbs a wall or tree with great ease, and even runs across a ceiling, provided neither wall nor ceiling has a highly polished surface; the ceiling must be rougher than the wall. The mention of ceilings and walls is entirely appropriate because in tropical countries geckos frequently live in houses, where they come out at night to feed on insects. I do not refer only to primitive types of jungle houses, but to well-constructed modern kinds as well.

Next in order of interest comes the gecko's voice. Here again, the gecko can scarcely be looked upon as primitive among lizards, for it is the only type that can make itself heard above a hiss or other simple sound. No other family of reptiles has succeeded in naming itself: the very sound on which the English name is based was derived from the call of the Old World tokay (*Gekko gecko*). All members of the family are believed able to make at least a squeak. An extreme development of the voice is found in the appropriately named *Ptenopus garrulus* of southern Africa. This gregarious three-inch lizard lives on dry, sandy dunes or flats, where it digs almost perpendicular burrows about a foot deep. In the late afternoon countless numbers call from the entrances to their homes. The din of their persistent *whick whick* has been described as almost deafening. Just what specific use the geckos make of their ability to utter a variety of sounds has never been definitely determined, although there is some evidence that the call is a love song. The mating habits of these fascinating lizards have been studied very little.

The eyes of geckos, though perhaps less remarkable than the feet, and not unique like the voice, have their special points of interest. Ordinary movable lids are usually lacking, a lack that gives the gecko eye its snakelike stare. But the catlike appearance of the great majority of gecko eyes is due to vertical-slit pupils. This type of pupil is well known to be associated with night life, which is something that most geckos indulge in. The gecko has not been satisfied to have an ordinary, run-of-the-mill slit pupil; the slit is often lobed, a condition thought to be the last word in gecko eye development.

Eye specialists tell us that when a lobed, vertical-slit pupil is brightly lit, the pupil closes completely to leave a series of pinholes made by the apposed extremities of the lobes. Each of these holes forms its own image on the retina without benefit of lens or cornea, and does so for objects at various distances, not requiring the usual adjustment for distance known as accommodation. Although insufficient light gets through any one pinhole, the combined light of all suffices to stimulate the retina. Thus the jagged edge of the gecko pupil is not madness without method.

If the lizard families ever decided to have a circus, I am sure they would call on the geckos to be the clowns, and these reptiles could easily bring the house down by a mere show of tails. The tail of a gecko is usually simple enough; it is thick at the base, but tapers to a point. It may, however, be varied in shape and form: slender and ratlike; leaf-shaped; carrot-shaped; globular at the end; sharply constricted at the base; fringed on the sides; crested above and below. All gecko tails, except the ratlike ones of a single genus (*Agamura*, with its two species of southwestern Asia), are fragile but easily reproduced when lost. Secondary tails are often bifid, occasionally trifid. Sometimes more than half of a lot of individuals caught wild will have new tails. The capture of a gecko without breaking its tail is often very hard to accomplish. In a few geckos the tail is useful as a grasping organ, being slightly prehensile.

Some final and unique characteristics of certain geckos will be briefly commented on. No other lizards have post-anal sacs and their accompanying bones. The sacs lie on the under side of the tail just behind the vent and, on casual examination, appear as two crescentic slits. They are not constructed like glands, and the bones, usually curved, are present only in males; the sacs of the females are not as well developed as are those of the males. This sexual difference suggests a sexual function, and experiments have suggested that the sacs are stimulating organs used by the male in quieting the female during the mating act. Most geckos also have a spur on either side of the base of the tail, and these are much larger in the male. Their function is dealt with on page 251.

With the exception of the species of two New Zealand genera, all geckos are believed to be egg-laying. Two eggs are nearly always laid at a time, although only one may be deposited. When more than two are found together, it is the result of collective laying, a habit well known to exist among these lizards. An observer even found 186 eggs in a single window-shutter. It should be explained that the eggs, when laid, are covered with a sticky substance that soon dries and causes the shells to stick not only to one another but to certain materials on or against which they are laid. I use the word "against" advisedly, because gecko eggs are frequently attached to a vertical surface, as suggested by the remark about the great number found on the single window-shutter in Canton, China. It is not unusual to find fertile eggs stuck beside remnants of obviously long-hatched ones. The eggs are round or nearly so, and the shell is white. The pinkish hue of some living eggs is apparently due to the contents showing through the thin shell.

More than 400 species of geckos are known. About 140 occur in Africa and as many live in the New World. At least 100 species inhabit tropical southern Asia. We have Loveridge to thank for the only recent and comprehensive treatment of the geckos of an entire continent: Africa (published in 1935). Europe, with 5 species living in its southern part, is a little better off for geckos than is the United States.

As already stated, only two species of geckos are native to this country. One of these, a lizard of Baja California, barely enters our country where Mexico and California meet. It is known as the Mexican leaf-fingered gecko (*Phyllodactylus tuberculosus*) because of the shape of the well-developed toe pads. This gecko is a denizen of dry, rocky country, where it lives on and near boulders. During the day it hides in cracks of the boulders. Our other gecko, in strong contrast, lacks toe pads and has ordinary eyelids. It is found in northern Mexico and from southern Texas through extreme southern California and over much of the intervening territory. As the banded gecko's scientific name, *Coleonyx variegatus*, indicates, the species is variable in coloration. Distinct bands cross the body of specimens from some areas; in individuals from other places these bands are more or less obscured by age or by the presence of spots and blotches. It has been given several scientific names on the basis of these and less obvious differences between the populations of various regions. The banded gecko is found in dry, rocky country or in deserts. It comes out after sundown and may often be seen between seven and ten at night crossing the road.

Two eggs are laid at a time, this, as already explained, being the usual number for the family. Courtship and mating are described on page 250.

Geckos have never gone in for size. The vast majority are from 4 to 6 inches in total length; a few reach a length of 10 to 12, and the gigantic tokay, already mentioned, may grow to be 14 inches long. This remarkable reptile makes a handsome but noisy pet. On the other extreme, geckos may be true midgets: one West Indian species is not nearly so long as its technical name—*Sphærodactylus elegans*—printed here, the adult length being but 1.3 inches.

IGUANIDS
(Family Iguanidæ)
PLATES 174, 175, 176, 177, AND 178

FOR TWO reasons I shall not dwell at length on the general aspects of the iguanids. One of these is because of their similarity to the agamids, which are described in some detail, and the other is because half of the species of the lizards of the United States are iguanids and need to be considered at length.

Why are two assortments of lizards so much alike placed in different families? The answer, put simply, is that there are constant differences sufficient to warrant the separation, the major one being the way the teeth are fixed to the jaws. The extensive distribution of the agamids in the Old World is described on page 284 and their absence from Madagascar noted. The iguanids are just as widely distributed in the New World, including the Galápagos Islands, and the agamids are entirely absent from these iguanid areas. Madagascar has two genera of iguanids made up of seven species, enough to prove that iguanids really belong there. The next odd thing about iguanid distribution is the presence of a lone species in the remote Fiji and Tonga islands of the Pacific Ocean. This handsome animal (*Brachylophus*) reaches a length of three feet, and is nearing extermination.

When the ranges of the iguanids and agamids are combined, the reptile world is well covered. The fossil record carries these families back to Cretaceous times (some hundred million years ago) and suggests that the iguanids, with their fossil record in Europe, were once present in the African region, where they were replaced by the agamids on the continent, but survived on Madagascar.

The Galápagos Islands, situated at the equator, six hundred miles west of South America, have an iguanid fauna much richer than that of Madagascar. The most remarkable part of this is the marine iguana (*Amblyrhynchus cristatus*), a powerful reptile that eats only seaweed, which is largely exposed at low tide. The marine iguana feels at home in the sea, although it lives strictly on beaches and in the immediate vicinity of the islands. A length of four and a half feet is attained by this lizard of unique habits. Another kind of iguana (*Conolophus*), a somewhat shorter, stockier species, is not so unusual in habits; it is terrestrial, and eats plants, including cacti, spines and all. Several species of *Tropidurus*, a genus well represented in South America, and a few geckos complete the Galápagos lizard fauna, one of the herpetological surprises of the world. Early travelers tell of finding the two gigantic species in astounding abundance.

The similarity between iguanid and agamid will be briefly summarized here from the iguanid point of view. Although no iguanid has taken to the air as did the flying dragons, the basilisks (*Basiliscus*) of tropical America have developed a novel type of locomotion. They are able to make short dashes across the surface of water. To do this, they rear on the hind limbs. The iguanids of forested tropical regions are predominantly arboreal, those of open, sparsely vegetated ones largely terrestrial. Bodies flattened from side to side are the rule among the climbers, whereas the ground-living species are flat in the usual sense of that word. The comical horned toads (*Phrynosoma*), to be considered in detail below, admirably illustrate the latter type, a small genus (*Corythophanes*) of tropical America the other. The three arboreal species of this genus have an odd-shaped, crested head rivaling that of certain agamids, a throat fan, and body flattened from side to side. They enhance their grotesque appearance and exaggerate their size by turning broadside to an enemy just as do the true chameleons, close relatives of the agamids.

Like the agamids, the iguanids have kept their limbs to make good use of them, and the iguanid tail is usually tough, sometimes very spiny. The color changes of the American chameleon (an anole), a member of the enormous genus *Anolis*, are so pronounced that great confusion of it with the true chameleons has resulted. Iguanids are mostly carnivorous, but there are notable exceptions, perhaps more than among the agamids. Most interesting of all is the parallel in method of reproduction. The iguanids are egg-laying, with the exception of certain species of two groups (*Phrynosoma* and *Sceloporus*) that bring forth the young directly.

Finally, by way of statistics, the family Iguanidæ has about 700 species divided among some 65 genera. Fully two fifths of the species are placed in the genus *Anolis*. Two other large genera, roughly equal in size, together comprise about 100 species, or nearly a quarter of the remainder. One of these is the familiar genus of spiny lizards (*Sceloporus*) of North America, the other a South American genus named *Liolæmus*. As to maximum length, the common iguana (*Iguana iguana*) of tropical America, including the Lesser Antilles, attains one of 6 feet 7 inches. It lives near water, into which it may drop from high, overhanging branches of jungle giants. It swims well, without using the legs.

IGUANIDS OF THE UNITED STATES

Half of the species and nearly half of the genera of lizards of the United States are iguanids. In spite of this, only two species of iguanids (the American chameleon and the common spiny lizard) are found east of the Mississippi River and north of peninsular Florida; two additional iguanids live in peninsular Florida. In the western, especially the southwestern part of our country, iguanids are by far the most conspicuous of lizards. Their competitors in this respect would be the race runners, often extraordinarily abundant in number of individuals per acre, though the race runners are too wary and speedy to be conspicuous. There are also many species of skinks, but skinks are secretive.

All of the iguanid genera will be considered one by one. It will be seen that there is difference of opinion as to the number of genera into which our forty species should be divided. This is a matter of importance only to the specialist in classification, the taxonomist.

As Canada has no lizard that is not also found in the United States, the following account completely covers the iguanids of that country.

ANOLES
(*Anolis*)
PLATES 159, 160, 161, AND 162

It is explained elsewhere that the American chameleon (*Anolis carolinensis*) is not really a chameleon; it was given this name because of an ability to change color rapidly. This anole is interesting as being almost our sole representative of the most unwieldy lizard genus; its hundreds of species literally swarm throughout the American tropics. For the combination of being difficult to classify and having a great number of species, the genus is probably unmatched among reptiles. The only other anole found in this country lives in the Florida Keys.

In contrast to this, *Anolis carolinensis* ranges widely over the southeastern states from North Carolina well into Texas. It is our one lizard commonly sold as a "pet." The unfortunate but widespread belief that it will live on sugar and water with an occasional housefly thrown in for good measure, requires the placing of the word pet in quotation marks. Captives require warmth and a substantial diet of insects, spiders, and other small, lively invertebrates. Weekly feeding should suffice. A little water sprinkled on leaves will supply all the water needed, although a well-fed individual gets along without much water.

A recent study by Dr. George W. D. Hamlett, of the Louisiana State University School of Medicine, establishes beyond doubt certain surprising aspects of its reproduction. In the region of New Orleans, Louisiana, this species mates from mid-spring throughout the summer, and eggs are laid singly, a female depositing one about every two weeks from late spring through the summer. Females mature rapidly and may lay during the first summer following hatching; the males grow less rapidly, requiring an additional year to attain sexual maturity. Large adult American chameleons are about seven inches long. The species is strictly arboreal in habits.

CRESTED LIZARD
(*Dipsosaurus dorsalis*)

The crested lizard is our single species of its small genus, the others, two in number, living in northwestern Mexico. Our kind occurs in arid country from extreme southern Nevada and adjacent territory southward into the northwestern corner of Mexico. It demonstrates an adaptation to desert living by voluntarily standing the highest body temperature (115.5° F.) of any desert reptile of North America. The body cavity has a black lining that appears to afford protection from the ultra-violet radiation of the desert. Over much of its range the crested lizard is closely associated with the creosote bush, the spring diet consisting predominantly of the flowers of this plant. When these are not available, other plants are eaten; in the summer insects and carrion enter into the diet. It runs with astonishing speed and occasionally may use only the hind legs. Mammal burrows are often occupied, or the crested lizard may dig its own home. Reproduction is by means of eggs. A length of sixteen inches is attained.

CHUCKWALLA
(*Sauromalus obesus*)
PLATE 179

The word "chuckwalla" somehow suggests a chunky, flattened creature, and our single species of the genus *Sauromalus* is just that. The technical name of the species, *obesus*, is even better. The range extends from extreme southern Utah and the southern tip of Nevada southward into the northwestern corner of Mexico. Six other species of chuckwallas are found in territory bordering the Gulf of California, but all have extremely limited ranges.

Arid, relatively barren, rock-strewn slopes are the preferred habitat of our chuckwalla. When alarmed, one of these reptiles retreats into a narrow crevice and fills its lungs with air until the body has increased about sixty per cent in volume. This inflation makes extraction very difficult unless the lungs are pierced and thus deflated. The local Indians, liking the meat of the chuckwalla, used to effect capture by doing this with a sharp stick. No other lizard of the United States except the Gila monster compares with the chuckwalla in bulk, although the slender glass snakes are much longer than either. A large chuckwalla is 16 inches in total length and about 3.5 wide; the thick tail is as long as the head and body.

It is surprising to see a lizard of so gross an appearance slowly and deliberately eating yellow flowers, but anyone who works with chuckwallas will have this novel experience. The leaves as well as the flowers and fruits of various plants are devoured, although yellow blossoms seem to have a special appeal. Reproduction apparently is by means of eggs; little is known about this and other aspects of the life history.

EARLESS LIZARDS
(*Holbrookia*)

The smaller species of lizards of the western United States are extremely confusing to the novice; for the most part, their differences are not the kind that lend themselves to brief diagnosis. The earless lizards constitute a happy exception, for, despite the fact that they never exceed 6.5 inches in length, the lack of an ear-opening will distinguish them at once; their coloration may be annoyingly similar to that of species in other genera. The group can be claimed by the United States; although its range includes a considerable part of northern Mexico, only one of the four or five species does not occur in the United States. The combined ranges of our species fall west of the tier of states bordered on the east by the Mississippi, south of those touching Canada, and east of Oregon and California. Unlike that of so many other groups, the center of distribution is not in the southwestern deserts, but just east of them; typically, the earless lizards frequent moderately dry, fine, or sandy soil with or without rocks. Places of low vegetation rather than grass ones are preferred. In suitable areas they are extraordinarily abundant, and their inquisitiveness makes them conspicuous as well. Earless lizards often appear to be about as interested in the habits of *Homo sapiens* as that mammal sometimes is in the behavior of earless lizards. These little reptiles are chiefly insect- and spider-eaters. Reproduction is by means of eggs.

GRIDIRON-TAILED LIZARD
(*Callisaurus draconoides*)

The range of the gridiron-tailed lizard is similar to that of the crested lizard, though somewhat more extensive, especially in Mexico. The genus *Callisaurus* has a single species. There are black spots on the underside of the tail that become encircling bands toward the tip. The gridiron-tailed lizard is a desert inhabitant with a short, sharp-edged snout that it uses when burying itself in the sand. This reptile often runs away swiftly with the conspicuously marked tail curled over the back; when the dash abruptly ends, the tail may be waved from side to side while yet curled, producing, because of the black spots, an interesting effect. The maximum speed has been estimated at about fifteen miles an hour, or considerably slower than that of a man (about twenty-one miles an hour). The food consists largely of insects and spiders; some plant matter is also taken. Reproduction is by means of eggs. Fully grown adults are about nine inches long.

FRINGE-TOED LIZARD
(*Uma notata*)
PLATE 180

Life in loose sand has its disadvantages, but these have been overcome to such an extent by the fringe-toed lizard that it actually prefers shifting dunes to sandy country with vegetation. The structure of the fringe-toed lizard, the only one of this country so thoroughly adapted to contending with sand, is modified in the following ways, beginning with the head. The snout is wedge-shaped and the lower jaw countersunk; the nasal passages are provided with special valves; the eyelids are thick and serrated; the toes are fringed to form what might be called "sandshoes." But this is not all, because the behavior of the lizard is as truly helpful in coping with sand as is the structure. When pursued, a fringe-toed lizard will literally dive into the sand and "swim" under it to complete concealment. The front legs do not assist in this submergence but are held against the body; pushing movements of the hind limbs together with undulatory movements of body and tail accomplish the feat.

The range of the fringe-toed lizard is confined to deserts of southern California, extreme southwestern Arizona, and the adjacent border region of Mexico at the head of the Gulf of California. Little is known about reproduction except that eggs are laid. The diet consists chiefly of insects; a limited amount of succulent plant parts is also eaten. The only other species of the genus *Uma* lives in the Mexican state of Coahuila.

COLLARED AND LEOPARD LIZARDS
(*Crotaphytus*)
PLATES 181 AND 182

The collared and leopard lizards are sometimes placed together in the genus *Crotaphytus* and sometimes separated, the latter being assigned to the genus *Gambelia*. It merely depends on the point of view; there are differences, but for our purpose they would best be considered together; I shall point out their similarities and then a few differences. Both are large, swift, pugnacious lizards that range widely over the southwestern quarter of the United States (nowhere do they occur in the Pacific coastal strip) with a northward extension in the west to southern Idaho and southeastern Oregon. They are voracious eaters of insects and lizards of other species. Reproduction is by means of eggs.

Coming to the differences, the leopard lizard (*C. wislizeni*) is more slender in build, and reaches a length (sixteen inches) about two inches greater than that of the collared lizard (*C. collaris*). The latter ranges much farther eastward, even to the Mississippi valley in southern Missouri and adjacent Arkansas. The leopard lizard frequents flat, sparsely grown desert areas that are not shifting dunes or strewn with boulders; the other prefers boulder-strewn, rugged regions, or, in the prairies, canyons. The collared lizard lays at one time from four to twenty-four eggs, the leopard lizard from two to four. When indulging in its characteristic dashes to safety, the collared lizard often rears on its hind legs.

The reticulated lizard, *C. reticulatus,* a close relative of the collared lizard, lives in the Rio Grande valley of Texas and Mexico. Little is known about its habits. Two additional species are found on islands in the Gulf of California.

SPINY LIZARDS
(*Sceloporus*)
PLATE 183

The spiny lizards are perhaps the dominant lizards of the elevated, dry region of North America from the southwestern United States through central Mexico. In the north they range into extreme northern Washington, to the south as far as Panama. One species (*Sceloporus undulatus*) has crossed the Mississippi to spread itself over the eastern United States except its northern third, and another (*S. woodi*) lives in peninsular Florida, where it largely replaces the other. But the true spiny-lizard country is the region first outlined. Fifteen species are found in the United States, about three and a half times that many in Mexico.

These lizards are not only dominant, but even appear to be so to the casual observer. There are several reasons for this. The spiny lizard, or "swift," as it is often called, is active in daylight and relatively bold, so that it is easily observed. Although all types of country are frequented by one species or another, rock- or tree-climbing habits are prevalent, a kind of behavior that constantly brings animals into human view. Populations of swifts can be extraordinarily large; in certain areas every rock, tree, or even post has its individual. Incidentally, it might be remarked here that spiny lizards have never become burrowing or water-loving; it is dryness and warmth that appeal to them. The species found in the eastern United States, where it is commonly called "fence lizard," wanders farthest from dry country, but compensates by frequenting situations where there is the least amount of moisture: openings in heavy forests, upland pine woods, and fences in pastures more or less adjacent to wooded areas.

The method of reproduction is not fixed in the spiny lizards; about two thirds of our fifteen species lay eggs, the rest produce the young directly. Insects form the bulk of the diet. There are exceptions to this insectivorous diet. For example, the desert spiny lizard (*S. magister*), widely distributed in our far southwest and in northern Mexico, devours other kinds of lizards as well as some plant matter. This species shares with the blue scaly lizard (*S. cyanogenys*) of the lower Rio Grande valley honors for greatest size among all recorded from the United States: both attain a maximum length of thirteen and three quarters inches.

UTAS
(*Uta*)

About twenty species of lizards found in the western United States and northern and western Mexico are notoriously hard to classify; sometimes they are placed in a single genus, *Uta*, sometimes divided about equally between *Uta* and *Urosaurus*. The differences in structure between these groups are technical; it is hard enough for the amateur to be sure an individual represents either type. For our purposes, the whole lot may be put in the single genus *Uta*. The total range covers the western United States and northern Mexico, with an extension to the state of Chiapas on the Pacific side. In the United States all of the five species of utas are confined to the southwest, except one that occurs as far north as Washington. It differs also from the other four in living on the ground or among rocks, and is known as the side-blotched uta (*U. stansburiana*). The other species are climbers that may do their climbing on bushes, trees, or boulders. They do well enough on the ground, but have an irrepressible desire to be in a more or less vertical position. Much the largest of all our utas, the California collared uta (*U. mearnsi*) of southern California and adjacent Baja California, reaches a length of about eleven inches. It is usually seen peering over rock or boulder for it is truly a rock-dwelling lizard. Utas lay eggs, and live chiefly on insects and spiders.

HORNED TOADS

(*Phrynosoma*)

PLATES 184 AND 185

Classifiers of animals are divided into two groups: the "splitters," those who magnify the differences, and the "lumpers," who emphasize the similarities. The horned toads have succeeded in splitting the classifiers. Herpetologists are divided between those who follow common usage in calling these reptiles "horned toads," and those who insist on trying to change the name to "horned lizards." Perhaps it is a division between the pragmatists and the idealists. It is easy to see how the early settlers of North America looked on these broad, flat, short-tailed creatures as toads. In fact, these reptiles have carried to its ridiculous extreme this business of being flattened and widened for ground living; their only rival is the strikingly similar moloch (*Moloch horridus*) of the arid parts of Australia. The heads of the fifteen species exhibit a most beautifully graduated series from the hornless head of the rare kind *Phrynosoma ditmarsi*, named after the late Raymond L. Ditmars, to heads completely and evenly crowned on the back and sides with enormous spines.

The grotesqueness of horned toads makes their bluffing antics ludicrous in the extreme. If instead of reaching a maximum body length of four and a half inches, our horned toads attained one of five or six feet, we should have to speak of warning behavior rather than of bluffing antics; an aroused horned toad will actually attack, and bite as it does so. I need not add that the bite is nothing more than a harmless pinch. The behavior of a short-horned horned toad

282

(*P. douglassi*) that I encountered in northern Arizona illustrates its bluffing method and that of other species. The miniature monster puffed itself up, stood high on the tips of its toes, rocked its body back and forth, opened the mouth to reveal a dark lining, and, finally, hissed as it charged. I was disappointed that it did not squirt blood from the eyes, the ultimate in horned-toad aggressive tactics.

Various kinds of horned toads have been seen to eject blood from the eyes up to a distance of seven feet. The anatomical basis of the phenomenon involves an especially thin nictitating membrane as well as an ability to increase the blood pressure of the head, an ability primarily associated with the process of shedding the old skin. The blood of a horned toad is entirely harmless.

Although the horned toads range from extreme southwestern Canada to Guatemala, they are typical of the elevated, arid region extending from the southwestern United States well into Mexico. In the former country, they are widely distributed west of the tier of states bordered on the east by the Mississippi River, though they just enter some of these states from the west. Seven species are found in the United States. Horned toads are versatile in reproduction, some producing the young directly, others laying eggs. The short-horned horned toad may give birth to as many as thirty young at one time, and even more eggs (forty) have been recorded for one egg-laying species. In spite of a broad body, the horned toads bury themselves in sand or loose soil to escape the cold of the desert night. When warming themselves in the sun, they flatten and tilt the body so that it receives full benefit of the rays. The diet consists chiefly of insects and other arthropods. Ants are eaten in great numbers (see page 247). Food is taken only when the temperature is high.

AGAMIDS
(Family Agamidæ)
PLATES 173, 186, 187, AND 188

THERE IS no generally used common name for the species of this family, which number nearly three hundred. The technical name is simple enough and might as well be used.

This family has the distinction of including the only living lizards that have taken to the air. These air-minded agamids belong to the genus *Draco* and are commonly called "flying dragons," a term not entirely suitable because they only volplane by means of a winglike structure on either side. This structure is nothing more than skin supported by prolonged ribs. When not in use, the "wings" are kept against the body. The flying dragons are entirely arboreal, and their "wings" greatly facilitate progress in the tropical forests where they live. The species, long reckoned as about forty in number, are found from southeastern Asia through the Malay and Philippine islands, with a lone species in peninsular India. A revision published in 1936 greatly reduced the number of species.

I cannot resist pointing out again how Mother Nature often makes secondary uses of a structure, in this case the appendages of the flying dragons. While contesting for a female, the males of certain kinds repeatedly open and close the "wings," which are often brilliantly colored. The other use I noticed quite by accident after placing in a box nineteen living individuals of *Draco maculatus*, the only species that occurs in China. The following day I was dumfounded to find nearly all of the lizards gone. Only close scrutiny enabled me to see one by one the missing dracos, each of which had closely applied itself to a twig of the limb that I had placed in the box. The camouflage was accomplished by moving the "wings" slightly downward until the body was lost to sight in appearing to be an enlargement of the twig, which it matched in color. The head and legs also were carefully placed so as to blend with the outline of the twig, and all of the long tail was precisely extended along the same. The fact that not a lizard moved during my search made the deception all the more bewildering. *D. maculatus*, a flying dragon rather small in size, is about eight inches long when adult.

Where the flying dragons live, the great majority of agamids are also arboreal, the dracos expressing the highest development in this direction. In Africa, where the family is represented by one ubiquitous genus (*Agama*) and a few groups confined to the northern half, conditions are reversed: with rare exceptions the African species are ground-dwellers of savannas, deserts, and rocky terrain.

A tendency toward aquatic habits crops up here and there among the genera found from southeastern Asia throughout Australia. The range of the family includes southeastern Europe and the vast region extending thence eastward across central Asia to northern China and adjacent territory. Only two genera inhabit this northern stretch, species of *Agama* in the west, and the species of the genus *Phrynocephalus*, some forty in number, from southeastern Europe (three species) right through central Asia. The agamids of this northern stretch are terrestrial lizards of arid country, like those of northern Africa. No members of this family occur on Madagascar, where they are replaced by iguanids.

In contrast to many other lizards, the agamids have kept their limbs and always made good use of them. Their tails are long as well as unusual for lizards in being tough and not easily broken. We might expect reptiles with non-fragile tails and arboreal habits to possess grasping tails, but the agamids, with few exceptions, do not. The exceptions are two species of the genus *Cophotis;* one lives on Ceylon, the other on Sumatra and Java. The well-developed agamid eyes have movable lids, and the teeth of some groups show an extraordinary diversity in shape and size.

So far I have mentioned nothing that would set this family aside sharply from others. It is not easy to characterize the agamids, and, indeed, they are in many ways similar to the iguanids, a predominantly New World family. The iguanids and the agamids show remarkable parallels in form, structure, and habits. Both of them include large species of grotesque shapes. Among the agamids, this grotesqueness may take the form of odd-shaped skulls, spines, or other structures on the snout, fringed flaps on the side of the head or neck, high crests extending down back and tail, and the wings of the flying dragons. The shape of the body comes in two types, one more or less flattened from back to belly, the other more or less compressed from side to side. I have repeated the qualifying phrase for emphasis because these types are not recognizable in all agamids. The first type is seen in the ground-living groups, the second in the arboreal ones. The agamids have never taken to a sub-surface life, although many species of arid, sandy regions (genus *Phrynocephalus*) are adept at burying themselves in the sand by rapid sidewise movements of the body, and Hardwicke's spiny-tailed lizard (*Uromastix hardwicki*) of West Pakistan and northern India lives in a hole that it digs to a length of eight or nine feet and a depth of four or five below the surface. This species grows to be about a foot long. When the nights are cold, this reptile, upon retiring for the night, carefully closes the entrance to its burrow. It, of course, is by no means the only agamid that digs a hole to live in.

A slight digression is justified here to relate how a hungry snake, attempting to capture a Hardwicke's spiny-tailed lizard in its burrow, is frustrated by that wary reptile. Upon becoming aware of the enemy's approach, the lizard, instead of retreating to the depths of its home, where it would be at a great disadvantage, sticks its formidable tail out of the burrow and violently switches it about. The spines of this organ are too much for any small animal to contend with, let alone a mere snake.

A characteristic that the agamids share with the iguanids and the closely related true chameleons is the ability to change color with astonishing rapidity. This ability is put to double use and associated with the grotesque shapes just enumerated. One of these uses is bluffing an enemy, the other winning a mate. The frilled lizard of Australia and New Guinea (*Chlamydosaurus kingi*) is the classic example of a great bluffer. This lizard, which grows to be about three feet long, has on the neck a cape or frill that can be spread out on either side until its diameter is eight or ten inches. During a display, loud hissing and an open mouth with a bright yellow lining and a pair of enlarged teeth enhance the alarming appearance of this inveterate pretender. The Australian region has other great bluffers, such as the bearded dragon (*Amphibolurus barbatus*), whose display has been definitely shown to be associated with sexual behavior as well as with defense. Its antics include rapid color changes and tactics much like those of the larger and more forbidding frilled lizard. There are other gigantic and adorned agamids of this region, some of them reaching a length of from three to four feet. I can think of nothing more fascinating than a study of the sexual behavior of these huge lizards, first in a laboratory, and then, for confirmation, in the wilds where they abound.

The agamid rule of reproduction by means of eggs is proved by few exceptions; one is the little prehensile-tailed Ceylonese lizard *Cophotis ceylanica*, the other, allegedly, a species of the large Asiatic genus, *Phrynocephalus*. The feeding habits are less uniform: the great majority of genera live on insects and other small invertebrates, a few are animal- as well as plant-eaters, and at least one is almost entirely plant-eating. This is the genus of spiny-tailed lizards (*Uromastix*) with several species frequenting the arid parts of northern Africa and southwestern Asia. The adults are well known to be herbivorous, whereas the young, whose teeth differ from those of the adults, may take insects.

Some of the agamids, when pressed, run on the hind legs, an act that seems to remind all observers of pictures of bipedal dinosaurs. The frilled lizard, already described, and the gigantic water dragon (*Physignathus lesueuri*), also of Australia, are examples.

I have told something about the three largest groups of agamids, the flying dragons (*Draco*), the agamas (*Agama*), and the genus *Phrynocephalus*, the species of which, because of a rather squat shape, often are called "toad lizards." The first and last of these genera have, as already stated, about forty species each, the remaining genus more than fifty. The only other large group, *Calotes*, comprised of only half as many species as *Agama*, is distributed from southeastern Asia through the Malay and Philippine islands. The species of *Calotes* are spiny lizards of moderate size not readily distinguished from their numerous relatives, which are set off into many small genera. The four large genera include well over half of all the agamids.

TRUE CHAMELEONS
(Family Chamæleonidæ)
PLATES 189, 190, 191, 192, 193, 194, 195, AND 196

IN THE United States at least, the lizards about to be considered must be called "true chameleons" to avoid confusion with an ordinary little lizard of this country that I designated as the American chameleon (see page 275). This confusion of names is most unfortunate, because the American chameleon shares none of the many unique and extraordinary features of the true chameleons, which abound in Africa and Madagascar, with a slight spillover into territory immediately adjacent to Africa and a single errant species in peninsular India and Ceylon. Included in this spillover is the one species of Europe, which occurs on the mainland of this continent only in southern Spain. Unfortunately, this species has two widely used technical names: *Chamæleo chamæleon* and *C. vulgaris;* the generic name, now *Chamæleo*, was long spelled *Chamæleon.*

Scrutiny of a true chameleon might well bring forth the remark that no lizard has the right to be so grotesque. A true chameleon may be recognized at a glance by its blunt head, its body greatly flattened from side to side and deep from top to bottom, its turret eyes, tweezerlike feet, and more or less curling tail. The other characteristics require time for their discernment; the striking color changes, the tongue action, which is beyond belief, the ridiculously slow movements, and the amusing antics that make up the bluffing, fighting, and courting behavior. In some species the head is developed into forms that suggest huge, odd-shaped casques or helmets; as many as three long horns may project straight forward, or the snout may be produced to form a bulbous, pointed, or even forked appendage.

Some of these characteristics are unique, whereas others are just as worthy of comment or explanation. Let us first consider a few of the unique attributes, those that are chiefly responsible for the setting off of the chameleons as a category higher than that of a mere family. I shall first mention head characters and shapes. The tongue reminds one of a popgun in action, although the propulsive force is entirely muscular. It has a sticky tip that can be projected to a distance considerably greater than the length of the head and body. The speed of projection is too fast for the human eye. The chameleon's eyes are mounted on protruding hemispherical turrets that move independently of one another, giving weird effects when one is directed straight forward, the other backward, or one upward, the other downward. The toes are united into two groups that oppose each other and form a grasping foot of the most efficient kind.

Now let us consider other characteristics; the first of these may be unique, but it is too intangible to be included above. The slow body and limb movements of the chameleons are in strong contrast to the usual quick ones of lizards in general. A chameleon, it would seem, makes comparatively little progress from birth to death; its movements are painfully slow to watch, and there is considerable evidence that its usual span of life is less than three years, the shortest span among reptiles (see page 238). The ability to change color, though well developed, is by no means unique among lizards; perhaps no others surpass the chameleons in this feat. The common belief that the chameleon simply matches in color the object on which it rests is false; other factors such as temperature and emotional state enter into the picture. The prehensile or grasping tail of the chameleon, though characteristic enough, is, like color change, seen in other lizards.

The chameleon peculiarities are not without purpose; in fact, these lizards might be thought of as deadly practical fellows who have decided to fit themselves for every contingency. The chameleon is first and foremost arboreal, descending to the ground only to lay (the young of the non-egg-layer are born aloft). Correlated with this type of life are the grasping feet and tail. The slow movements, rolling eyes, long-range tongue, and body flattened from side to side (presenting a deceptive front) work together beautifully in the stalking of insects and other prey. It must take a lot less energy to get a breakfast the chameleon way than by the cruder rushing or overpowering methods. The casque and horns of the head are used by the males in contesting for a mate. But the chameleon has shown real cleverness in making triple use of the flat body, a flatness that is under voluntary control allowing the body to be made so flat that the animal appears to stand on edge. When attacking an enemy, the chameleon first flattens itself and then turns its broadside, thus enhancing its size; when stalking prey, it flattens to present a narrow front; when attempting to escape, it does the same, with the delicate touch of swaying as it retreats, making itself look like a leaf in a breeze. Inflating the body and hissing are also included in the chameleon's repertoire.

The chameleons are grouped into one very large genus (*Chamæleo*) and a few small ones, there being some difference of opinion about how many of the latter should be counted. A grand total of somewhat more than eighty species is known, about half of which live on Madagascar, where these lizards run riot. A Madagascan midget is credited with the unbelievable total length of only one and a quarter inches, whereas a giant of the genus, such as Oustalet's chameleon (*C. oustaleti*) of Madagascar, may reach a length slightly in excess of two feet. Chameleons are related to the agamids. The few fossil chameleons in the records are of somewhat doubtful identity, and therefore the past history of these lizards is virtually unknown.

NIGHT LIZARDS
(Family Xantusidæ)

THE ASSEMBLAGE of eleven strong-limbed species known as night lizards includes only small reptiles of ordinary appearance that, nevertheless, have their points of interest. Six of these live in Central America and the southern half of Mexico, a seventh in Cuba, where it is known from an area but a few square miles in extent. I shall spare the reader the technical names of these seven, remarking only that they are different enough to be placed in two or even three genera; little is known about them anyway. The genus *Xantusia*, with four species, lives in the Mexican state of Baja California and the extreme southwestern corner of the United States; it is on this genus that I shall dwell.

Our night lizards have well-developed limbs and a normal, though somewhat flattened, shape. In spite of this, they can be recognized at a glance by lidless eye and catlike pupil, the latter bespeaking nocturnal habits. Until recent years they were believed to be rare, but improvement of hunting methods quickly dispelled this belief. Two of our three mainland species, the Arizona night lizard (*X. arizonæ* of central and western Arizona) and the granite night lizard (*X. henshawi* of extreme southern California and northern Baja California), live on and among granite boulders. To find night lizards with such a home, the collector has to pry off the thin flakes of granite that form so quickly under desert conditions of rapid

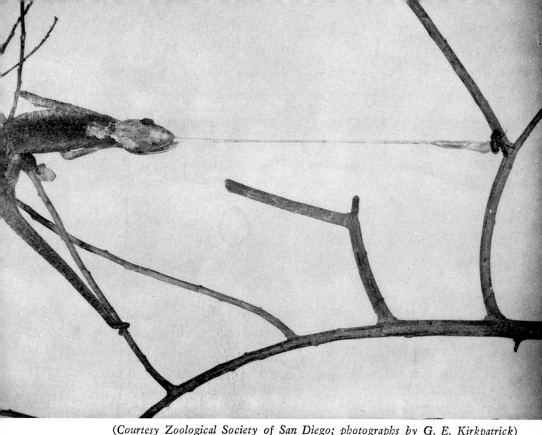

(Courtesy Zoological Society of San Diego; photographs by G. E. Kirkpatrick)

191. ABOVE: without benefit of electronic device, the photographer took this remarkable picture of a chameleon (*Microsaura pumila*) in the very act of making a successful shot with its tongue. 192. BELOW: the same chameleon withdrawing the tongue with prey stuck to its bulbous end.

(Courtesy Bernard Greenberg and Chicago Natural History Museum)

193. A chameleon from the mountains of eastern Africa (*Chamæleo bitæniatus*).

194. A male Owen's chameleon (*Chamæleo oweni*) displays his three horns. The female of this species of tropical African forests is seen upsidedown. She is not so formidably armed.

(Zoological Society of Philadelphia)

(*Courtesy Zoological Society of San Diego*)

195.   This chameleon (*Microsaura pumila*) gave birth to eighteen young, many of which are shown with her. The photograph does not imply parental care.

196.   A gigantic chameleon (*Chamæleo verrucosus*) reposing on the arm of Dr. Medem.

(*Photograph by Hymen Marx*)

(*Zoological Society of Philadelphia*

197. Cunningham's skink (*Egernia cunninghami*). This species, widely distributed in Australia, commonly attains a length of one foot.

198. Schneider's skink (*Eumeces schneideri*). This species occurs in extreme northern Africa, adjacent southwestern Asia, and on the island of Cyprus. It attains a length of sixteen and a half inches.

(*Photograph by Isabelle Hunt Conant*

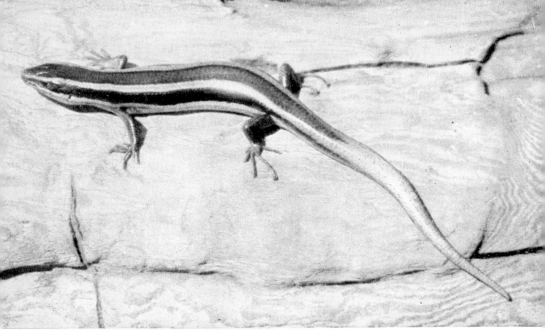

(Courtesy The American Museum of Natural History)

199. Western skink (*Eumeces skiltonianus*).

(Courtesy New York Zoological Society)

200. Sand skink (*Neoseps reynoldsi*).
The limbs of this degenerate burrower are useless in locomotion.

201. Viviparous lizard (*Lacerta vivipara*) with six of
her young. The photograph does not imply parental care.

202. Eyed lizard (*Lacerta lepida*).

(*Photograph by Isabelle Hunt Conant*)

203. A lizard (*Lacerta sicula*) from southern Italy. It is green.

204. Digging out nests of a common teiid, *Ameiva chrysolæma*, of Hispaniola.

205. Nest of the common teiid, *Ameiva chrysolæma*, of Hispaniola.

(*Photographs by William G. Hassler*)

206. Northern tegu (*Tupinambis nigropunctatus*).
This species reaches a length of slightly more than three feet.

207. Caiman lizard (*Dracæna guianensis*). This species attains a length of four feet. It eats mussels and snails, which it readily crushes with the powerful jaws.

(*Courtesy The American Museum of Natural History; photograph by Charles M. Bogert*)

208. Tessellated race runner (*Cnemidophorus tigris*). This handsome species ranges widely over somewhat more than the western third of the United States, except in the more northern portion. It also occurs in northern Mexico.

209. Blue-bellied race runner (*Cnemidophorus sacki*). This species is widely distributed over the southwestern United States and ranges southward through Mexico to Guatemala. It does not occur in California.

(*Photograph by Isabelle Hunt Conant*)

210. Nest of six-lined race runner (*Cnemidophorus sexlineatus*) from Maryland. This species lays from four to six eggs at a time.

(*Photograph by William G. Hassler*)

(Courtesy Frederick Medem)

211.   White-bellied worm lizard (*Amphisbæna alba*) from the Alto Llano
Oriental, Colombia. The similarity of head and tail is clearly demonstrated.
This gigantic individual was about two feet long and astonishingly hard to hold.

212.   Florida worm lizard (*Rhineura floridana*).

(Courtesy The American Museum of Natural History)

213. The monitors look much alike to the unpracticed eye.
This species of *Varanus* serves to illustrate the typical
appearance and gives the specialist a chance to test his
knowledge.

214. Komodo dragon (*Varanus komodoensis*), largest of living lizards.

215. Gila monster (*Heloderma suspectum*).
This is the only poisonous kind of lizard found in the United States

216. Captive Gila monster eating a hamster.

(*Courtesy The American Museum of Natural History*)

2 1 7.   Mexican beaded lizard (*Heloderma horridum*) nearly thirty inches long
(San Antonio Zoo). This species, like the Gila monster, readily becomes tame.

2 1 8.   Red-backed alligator lizard (*Gerrhonotus multicarinatus*)
from the northern part of its range.

(*Courtesy The American Museum of Natural History; photograph by Charles M. Bogert*)

(*Photograph by Isabelle Hunt Conant*)

219. Eastern glass snake (*Ophisaurus ventralis*).
This is one of our two widely distributed species of glass snakes.

220. The European glass snake (*Ophisaurus apodus*) occurs in southwestern Asia as well as in southeastern Europe. It commonly attains a length of a yard and may considerably exceed this length.

(*Zoological Society of Philadelphia*)

221. Giant girdle-tailed lizard (*Cordylus giganteus*).

temperature changes. Incidentally, the habit of secreting themselves in deep cracks saves night lizards from destruction by the fires that often sweep their arid country as well as from man and other animate enemies. The yucca night lizard (*X. vigilis*), the only species with a large range, which extends from extreme southern Nevada and adjacent territory southward throughout Baja California, does not share this love of granite, but hides chiefly in and under decaying debris of yucca plants. To collect it one needs a machete rather than a crowbar.

The fourth species, the island night lizard (*X. riversiana*), lives on the southern group of Channel Islands off the coast of southern California. Apparently it is found under stones and wood. This kind reaches the respectable length of eight inches, strongly contrasting with the little yucca night lizard, whose maximum length is only half that, and whose length at birth is but two inches. This same island species has other notable differences in its habits. It has been seen to feed during the day, and it is known to be the only species that eats a lot of plant as well as animal food. Island life must have gone to the head of this reptile. The Arizona night lizard eats only insects, whereas the other two mainland kinds include a lot of spiders in their predominantly insect diet. Ants are the mainstay of the diet of the species taken as a whole.

The three mainland night lizards bring forth their young directly, producing one or two at a time (see page 254). Careful experiments have shown that the yucca night lizard has unusual and therefore interesting color changes correlated chiefly with differences in temperature. When concealed during the day, this species is dark in color, whereas it becomes lighter with the approach of darkness; excitement may also make it lighter.

SKINKS
(Family Scincidæ)
PLATES 197, 198, 199, AND 200

IN SPITE of being the largest and most widely distributed family of lizards, the skinks are among the least familiar of reptiles. This can be largely explained by their general shyness, secretive habits, quick movements, and the small size of many species. To the specialist, they are the most confusing of lizards because they fall into very unequal groups of genera, several of which are unwieldy, to put it mildly. The species in some of the genera can be distinguished only by using a strictly modern, statistical approach based on counts of "characters" of the scale covering. Even the assortments of species are not easily divided into genera, for they, as units, merge just as do the species. There is of course great difference of opinion as to the number of genera and species that exist. The highest estimates put the genera at about sixty, the species as more than six hundred. This great profusion of kinds indicates rapid evolution of a progressive group. The skinks have not left a helpful fossil record; we know nothing about their ancestry.

There is no great amount of confusion over the skinks of the New World, because a mere fifty species occur on this side of the globe. Seventeen of these live in the United States, approximately twice that many in North America south of our boundary, and still fewer in South America, where about six species of the genus *Mabuya* are widely distributed. (A single Pacific skink has been introduced to the western coast of South America.) It is in the tropical parts of the eastern hemisphere that skinks come into their bewildering own. Europe, with but seven species, is on a par with the New World.

Evasiveness and disconcerting similarities notwithstanding, the skinks have their own attractiveness and scientific interest. A skink, with its firm, smooth, polished coat of scales, is beautiful to look at if less pleasant to handle than a soft gecko. The skink is scratchy, aloof, and indifferent; the gecko alert, cozy, and clinging. A skink's beauty is often enhanced by a brilliant color pattern. As the skinks can never be the nice pets that geckos will someday make, we may as well forget the human relations of the skink, and look into some of its more scientific aspects. Even here the skink must take second place to the gecko, except in the United States, where the former is readily available, the latter all but lacking.

Perhaps the most outstanding thing about the skinks is the typical lizard trait, carried to its extreme, of not being able to decide what to do about limbs. These are normal in size, or reduced in many degrees proportionate to size of the possessor. The front and rear pair may be alike, or one may be much larger than the other. Not infrequently the limbs are lost entirely, or reduced far beyond the point of usefulness. Degrees of reduction may take place in species that obviously are closely related; reduction and loss have occurred over and over again. Even the limbless skinks have kept their foot in the door, so to speak: the limb-supporting bones, or shoulder and hip girdles, have never been completely lost. The loss or reduction of limbs has been correlated with a way of life, a sub-surface or even burrowing existence. This alone is evidence that the skinks are a very vigorous group ready to take advantage of every possibility.

Although the great majority of species lead the sort of existence just referred to, a limited number have taken to special habitats. Closely related to ground living is life in desert sands, where the extreme types almost swim in this medium. The sand skinks (*Scincus*), some seven in number, are typical of the deserts of northern Africa and adjacent southwestern Asia. They have fringes on the toes, wedge-shaped snouts, and countersunk lower jaws that help greatly in progress through sand. Other types of skinks dwell among rocks, and a few have even become aquatic to the extent of living along streams and taking to the water when alarmed. There are some twenty species of these water-loving skinks (*Tropidophorus*) distributed from southeastern Asia to northern Australia, including the Philippines. Climbing habits of certain skinks will be noted in the discussion of our own species. There is almost no type of country well suited to reptile life that does not have its skink, but, for the sake of emphasis, I shall repeat that the typical skink should be thought of as a small lizard scurrying for cover on the forest floor or on other ground with good cover.

The skinks do not have special feet for climbing that compare with those of the geckos, but they did make a beginning along that line; a sort of forerunner of the gecko pad is seen in a few skinks. Considering the fact that the skinks went underground rather than up into the trees, they did very well. The reduction or loss of limbs admirably suited them to the sub-surface life, and there they did not stop short of extremes, a fact that has already been dealt with. This burrowing habit is strongly reflected in the structure of the eye. In certain burrowers this organ has become small; its lower lid has thickened and partly lost mobility. In contrast to this is the development of a "window" in the lower lid of some skinks, a condition that cannot be associated with any special type of existence. The transparent area or "window" becomes larger and larger, finally occupying most of the lid, which in turn grows to cover the entire eye and unites with the small upper one to form an immovable unit (see page 236). In all reptiles the lower lid is the one that moves. The extreme development of this "window" is seen in some species of the snake-eyed skinks, a genus (*Ablepharus*) widely distributed in the eastern hemisphere and having about twenty-five species.

Reproduction in skinks is as complex and variable as are body and limb form, a lack of uniformity that has led to conflicting statements about the development of the young and the method of bringing them into the world. There are three types of development, two of them resulting in birth, the other in egg-laying. In one birth type, the mother develops a primitive placenta and thus nourishes the young (before birth) somewhat as mammals do. The eyed skink (*Chalcides ocellatus*) of southern Europe, northern Africa, and southwestern Asia has the best placenta, although several other skinks are provided with one of inferior quality. This question is discussed further on page 252. In the other birth type, the young presumably derive no nourishment from the parent. So few lizards have been studied that no one knows how many of the numerous live-bearing skinks belong to this or to the placenta type. Egg-laying in skinks is, apparently, not very common, although here again information is lacking.

Skinks vary so much in size that it is next to impossible to generalize. Great hordes of species only a few inches in length live on or in the ground and its cover; species of some groups often grow to be 8 or 9 inches long, and in the Australian region giant skinks exist, some of the kinds measuring from 18 to 22 inches long. The giant among them is usually conceded to be the blue-tongued skink (*Tiliqua scincoides*) with a maximum total length put at slightly less than two feet. The only skink that surpasses this one in length is the prehensile-tailed skink (*Corucia zebrata*) of the Solomon Islands; its tail is a great deal longer than the head and body, which alone may be a foot long. This long-tailed animal is most remarkable for its grasping tail, which is unique among skinks and hard to measure in preserved specimens (it comes curled and brittle).

Finally, before taking up the skinks of the United States, I shall give a few facts about the three great, widely ranging groups of skinks. One of these, the genus *Eumeces*, without a good common name, is comprised of about fifty-eight species with three widely separated areas of distribution: one stretching from the southern edge of Canada southward into Central America; another extending across extreme northern Africa and on into southwestern Asia as far as West Pakistan; a third in extreme eastern Asia from Thailand (Siam) and Cambodia northward to Manchuria and Japan. Dr. Edward H. Taylor of the University of Kansas has written a comprehensive monograph of these lizards (see bibliography). The next genus, *Mabuya*, is much larger, having about eighty-five species. Its range is staggering: southern Mexico southward over most of South America; the West Indies; Africa and Madagascar; southern Asia; the Malay Archipelago, the Philippine Islands, and New Guinea. The final assortment of skinks, including about half of all the known species, was long placed in a single unwieldy genus, *Lygosoma*, but is now broken down into smaller groups, which may be called either genera or subgenera. These groups are separated one from the other with some difficulty; the species making up the various groups are often distinguished with as much difficulty. The resulting confusion has been referred to at the beginning of the treatment of skinks; it can well stand repetition here for the sake of emphasis. The distribution of the genus in its old, broadest sense is virtually cosmopolitan.

In spite of the fact that the skinks are not abundant in the western hemisphere, the number of United States species of *Eumeces* surpasses that of any other lizard group except the genus of spiny lizards (*Sceloporus*). Both of these genera are widely distributed and both have fifteen species in the United States, but the spiny lizards are known to every country person, whereas the skinks are unrecognized by most. Many a person has secretive skinks in the back yard without knowing it; few can overlook a spiny lizard as it suns on rock, fence, or tree.

Some species of *Eumeces* is found in every state except the three northeastern ones, and a few even reach extreme southern Canada. The two familiar and most broadly distributed species of the eastern half of the country are the five-lined and the greater five-lined skinks (*E. fasciatus* and *E. laticeps*). The former attains a length of about nine and a half inches, the latter grows to be fully three inches longer. The young of these two are striped and have a brilliant blue tail, which loses its blue with growth. Both are woodland species, the larger one being much more of a climber than the smaller. See page 253 for an account of their brooding habits. In the central part of the country, the prairie and Great Plains skinks (*E. septentrionalis* and *E. obsoletus*) abound, the latter the more southern and western in distribution. The prairie skink is about the size of the five-lined skink, and is also striped. The Great Plains skink is large like the greater five-lined skink, usually spotted rather than striped, and with a bad disposition. Its bite is painful but in no way dangerous. In the far west, the western skink (*E. skiltonianus*) ranges from an extreme corner of Canada to northern Baja California, although absent from the southern Sierra Nevadas. It is not large and is readily recognized by the pair of bold light stripes extending down the back, one on either side.

All of the species of *Eumeces* of the United States lay eggs, though certain of the twenty-two Mexican species produce the young directly.

The little brown skink is our single representative of that great world-wide assortment of some three hundred skinks that until recently has defied all efforts to be classified. Our member is typical of a subgroup of some fifty small species that slither around in and under leaves and other debris covering the ground of various types of country. The little brown skink is partial to woodland areas of the southeastern states, where it is widely distributed. From one to five, usually three, eggs are laid at a time. The size (large adults are about five inches long) of this lizard scarcely warrants the bewildering number of technical names that it has been given: *Lygosoma*,

Leiolopisma, or *Scincella laterale* or *unicolor;* it has masqueraded under no fewer than nine combinations of these. This is another case in which the system of scientific christening broke down; the common name has been stable enough. The history of all this naming would fill a chapter by itself, and be understood (but probably not enjoyed) only by a taxonomist. The taxonomist names what the taxidermist later "stuffs." Sometimes the stuffing comes first.

The sand skink (*Neoseps reynoldsi*) of peninsular Florida is a fine example of a degenerate, burrowing skink with each of the ridiculously small front legs reduced to a single, clawed, toelike structure that fits into a groove; presumably it can in this way be kept from interfering with the animal's locomotion. The hind limbs are bigger but quite as useless. The sand skink lives in sand or other loose, dry soil of rosemary scrub and high pine woods. It reaches a length of four and three-quarters inches, half of which is taken up by the tail. The life history is not known.

DIBAMIDS AND OTHER RELATIVES OF THE SKINKS
(Families Dibamidæ, Feyliniidæ, and Anelytropsidæ)

THE DIBAMIDS, a family of a single genus with but three species, all worm-shaped, have carried to extreme this business of playing free with limbs: only the males have any, and these tiny flaplike appendages are the rear pair, which the males probably use as claspers while mating. Vestiges of the bones that must once have supported the front limbs remain to be detected only by dissection. The family range extends from southern Indochina to New Guinea and includes the Philippine and Nicobar islands. The widely distributed species, *Dibamus novæ-guineæ,* grows to be about seven inches long; it is known to reproduce by means of eggs.

A few species of degenerate, limbless, worm-shaped lizards, obviously closely related to the skinks, live in Africa and Mexico. These have been variously classed as skinks, and as members of two other families: the Feyliniidæ and Anelytropsidæ. It is patent that their exact relationships are unknown. I mention them merely for the sake of completeness. The single Mexican species (*Anelytrop-sis papillosus*) really looks much like a blind snake about the size of an ordinary earthworm. To my knowledge, it has been found but three times and is known from only a few individuals. My wife and I were fortunate to number among its collectors. While working seventeen miles southeast of Jalapa in the central part of the Mexican state of Veracruz, one of our party found a specimen of *A. papillosus* under a stone on a steep, rugged, bush-grown hillside. It was a discovery that richly compensated for hours of work in a drenching rain. This individual is now in the hands of a specialist who undoubtedly will be able to decide just where it belongs in the lizard firmament.

GERRHOSAURIDS
(Family Gerrhosauridæ)

THE TWENTY-FIVE species of this family, which, for want of a better name, we shall call "gerrhosaurids," need not detain us long. Although they have an abundance of interesting things about their structure, to the layman they resemble skinks and are actually considered by the specialist to be a link between the skinks and the lacertids. One species has a "window" in its lower eyelid, as found in both of those families. For those willing to make a close examination, a deep fold extending along each side near the belly serves to distinguish gerrhosaurids. This fold is present only far forward in two rare Madagascan species.

The one obvious remarkable characteristic of the family is the way it has been willing to dispense with limbs. The case is astonishingly similar to that of the girdle-tailed lizards (see page 320). In both cases extremes of limb development are seen, and, in both, one extreme is represented by a snake-shaped species that has lost the front limbs entirely and reduced the hind ones to mere stumps. The similarity is more striking when we compare these two families as to size and range. The gerrhosaurids have a slightly more extensive range: Madagascar (where nearly half of the species live) and Africa south of 13° north latitude. In both families the number of species increases toward southern Africa, the part of the continent where the species abound and come in a great variety of forms. The fact that all of the four African gerrhosaurid genera are found in southern Africa, whereas only one occurs in its central part, illustrates this point. Two of the six genera are Madagascan.

On the whole, these lizards like rugged, hilly country with plenty of rocks, where they are quick to hide in deep crevices between boulders. The few snake-shaped ones prefer less rugged, grass-grown country, and savannas are frequented by species of normal shape that live in the flat parts of central Africa. One of these (*Gerrhosaurus major*) plays the trick of running a distance and then suddenly halting, usually with the tail raised. This sudden stopping is confusing to a pursuer, especially if done when cover has been reached.

The young hatch from eggs. The largest species grow to a considerable size, one reaching a length of twenty-six and three-quarters inches. There is no fossil record that helps us reconstruct the history of this ancient family. We have Loveridge to thank for a revisionary study of the African gerrhosaurids (see bibliography).

LACERTIDS
(Family Lacertidæ)
PLATES 201, 202, AND 203

THE LIZARDS of this family are unknown in the New World and have no generally used common name there. In contrast, they make up the great body of the European lizard fauna, and are thought of in Europe simply as "lizards." In default of a better term, I shall refer to them as "lacertids," a name not too difficult; the word "lizard" is Middle English, and was derived from the Latin *Lacerta*, the technical name of the common European genus of lacertids. The range of the lacertids is much like that of the true vipers: Africa and all of Eurasia south of its northern part with permanently frozen sub-soil. Half or more of the Scandinavian peninsula is inhabited, and there is a spillover of a single species into the Malay Archipelago, including Sumatra, Java, and Borneo. Africa is the headquarters of the family. Approximately one hundred and fifty species are divided among some twenty-two genera. These lizards were monographed in two volumes (see bibliography) by the late George Albert Boulenger of the British Museum (Natural History), London. Dr. Boulenger is the most renowned of herpetologists.

The lacertids have not gone to extremes in developing odd shapes, nor have they lost, or even tended to lose, the limbs. There is nothing unusual about their appearance. Although no lacertids live in the New World, their place is taken there by another family (Teiidæ). The superficial resemblance between the members of these two families is startling, and would fool all but the lizard anatomists. As the difference in distribution is such a simple and convenient distinction, I shall not include the characteristics of structure.

One small variation in the lacertid eye-covering found in this family deserves brief mention. A few species have a window in the lower eyelid. In one group (two species of the genus *Cabrita* of the Indian peninsula and adjacent territory) the lower eyelid is movable, so the possessor presumably has the choice of either looking out with open eyes or peering through its eyelid window. In the other group (*Ophisops* of the region where Africa, Europe, and Asia approach one another) the lower eyelid is united with the upper, and the window is very large. These lizards have no choice but to look through the window. Such lids, found in other families, are discussed in detail on pages 236 and 294.

Although the lacertids are not known to have many defensive tricks, the tiger lizard (*Nucras delalandi*) is reported by Dr. Rose to use one that works well. When a sand snake attacked a large individual it made a stiff ring of the body and took a firm grip on its own hind leg. The frustrated snake first tried to swallow the lizard from the head end, but of course could not do so. Next it began with the tail and could not go beyond the ring. Disgorging the tail, the snake once more worked on the head. This fruitless alternation went on for so long that the patience of the observer gave out, and the predator was separated from its victim, which ran away apparently none the worse for its experience. The tiger lizard grows to be a foot long and is extremely agile; one might think it able to escape without resorting to such trickery.

An unusual way of life is seen in a Chinese grass lizard (*Takydromus septentrionalis*). In the province of Anhwei I frequently saw these little reptiles making their way through thick, high grass by nimbly jumping from stem to stem. They kept themselves well above the ground, and were prone to take sudden sharp turns that made them seem to vanish as if by magic. This trick was responsible for the difficulty in catching them, as their speed was not great. It might well be asked how ordinary grass can support an animal about a foot long, and the answer is most interesting. The extremely slender tail is three or a little more than three times as long as the head and body, and helps the lizard to spread its weight over enough stems to support it. A special word should be coined to describe this type of progress through grass; such a reptile could not be called arboreal, nor is it truly terrestrial. Other species of this genus, characteristic of eastern Asia and the Malay Archipelago, have similar habits.

In the choice of open country as a home, grass lizards of Asia and the Malay islands are fairly typical of the whole family. Although forest-loving lacertids do exist, the vast majority live in bushy, grassy, or rocky country that may be either flat or mountainous. On one extreme, desert sands are frequented. For example, the species of the genus *Acanthodactylus*, some twelve in number, inhabit southwestern Europe, northern Africa, and southwestern Asia, and include true desert types. Fringes extending from the sides of the toes help these lizards to move about over the shifting sands.

The greatest lot of lacertids is the genus *Eremias* with some forty-five species found all over Africa, and from southeastern Europe right across central Asia as well as southeastward to Afghanistan and West Pakistan. These ubiquitous lizards are characteristic of dry, open, bushy, or rocky country, where they often occur in vast numbers. Many kinds prefer regions with conditions approaching those of a desert; this would include the edges of true deserts.

Next to *Eremias* comes the big assemblage placed in the genus *Lacerta*, the thirty species of which might as well be called simply "lacertas." These make up the body of that majority of European lizards referred to at the beginning of the treatment of this family. The chief characteristic of these normal-looking lizards is their variability. The European students of reptile classification have so intensively collected and compared certain species and their local populations that no fewer than one hundred and fifty technical names have been given to these various populations. Some of the common species have been divided into numerous "races," which may number from twelve to twenty-four, the greater number being found on small Mediterranean islands. Jokers have been known to say that every rock in the Mediterranean has its own race of lacerta of one kind or another. The same jokers might add that the number of races is directly proportional to that of herpetologists willing to concentrate their efforts on lacerta distribution. Although to the layman this excessive giving of names may seem futile, from the point of view of pure science it has real value in showing the great plasticity of these lizards when considered from an evolutionary point of view. The layman will do well to recognize the species without bothering about their subdivisions. In the case of island "races," no problem exists; if the lizard is found on an island for which it is named, it undoubtedly belongs to that island race.

Perhaps the most familiar lacertid of Europe is the wall lizard (*Lacerta muralis*). It is one of the species that has been given many technical names. Adults are usually six or seven inches long. As the word *muralis* implies, this species is a good climber; it is often seen on rock walls in the vicinity of human habitations. The viviparous lizard (*L. vivipara*) is not only the most widely distributed member of the genus, being found right across central Asia to the island of Sakhalin, but is the single one of the three lizards of the British Isles to reach Ireland. In the method of reproduction this small lizard is remarkable. Normally it brings forth directly from five to eight young, whereas in the Pyrenees it lays eggs. Since all other lacertas are strictly egg-laying, the dual ability of this species calls for explanation. It has been suggested that the oviparous population of the Pyrenees simply retains the primitive reproductive method of the species.

The sand lizard (*L. agilis*), the only other lacertid found in the

British Isles, is another common European lacerta. It ranges across Europe into central Asia. In spite of the technical name, it is anything but agile, being a good digger but poor climber. The largest of all the lacertas, and apparently the largest species of its entire family, is the eyed lizard (*L. lepida* or *ocellata*) of southwestern Europe and adjacent northern Africa. This beautiful, predominantly green reptile attains a length of two feet. But *Lacerta goliath*, a Canary Islands species that has recently died out, apparently reached the astonishing length of three feet and three inches. A rare fossil lacertid (*Nucras*) has been found in European amber of some thirty-five million years ago (Oligocene), and the fossil record of the genus *Lacerta* goes back to Eocene times. Reptiles, in contrast to insects, are rarely preserved in amber.

TEIIDS
(Family Teiidæ)
PLATES 204, 205, 206, 207, 208, 209, AND 210

ALTHOUGH THE reptiles of the present assortment are the most American of all the important lizard families, there is no common name for them; the best we can do is call them "teiids."

Thanks to the students of geology and of the evolution of mammals, we have good evidence that for millions of years South America was an island just as Australia is today. The separation from North America fell along the line of the often-proposed interoceanic canal that would have taken the place of the Panama Canal. This line follows rather closely the southern boundary of Nicaragua, where a morning's hike plus travel through natural waterways will take anyone from Pacific to Atlantic. Now, that long period of isolation ended in Miocene times some twenty million years ago, since when Central America has been an isthmus, North and South America a continuous land mass. The many odd South American animals of various types (mammals, birds, reptiles, fishes) amply confirm the geologic evidence and tell us that evolution had its undisturbed day.

How do the teiids fit into this picture? The family is comprised of about forty genera. All of these groups occur in South America, and eight of them have species in Central America, but only three of the eight pass that old separation line near the southern boundary of Nicaragua. These three are represented also in Mexico, one (*Cnemidophorus*) reaching the United States.

The mental picture of this increase in density of teiids is almost like a road sign pointing southward. There can be no doubt that these reptiles swarmed in South America and were blocked by the strait in Central America until that was closed. Then the pressure from the south pushed a few northward, one species finally reaching the Atlantic coast of the United States. It is also tempting to calculate the speed of travel, about twenty million years to go so many thousand miles. The catch here is that we do not know how long ago that lone species arrived at our eastern seaboard. The sight of a teiid in a hurry certainly leaves the impression that it will arrive on time wherever its destination may be. The great diversity of race runners (*Cnemidophorus*) in northern Mexico, and fossil remains of this genus from the Pliocene deposits (some five million years old), indicate that teiids wasted little time in spreading northward. Unsuitable terrain and heavy southward traffic of various other animals must have kept the rest of the teiids back.

The diversity of the teiids is additional evidence of their long evolution in South America. The species number only about two hundred; most of the genera are small, a few are moderate in size, and one is large. This one (*Ameiva*), though widely distributed from Mexico through South America, is large (about forty species) only because of the diversity of species in the West Indies, a diversity that parallels but does not come up to that of the lacertas (*Lacerta*) on the Mediterranean islands (see page 302). Probably, when the ameivas have been studied as thoroughly as the lacertas have been, the number of species will diminish, as the subspecies increase, and the genus *Ameiva*, as well as its family, will be left with fewer rather than more species.

The teiids have to a limited degree taken advantage of their rich environment; they seem almost entirely to have passed up the possibilities offered by trees, and become adapted to surface and subsurface life. However, the northern tegu (*Tupinambis nigropunc-*

tatus), widely distributed in central and northern South America, may lay its eggs twelve feet above the ground in termite nests, an interesting fact discovered in British Guiana by Dr. William Beebe, the noted writer and explorer. It is odd that this tegu (it often slightly exceeds three feet in length and may weigh two pounds) should be the exception to the ground-living habits. It must be emphasized that tegus are nearly always found on the ground. There is a whole fauna, the "micro-teiids" of specialists, that lives on the ground or just under the surface. Some micro-teiids have limbs considerably reduced, though never lost. In size, they contrast sharply with the gigantic tegus and caiman lizards (about to be discussed). For example, the common, long-tailed denizen of the jungle floor, *Leposoma percarinatum*, is only three and five-eighths inches long and weighs but one twenty-eighth of an ounce (one gram) when fully grown. It lives in British Guiana, Venezuela, and adjacent Brazil.

Open country has by no means been neglected; teiids of moderate size make great use of it, as we shall see below in the account of our race runners. The ameivas are also lovers of unshaded areas. Although teiids on the whole are anything but aquatic, a few of them have taken up an amphibious existence. The most noteworthy of these is the caiman lizard (*Dracæna guianensis*), a creature that looks as much like a crocodilian as the name implies. Its maximum recorded length is four feet, and it abounds in the tidal marshlands of the Guianas and the lower Amazon. This reptile is also unusual in possessing broad crushing teeth in the sides of the jaws, teeth admirably suited to deal with the mussels and snails that the caiman lizard feeds on. Surprisingly enough, a brand new caiman lizard (*D. paraguayensis*) has been recently (1950) made known to science by Dr. Afranio do Amaral. It lives in the great swamps of the upper Paraguay River. The feeding habits are like those of the other species, but the new one is less aquatic, as one might expect. The brown water lizard (*Neusticurus rudis*) of northeastern South America is of moderate size and lives along jungle streams. It swims well and is known to eat fishes, tadpoles, and water beetles, a diet that well confirms its aquatic habits.

One of the big zoological surprises of the last few decades was made by Ivan T. Sanderson, noted naturalist and explorer, when he discovered in a cave on the island of Trinidad what may well be the first luminous terrestrial vertebrate on record, a little teiid lizard with the formidable name *Proctoporus shrevei.* When first seen in a crevice beneath a ledge, the lizard lit up for a few seconds a series of lights along its side, suggesting to the observer portholes of a ship at night. It is further interesting that this ability to light up is possessed only by the males, and thus suggests a sexual function of some kind. A careful study (*Luminous Organs in Lizards;* Parker, 1939) of a series of specimens confirmed the field observation and revealed the fact that the light-giving organ is of a simple type lacking nerve supply as well as complex lenses and reflectors. Just how it works has yet to be determined, there being various familiar types of luminescent organs of fishes. Other teiids have spots somewhat like those of *P. shrevei,* so it is highly probable that they, too, can light up. It must be admitted that these lizard "portholes" may prove to be merely reflectors of light like the "reflection pearls" of certain nestling birds. At any rate, whether the lizard merely reflects light or actually produces it, the discovery remains one of extreme interest, giving the teiids claim to everlasting glory.

Before taking up the teiids of the United States, I want to point out again (see page 300) the striking similarity between the teiids (New World) and the lacertids (Old World). This case of parallelism is strongly remindful of that shown by the iguanids and the agamids, which did not have such completely separated ranges. In both cases, the amateur would be hard pressed to find a difference, but anatomists have determined constant ones between teiid and lacertid head: one in the way the teeth are united to the jaws, the other in the superficial covering of the skull. The teiids are the more diverse in structure, their species more numerous. Modifications of the eye-covering seen among teiids are strikingly like those of the lacertids: a movable lower lid with a window may occur, as well as a transparent lower lid fused to the upper (see page 300).

The teiids, in sharp contrast to the lacertids, show strong tendencies to reduce the limbs and develop a serpentine form. This is carried to its extreme in the genus *Bachia* with about a dozen species of northern and western South America. In these wormlike reptiles, the limbs are tiny and their usefulness is in proportion to the speed of progress: when moving along leisurely, *Bachia cophias*, according to Dr. Beebe, makes good use of the limbs, especially the front pair; if alarmed, snakelike crawling is begun, the limbs fanning the air all the while. Extreme excitement may cause this slender lizard, which is only four or five inches long, to leap to a height as great as three times its length, and advance even farther. Such gymnastics, apparently accomplished by flexion of the long tail, are undoubtedly useful in the performance of a vanishing act before an enemy.

The only teiids of the United States are race runners (*Cnemidophorus*), seven species of which are widely distributed over the southern two thirds of the country with a few limited intrusions somewhat farther to the north. One of these intrusions is into the Mississippi valley, another into the midwest, and a third into Idaho and Oregon. A single species, the six-lined race runner (*C. sexlineatus*), is found east of the Mississippi River. The flat statement that we have seven species, or about a third of those usually recognized as comprising the genus, may call for revision, because the classification of race runners has long baffled students. Dr. Charles E. Burt made some order out of chaos when he published his monograph in 1931 (see bibliography), but much remains to be done. The variation exhibited by series of individuals is bewildering. To make matters worse, there is in most species a marked change in pattern that begins soon after hatching and continues indefinitely. The young may, for example, be distinctly lined, the somewhat older ones lined and spotted, the adults tessellated. In general, if the young are spotted, the change may not be so great, whereas if the young are lined, as is frequently the case, anything might happen to the pattern.

The race runners are typically lizards of dry, open country with loose soil. Deserts are not avoided. These reptiles attain their highest development in our southwest and the highlands of northern Mexico, although five species reach South America and the generic range terminates only in southern Brazil. The species that range into the tropical forests frequent open places such as clearings, trails, riverbanks, and other situations that admit an abundance of sunlight. The same may be said of our eastern species, which is widely distributed; it is found in fields, pastures, and in other exposed areas.

In rural districts the six-lined race runner is often called "streak-field," a name that well describes how one of these reptiles appears to the casual observer. The speed of retreat of a race runner is astonishing. Great patience well rewards the observer; he will see a slender, long-tailed reptile progressing in quick, jerky movements interrupted by frequent pauses. The head is moved about, indicating alertness, and the elevated fore limb is often twitched nervously before being placed on the ground again. In especially suitable places, several individuals can be seen at once from a single vantage point: race runners come in enormous populations. The race runners live largely on insects and reproduce by means of eggs, which are deposited in the ground. The largest species attain a maximum length of about seventeen inches.

WORM LIZARDS
(Family Amphisbænidæ)
PLATES 211 AND 212

THAT OLD joke about a door might appropriately be reworded here to read: "When is a lizard not a lizard?" The proper answer obviously would be: "When it is a worm lizard." The species of the present family, approximately one hundred and twenty-five in number, have such peculiar, compact, unlizardlike skulls that they should be, although they seldom are, set aside as a major group of their own, a group equivalent to all the true lizards. Not only is the skull peculiar, but the entire worm lizard looks like a huge earthworm, and its way of moving, either backward or forward, suggests the actions of one. The tail is blunt, the head either blunt or ending in a sharp-edged, wedgelike snout admirably suiting the creature to its burrowing existence. Limbs are lacking except for a ridiculously small pair of front ones in the three Mexican species (*Bipes*). The shoulder and hip bones are rudimentary; the former actually may be lacking. Usually the worm lizards are grouped into about twenty genera; there is considerable difference of opinion on this grouping. Nearly half of all the species are ordinarily assigned to the genus *Amphisbæna* of both the New World and the Old.

The fossil record, going back to Eocene times, shows that worm lizards have flourished without a great deal of change for some fifty million years. They once lived in the western central part of the United States, although now our single kind is confined to central and northern Florida. It is not surprising that such bony, hard-headed creatures make good fossils. At present worm lizards abound on two continents: Africa (except its great northern desert and southern tip) and South America (except its extreme southern part). More than a hundred species are found on these two continents, South America having a few more than Africa. About nine species live in the West Indies, and still fewer in the Mediterranean countries, including some territory just east of the southern Red Sea and another stretch at the head of the Persian Gulf. Only one species is certainly known to occur in Europe (the Spanish Peninsula).

Perhaps no other moderately large and widely distributed family of reptiles has been so successful in keeping its habits, which must be fascinating, concealed from the eyes of students. Loveridge, in monographing the African worm lizards (see bibliography), was able to quote observations on the breeding of only two species. The gist of these quotes is that one species gave birth to five young, whereas another laid four eggs. From these and other observations, we know that worm lizards have by no means confined themselves to a single method of reproduction.

Observers of the New World have been, especially in South America, a little more successful than have those of Africa. Our own single species (*Rhineura floridana*) has until the last few years kept its life history an almost complete secret notwithstanding the care with which the reptiles of Florida have been investigated. Now we know that one specimen apparently laid two eggs, and that spiders and earthworms form a part of the diet. The Florida worm lizard reaches a length of twelve inches (thirteen and seven-eighths maximum) and, judging by the little information available, may measure three and a half or four inches at hatching. This is a length commonly reached by members of the family, although a greater one is attained by some. The gigantic West African *Monopeltis jugularis* is, for example, known to grow to a length of twenty-six and three-eighths inches.

MONITORS
(Family Varanidæ)
PLATES 213 AND 214

THE MONITORS are enough alike to be placed in a single group (*Varanus*). This genus has the distinction of including the largest of lizards as well as some of moderate size; no other genus of reptiles can boast of such a difference between its smallest and largest members. The Komodo dragon (*Varanus komodoensis*), of Komodo and two other Malay islands, reaches a length of ten feet; a captive only eight feet two inches long weighed one hundred and sixty-three pounds. In contrast to this, two dwarf species of western Australia (*V. brevicauda* and *caudolineatus*) attain a length of only eight to ten inches. The largest kind of monitor may be fifteen times as long and weigh thirty-seven hundred times as much as the smallest, the tiny monitors looking like miniatures of the larger ones.

The fossil record tells us that monitors have a long history. Kinds not greatly unlike those of today flourished some fifty million years ago in Eocene times. Monitors have certain points in their structure that link them to the snakes, and, indeed, it seems that snakes and monitors have a common ancestor if we trace their lines back far enough. Even today the monitor's long neck, whiplike tail, and slender, forked tongue, which it constantly shoots out, remind one of a snake.

These reptiles are found over nearly all of Africa, all of extreme southern Asia (as far north as the Aral Sea in the west, but not so far north in the high Tibetan region farther to the east), the Malay Archipelago and Philippine Islands, all of Australia, New Guinea, and on the islands just east of New Guinea. Their presence on certain oceanic islands of the western Pacific Ocean presents a problem: the peoples of these islands like to eat monitors, and perhaps these lizards have been carried from island to island. The distribution of the species in the various areas is not uniform. Africa has but three, whereas thirteen are found in the region between Africa and Australia, and twelve in Australia alone.

Perhaps no other small, compact group of lizards makes such complete use of its environment. Monitors are found in all types of country from deserts, largely lacking vegetation, to tropical forests. Some kinds, partial to water and its vicinity, might even be called amphibious. These are of course good swimmers and do not hesitate to cover short distances in the sea from island to island. Several species are at home in trees, to the highest branches of which they may ascend. Anyone who has felt the grip of a monitor's claws on his leg realizes how safe such a powerful lizard is when clinging to a limb. I was told in Asia that robbers take advantage of this grip in scaling walls: a monitor with a rope tied about it is first thrown over a compound wall, and the robber soon follows. Not only do monitors as a group show great adaptability, but some individual species make remarkable use of varied situations, being good runners, divers, swimmers, climbers, and diggers. The common Asiatic region species *salvator*, the island *indicus*, and the African *niloticus* should be mentioned especially.

Large kinds of monitors gain a reputation for ferocity, just as any such powerful reptiles might be expected to do. The tail is said to be a dangerous weapon. As a matter of fact, a monitor is more of a bluffer than anything else. Such a creature standing at bay, puffing up the body, hissing loudly, and lashing the long tail would command respect from anyone. Experiments on the island of Hainan with *Varanus salvator* convinced me that the tail is unable to inflict appreciable damage on a well-clothed man, and that the lashing of it merely enhances the formidable appearance. The grip of the jaws is, of course, to be feared; fortunately, a monitor uses them only at very close range. It goes without saying that big individuals of the larger species should be treated with great respect until they become tame, which they readily do in captivity.

Almost any small animal that a monitor can catch, overpower, and swallow whole will fall victim to it. Reproduction is by means of eggs. There may be as many as thirty-five to a clutch, with one record of a somewhat larger batch, although usually only about half that number is deposited at a time. The Nile monitor (*V. niloticus*), in Natal, at least, has learned to lay its eggs in termite ("white ant") nests. This is accomplished during the rainy season when the nests are softened by the rain and the lizards can easily dig into them. The termites repair their nests, sealing in the eggs under conditions admirably suited for incubation. The hatchling monitors find no difficulty in scratching their way to freedom.

The hides of some monitors have great commercial value, and the larger species are killed by the thousands for their skins, which have small, beadlike scales.

One of the best of monographs on a small group of reptiles deals with the monitors. This work, written by Dr. Mertens, is listed in the bibliography.

SNAKE–LIZARDS
(Family Pygopodidæ)

SOME EIGHTEEN species of extremely odd, snakelike lizards are widely distributed over Australia, and occur also on New Guinea and Tasmania. With one possible exception, the tail is much longer than the head and body. There are no front limbs, the hind ones are reduced to mere flaps, which may be tiny, and, as might be expected, progress is snakelike. The pupil is vertical, the eyes without movable lids. Some kinds have an ear-opening, others do not; the latter seem to be burrowing in habits, whereas the former live in grass, or under bushes and stones. The loss of the external ear appears, then, to be correlated with the way of life. The largest species grows to be about two feet long. As far as known, reproduction is by means of eggs.

There is enough diversity in structure for the few species to be divided into nine genera, a condition that indicates antiquity. Fossils to confirm this are lacking. One of the most peculiar and familiar of all is the sharp-snouted snake-lizard (*Lialis burtoni*). The long, wedge-shaped snout and small scales on top of the head give this large species its characteristic look. It is frequently used to illustrate the family, a procedure that is misleading because the ordinary snake-lizard does not have such a long or wedge-shaped head. The more typical and still larger species, the scaly-foot, *Pygopus lepidopodus*, lives in nearly all of Australia and is found also on Tasmania. The tail, more than twice the length of head and body, is very fragile. When first broken, its lively movements may serve to confuse an enemy long enough to allow the scaly-foot to make good its escape.

GILA MONSTER AND MEXICAN BEADED LIZARD
(Family Helodermatidæ)
PLATES 215, 216, AND 217

THE GILA monster and the Mexican beaded lizard stand alone as being the only lizards definitely known to be venomous. An excessively rare lizard of Borneo (*Lanthanotus* [1]), placed in the same family, is naturally suspected of being venomous; absolutely nothing is known about its habits. The lizard method of inflicting injury differs widely from that of the viperine snakes. All the teeth of the Gila monster and Mexican beaded lizard are grooved, whereas only those of the lower jaw are closely associated with venom ducts, the glands of these ducts being located in this jaw. As grooved teeth are poor conductors, these lizards must chew in order to get an appreciable amount of venom into the wounds made by the teeth. This they do; a recent punch-by-punch account of a bite states that it took the victim and his friend, an experienced reptile man, literally five minutes to free the bitten finger from the slow chewing movements of the fifteen-inch Gila monster. Slamming the lizard to the floor was apparently at least partly responsible for discouraging its aggressive behavior.

Although a monograph on the venom of the Gila monster was published as long ago as 1913 (see Loeb in bibliography), there is still much difference of opinion as to the danger of a bite. The venom, chiefly nerve-affecting in action, can cause death in human beings. The most complete tabulation of results of bites indicates a

---

[1] *Lanthanotus* is now granted family rank (Lanthanotidae).

mortality rate of about twenty per cent. This figure is undoubtedly much too high, but serves as a warning for those who like to handle Gila monsters. I dare say that half the deaths were due to faulty treatment, others to bites of captives with infected mouths, and several probably were purely fictitious. Some readers will laugh at the suggestion that anyone would want to handle such a formidable reptile; the warning is justified because Gila monsters in captivity readily become tame and may be freely handled without showing the least sign of bad temper. Captives delight in a diet of raw hens' eggs mixed with a little chopped raw meat. It is a surprising fact, without reasonable explanation, that they also show a special fondness for soaking in a pan of water.

Gila monsters are found from the Mexican state of Sonora northward through Arizona to the tip of Nevada. The extreme southwestern corners of Utah and New Mexico must be included, the northeastern third of Arizona excluded. Its presence in California seems to be doubtful. The Mexican beaded lizard ranges from southern Sonora southward in western Mexico to the Isthmus of Tehuantepec. In general appearance these lizards are much alike, the conspicuous differences being in size, color, and shape of the tail. Big Gila monsters are approximately two feet long, whereas the other species grows about a foot longer. The lighter part of the pattern of the northern one is more or less white or yellow, that of the other pink. The Gila monster, when well fed, has much the thicker tail, and its head is not entirely black like that of the Mexican beaded lizard. The latter, in keeping with its essentially tropical distribution, prefers country with much more vegetation than that selected by its northern desert cousin. The beaded lizard, however, must not be thought of as a denizen of typical luxuriant tropical forests; much of western Mexico is arid as well as tropical.

The little information recorded on the feeding habits of the Gila monster indicates that it lives largely on reptile and bird eggs but also eats lizards and small mammals (see page 247). One individual disgorged Gambel quail eggs that patently had been swallowed whole. The heat of the desert sun is too great for this and other reptiles, which therefore must prowl chiefly at dusk or later. The eggs of the Gila monster are about two and a half inches long, and number from five to thirteen per clutch. The young are approximately four inches in length when they emerge after incubating some thirty days. An odd habit of assuming an upside-down position is ascribed to this lizard with such elusive habits. It has been said to sleep in this position and also to turn over for purposes of defense.

The technical names of these two lizards are rather interesting. In 1829 the Mexican one was christened *Heloderma horridum,* which might be freely translated "the terrible one with the studded skin." Oddly enough, ours was not named until forty years later. It was branded as a suspect (*"suspectum"*), no doubt because reliable information on the effects of its bite was lacking. These names, rather than being cold and scientific, are fraught with emotion.

GLASS SNAKES AND ALLIGATOR LIZARDS
(Family Anguidæ)
PLATES 164, 165, 218, 219, AND 220

THE LIZARDS of this small but far-flung family give the people of the United States a chance to see at first hand the favorite lizard stunt of playing free with limbs, either keeping them or giving them up entirely. Unfortunately, the legless glass snakes (*Ophisaurus*) are eastern, whereas the legged alligator lizards (*Gerrhonotus*) are western, the ranges barely meeting in Texas. Here is another case that fools the layman, who surely would not count the glass snakes and alligator lizards as allies. Members of these two genera do have a deep fold extending along the lower side that serves to distinguish them from other North American lizards, and might help to convince the casual observer of their close relationship. The specialist finds more fundamental evidence of alliance in the skull. This fold, it might be added, is not a characteristic of most of the genera of the family. It might also be remarked here that the species of this family do not have one good English name, hence my use of two that are widely applied to our own species.

It is unfortunate that our anguid legless lizards are universally called "glass snakes"; the first thing that the novice has to learn about them is that they are lizards with no legs and very long tails.

Examination of the lidded eyes may convince the skeptic, and the anatomist will vouch for the fact that both girdles (limb-supporting bones) are to be found by dissection. The false stories that have arisen about the glass snakes are endless; all are based on the fantastic belief that, when struck, a glass snake shatters like a piece of glass and, after danger has passed, joins together again. There is a grain of truth in this product of the human imagination: the long tail of these reptiles, like that of many other lizards, is very fragile. As already explained, this ability to survive loss of such a conspicuous appendage is advantageous, often promoting escape from an enemy. There are three species of glass snakes in the United States, two of them distributed over its eastern half, with the exception of the northeastern part. One is limited to the extreme southeast. None is found in Mexico or south of it. Extremely large individuals are about three feet long, and the record is set by a specimen from Raleigh, North Carolina, with a total length of 42.6 inches. Reproduction is by means of eggs.

The alligator lizards, so-called because of their alleged resemblance to an alligator, include five species that live in this country, two of them common and widely distributed. One of these, the northern alligator lizard (*Gerrhonotus cœruleus*), is, as the name implies, the more northern in distribution, actually reaching Canada. The food consists chiefly of insects, although other small creatures such as spiders and millipedes are readily taken. This species brings forth the young directly. The largest individuals barely exceed five inches in head-body length. The other familiar kind, the red-backed alligator lizard (*G. multicarinatus*), lays eggs, and grows to be about an inch longer. It likewise eats an abundance of insects, but also devours small backboned animals such as frogs and mammals. It has been found to relish the black-widow spider as well as its egg cases. In this way certainly it is a special friend of man. Our five species of alligator lizards are confined to the western part of the United States and the extreme southwestern corner of Canada. They avoid the central Rocky Mountains, but, in the north, occur as far eastward as western Montana; in the south, as far as central Texas.

Incidentally, the northern and red-backed alligator lizards show

how careful the classifier of reptiles must be in using the method of bringing forth young as evidence of kinship. This case is especially interesting because it is the species with the more northern range that produces the young directly, and suggests a correlation between latitude and method of reproduction.

Having used so much space on our own eight members of the present family, it will be necessary to deal with the remaining species, about fifty in number, briefly. The vast majority of these live in Mexico, the West Indies, and South America. In these areas also occur all but two of the genera (*Ophisaurus* and *Anguis*), which number a maximum of eleven for the entire family (some specialists do not recognize this many). The groups of the New World south of our border are limbed types relatively normal in appearance. Certain species are arboreal in habits. Little or nothing is known about the life histories of the majority.

The family is represented in the Old World by a few species, the members of which are either legless or with vestiges of hind legs, mere tokens of limbs. One, a legless species broadly distributed in Europe, including Great Britain, and found in southwestern Asia, is set off as a genus by itself (*Anguis*), and usually called "slow-worm." The remaining Old World species are placed along with our glass snakes in the genus *Ophisaurus*, which has an almost world-wide distribution: the eastern United States, an extreme tip of Africa (opposite Spain), southeastern Europe and adjacent southwestern Asia, a section of far southeastern Asia, and Borneo. Such a broken and extensive range bespeaks great age, and the fossil record proves that the genus is at least thirty million years old, going back to Oligocene times.

One Oligocene anguid lived in Wyoming and had a skull five inches long. It was appropriately named *Glyptosaurus giganteus*. The family itself is much older, with Cretaceous fossils to its credit. These must be more than seventy-five million years old. The ancestors are unknown, although relationships seem to be with the Gila monster, the legless lizards, and the xenosaurids.

While on the subject of age, it is interesting to note that the longevity record for lizards, thirty-two years in captivity, is held by the slow-worm (*Anguis fragilis*), and that a specimen of the European glass snake (*Ophisaurus apodus*) lived in the San Diego Zoo for twenty-five (see page 238).

XENOSAURIDS
(Family Xenosauridæ)

IT WOULD take a specialist to realize that the three small species of lizards assigned to this family are anything unusual. Although one of the three was discovered about a century ago, the other two were not made known to science until after 1940. The combined range of the species, all of which belong to the genus *Xenosaurus*, is limited to the area from eastern central Mexico to part of Guatemala adjacent to the Mexican boundary. A very recent study shows that the relationship is with the much larger Gila monster. It is only for the sake of completeness that this family is even mentioned. The technical name, of Greek derivation, means "guest" or "strange lizard," and makes a poor common name if translated. There are many strange lizards and few of them are ordinarily thought of as appropriate guests.

CHINESE CROCODILE LIZARD
(Family Shinisauridæ)

IN 1928 an expedition sent out by Sun Yatsen University of Canton, China, discovered in eastern Kwangsi Province a remarkable crocodile-like lizard that was later aptly named *Shinisaurus crocodilurus*. This species has remained the one and only member of a family, although Bogert writes that he considers it a close relative of the Xenosaurids; its isolated position probably will not hold. The largest specimen with a complete tail measured fifteen and five-eighths inches. This lizard's habits of holding on tenaciously after biting viciously and of sunning on branches overhanging mountain streams have won for it two picturesque local names: "thunderbolt snake" and "snake of great drowsiness." The first of these is an echo of our own rural belief that the snapping turtle will not release its grip until the thunder rolls. In China, recognition of the close relationship between snake and lizard, so well confirmed by scientific research, is age-old; lizards are often called "four-footed snakes." The crocodile lizard was found to be somewhat aquatic: it not only swims well, but seeks refuge in streams and eats, among other animals, tadpoles and fishes.

FOOTLESS LIZARDS
(Family Anniellidæ)

THE PRESENT family has a special interest for us because it is a legless group confined largely to this country; our other legless lizards, the glass snakes and the Florida worm lizard, are merely local representatives of widely distributed groups. The eyelids are well developed and movable in the footless-lizard and glass-snake families, whereas the former lacks an ear-opening, a structure possessed by the latter. The footless lizards have even lost all but the merest trace of the shoulder girdle, the supports of the front limbs. In this way they are like the Florida worm lizard, which does not have even a trace.

The family of footless lizards, sometimes known as the legless lizards, is comprised of but two species, one found in northwestern Baja California, and in western California from the region of San Francisco Bay southward (there is an extension from the south as far as Sequoia National Park); the other, a recent discovery, is confined to Isla San Gerónimo off the coast of Baja California.

The California footless lizard (*Anniella pulchra*) reaches a length of about ten inches, the tail, if complete, comprising about a third of the total. It prefers sand hills, beach dunes, or other places with soil of fine texture. There must be cover in the form of bushes, dead leaves, and other debris. One is seldom seen on the surface even in areas where numerous tracks crisscross the surface. When raked from the sand, a footless lizard disappears with astonishing rapidity. From one to four young are produced directly at a time in September, October, or November.

The footless lizards are related to the anguids and the xenosaurids.

GIRDLE–TAILED LIZARDS
(Family Cordylidæ or Zonuridæ)
PLATE 221

THE GIRDLE-TAILED lizards abound in southern Africa, and a few kinds are found in the eastern central part of that continent. If the twenty-three species were seen together, the casual observer would have to know a lot about lizard structure to understand why reptiles so varied in form are placed together in a family. The chief difficulty would be with four species (genus *Chamæsaura*) that are snakelike in shape, have ridiculously small limbs, and tails at least three times as long as the body. At one extreme the limbs, though having toes, are too small to be of use; at the other they are mere stumps; in one of the species the front ones have been reduced to "a minute clawed vestige," in another there actually are none. The next difficulty would be with a few species of normally shaped lizards of southern Africa only. But it is the remaining lot of species that give the family its name and chief characteristic: a spiny tail that, in certain kinds, is carried to an extreme almost beyond reason. In some of the thirteen species of the genus *Cordylus* (or *Zonurus*, as it was formerly called) we see this extreme development of the spiny tail. These thirteen species may be called the typical girdle-tailed lizards, and the use that at least some of them make of a remarkable appendage is worth describing in detail. It should first be explained that these spiny lizards usually live in or very near rocky areas.

For illustration I shall take a girdle-tailed lizard (*Cordylus cataphractus*) of extreme southwestern Africa; its life history has been more thoroughly studied than has that of any other species. At the slightest alarm, this reptile, which is usually seven or eight inches long and lives in arid sandstone country, enters the deepest crevice it can find. There, surrounded by rock, it curls the tail across the belly and seizes the tail with the jaws. Not only the sharp spines of the tail but those of the head and back give good protection, especially to the vulnerable belly. The lizard will coil in the same manner if headed off or removed from its retreat. Once it has coiled, it may even be rolled about on the ground without relaxing. If the tail is lost, another, but inferior, one will slowly grow out. As might be expected, such a useful tail is not easily broken off.

The formidable tails of these spiny lizards are probably used in more active ways. A captive individual of the most imposing member of the genus, the giant girdle-tail (*Cordylus giganteus*), which reaches a length of fifteen inches, was once seized and encircled by three coils of a hungry mole snake. After a brief period of constricting the spiny meal, the snake suddenly let go to retire a wiser but still hungry serpent. More interesting still is the encounter, related by Loveridge (see bibliography), between a puff adder and a giant girdle-tailed lizard. The snake seized the unresisting lizard and made good headway until it suddenly came to life, as it were, and with the tail belabored the snake so effectively that the latter was glad to disgorge the meal and escape.

The species of this family live almost entirely on animal matter, and, as far as definitely observed, bring forth the young directly.

Bibliography

✧

Amaral, Afranio do: "Two New South American Lizards." *Copeia* No. 4 (1950), pp. 281–4.

Angel, F.: "Les Lézards de Madagascar." *Mémoires Académie Malgache*, Vol. 36 (1942), pp. 1–193.

Anonymous: "Obituaries." *Zoonooz*, May 1948, p. 7.

Atsatt, S. R.: "The Storage of Sperm in the Female Chameleon *Microsaura pumila pumila*." *Copeia* No. 1 (1953), p. 59.

Barrett, Charles: "Lizards in Australian Wilds." *Bulletin, New York Zoological Society*, Vol. 21 (1928), pp. 99–111.

——: *Reptiles of Australia*. Toronto: Cassell & Company; 1950.

Barrows, Shirley and Hobart M. Smith: "The Skeleton of the Lizard *Xenosaurus grandis* (Gray)." *Science Bulletin, University Kansas*, Vol. 31, Part 2 (1947), pp. 227–81.

Beebe, William: "Field Notes on the Lizards of Kartabo, British Guiana, and Caripito, Venezuela. Part 3. Teiidae, Amphisbaenidae and Scincidae." *Zoologica*, Vol. 30, Part 1 (1945), pp. 7–32.

Boulenger, George Albert: "Monograph of the Lacertidae." *British Museum (Natural History)*, Vol. 1 (1920), pp. 1–352, and Vol. 2 (1921), pp. 1–451.

Brattstrom, Bayard H.: "The Food of the Nightlizards, Genus *Xantusia*." *Copeia* No. 3 (1952), pp. 168–72.

Burt, Charles E.: "A Study of the Teiid Lizards of the Genus *Cnemidophorus* with Special Reference to Their Phylogenetic Relationships." *United States National Museum*, Bulletin 154 (1931), pp. 1–286.

—— and May Danheim: "A Preliminary Check List of the Lizards of South America." *Transactions, Academy Science St. Louis*, Vol. 28 (1933), pp. 1–104.

Cagle, Fred R.: "A Lizard Population on Tinian." *Copeia* No. 1 (1946), pp. 4–9.

——: "A Population of the Carolina Anole." *Natural History Miscellanea, Chicago Academy Sciences*, No. 15 (1948), pp. 1–5.

Camp, Charles Lewis: "Classification of the Lizards." *Bulletin, American Museum Natural History*, Vol. 48 (1923), pp. 289–481.

Carr, Archie: "Notes on Eggs and Young of the Lizard *Rhineura floridana*." *Copeia* No. 1 (1949), p. 77.

Cowles, Raymond B.: "Parturition in the Yucca Night Lizard." *Copeia* No. 2 (1944), pp. 98–100.

Bibliography

Cullen, Lucy P.: *Beyond the Smoke That Thunders.* New York: Oxford University Press; 1940.

Davis, D. Dwight: "Behavior of the Lizard *Corythophanes cristatus.*" *Fieldiana: Zoology,* Vol. 35 (1953), pp. 1–8.

Duellman, William E.: "A Case of *Heloderma* Poisoning." *Copeia* No. 2 (1950), p. 151.

Dunn, Emmett Reid: "Notes on American Mabuyas." *Proceedings, Academy Natural Sciences Philadelphia,* Vol. 87 (1936), pp. 533–57.

——: "Los Géneros de Anfibios y Reptiles de Colombia, II." *Caldasia,* Vol. 3 (1944), pp. 73–110.

Fan, T. H.: "Preliminary Report of Reptiles from Yaoshan, Kwangsi, China." *Bulletin, Department Biology, Sun Yatsen University,* No. 11 (1931), pp. 1–154.

Fitch, Henry S.: "Natural History of the Alligator Lizards." *Transactions, Academy Science St. Louis,* Vol. 29 (1935), pp. 1–38.

——: "A Field Study of the Growth and Behavior of the Fence Lizard." *University California Publications Zoölogy,* Vol. 44 (1940), pp. 151–72.

Flower, Stanley S.: "Contributions to our Knowledge of the Duration of Life in Vertebrate Animals.—3. Reptiles." *Proceedings, Zoological Society London,* No. 60 (1925), pp. 911–81.

——: "Further Notes on the Duration of Life in Animals.—3. Reptiles." *Proceedings, Zoological Society London,* Series A, Part 1 (1937), pp. 1–39.

Gilmore, Charles W.: "Fossil Lizards of North America." *Memoirs, National Academy Sciences,* Vol. 22 (1928), pp. 1–169.

——: "Descriptions of New and Little-Known Fossil Lizards from North America." *Proceedings, United States National Museum,* Vol. 86 (1938), pp. 11–26.

Greenberg, Bernard: "Notes on the Social Behavior of the Collared Lizard." *Copeia* No. 4 (1945), pp. 225–30.

—— and G. K. Noble: "Social Behavior of the American Chameleon (*Anolis carolinensis* Voigt)." *Physiological Zoölogy,* Vol. 17 (1944), pp. 392–439.

——: "Social Behavior of the Western Banded Gecko, *Coleonyx variegatus* Baird." *Physiological Zoölogy,* Vol. 16 (1943), pp. 110–22.

Hamlett, George W. D.: "Notes on Breeding and Reproduction in the Lizard *Anolis carolinensis.*" *Copeia* No. 3 (1952), pp. 183–5.

Hennig, Willi: "Revision der Gattung *Draco* (Agamidae)." *Temminckia,* Vol. 1 (1936), pp. 153–220.

Hudson, Robert G.: "Maximum Length of the Glass Lizard." *Herpetologica,* Vol. 4 (1948), p. 224.

Knowlton, G. F. and M. J. Janes: "Studies of the Food Habits of Utah Lizards." *Ohio Journal Science,* Vol. 32 (1932), pp. 467–70.

Kopstein, Felix: "Ein Beitrag zur Eierkunde und zur Fortpflanzung der Malaiischen Reptilien." *Bulletin, Raffles Museum,* No. 14 (1938), pp. 81–167.

Laurent, R.: "Note sur les Amphisbaenidae d'Afrique." *Rev. Zool. Bot. Afr.,* Vol. 40 (1947), pp. 52–63.

Loeb, Leo: "The Venom of *Heloderma.*" *Carnegie Institution Washington,* No. 177 (1913), pp. 1–244.

Loveridge, Arthur: "Revision of the African Lizards of the Family Amphisbaenidae." *Bulletin, Museum Comparative Zoölogy,* Vol. 87 (1941), pp. 353–451.

323

Lizards

Lizards

Lizards

——: "Revision of the African Lizards of the Family Gerrhosauridae." *Bulletin, Museum Comparative Zoölogy*, Vol. 89 (1942), pp. 485–543.

——: "Revision of the African Lizards of the Family Cordylidae." *Bulletin, Museum Comparative Zoölogy*, Vol. 95 (1944), pp. 1–118.

——: *Reptiles of the Pacific World.* New York: The Macmillan Company; 1945.

Mertens, Robert: "*Lacerta goliath* n. sp., eine ausgestorbene Rieseneidechse von den Kanaren." *Senckenbergiana*, Vol. 25 (1942), pp. 330–9.

——:"Die Familie der Warane (Varanidae)." *Abhandlungen d. Senckenbergischen Naturforschenden Gesellschaft*, Abh. 462, 465, 466 (1942), pp. 1–291.

——: "Die Warn- und Droh-Reaktionen der Reptilien." *Abhandlungen d. Senckenbergischen Naturforschenden Gesellschaft*, Abh. 471 (1946), pp. 1–108.

Miller, Malcolm R.: "Some Aspects of the Life History of the Yucca Night Lizard, *Xantusia vigilis*." *Copeia* No. 2 (1951), pp. 114–20.

Mosauer, Walter: "The Reptiles and Amphibians of Tunisia." *Publications University California Los Angeles Biological Sciences*, Vol. 1 (1934), pp. 49–64.

Neill, Wilfred T.: "The Eyes of the Worm Lizard, and Notes on the Habits of the Species." *Copeia* No. 2 (1951), pp. 177–8.

Noble, G. K. and G. C. Klingel: "The Reptiles of Great Inagua Island, British West Indies." *American Museum Novitates*, No. 549 (1932), pp. 1–25.

—— and H. T. Bradley: "The Mating Behavior of Lizards; Its Bearing on the Theory of Sexual Selection." *Annals, New York Academy Sciences*, Vol. 35 (1933), pp. 25–100.

—— and E. R. Mason: "Experiments on the Brooding Habits of the Lizards *Eumeces* and *Ophisaurus*." *American Museum Novitates*, No. 619 (1933), pp. 1–29.

Norris, Kenneth S.: "The Ecology of the Desert Iguana *Dipsosaurus dorsalis*." *Ecology*, Vol. 34 (1953), pp. 265–87.

Oliver, James A.: "Ontogenetic Changes in Osteodermal Ornamentation in Skinks." *Copeia* No. 2 (1951), pp. 127–30.

——: "Caiman Lizard—a Reptile Rarity." *Animal Kingdom*, Vol. 54 (1951), pp. 151–3.

Pope, Clifford H.: "Notes on Reptiles from Fukien and Other Chinese Provinces." *Bulletin, American Museum Natural History*, Vol. 58 (1929), pp. 335–487.

Reeve, W. L.: "Taxonomy and Distribution of the Horned Lizard genus *Phrynosoma*." *Science Bulletin, University Kansas*, Vol. 34, Part 2 (1952), pp. 817–960.

Rodgers, Thomas L. and Viola H. Memmler: "Growth in the Western Blue-Tailed Skink." *Transactions, San Diego Society Natural History*, Vol. 10 (1943), pp. 61–8.

Romer, Alfred S.: *Vertebrate Paleontology.* Chicago: The University of Chicago Press; 1933.

Rooij, Nelly de: *The Reptiles of the Indo-Australian Archipelago. I. Lacertilia, Chelonia, Emydosauria.* Leiden: E. J. Brill; 1915.

Rose, Walter: *The Reptiles and Amphibians of Southern Africa.* Cape Town: Maskew Miller; 1950.

Bibliography

Ruibal, Rodolfo: "Revisionary Studies of Some South American Teiidae." *Bulletin, Museum Comparative Zoölogy*, Vol. 106 (1952), pp. 477–529.

Sanderson, Ivan T.: *Caribbean Treasure*. New York: The Viking Press; 1939.

Schmidt, Karl P.: "Contributions to the Herpetology of the Belgian Congo Based on the Collection of The American Museum Congo Expedition, 1905–1915." *Bulletin, American Museum Natural History*, Vol. 39 (1919), Part I.—Turtles, Crocodiles, Lizards, and Chameleons, pp. 385–624.

——: "Contributions to the Herpetology of the Belgian Congo Based on the Collection of The American Museum Congo Expedition, 1905–1915." *Bulletin, American Museum Natural History*, Vol. 49 (1923), Part II.—Snakes, pp. 1–146.

Shaw, Charles E.: "The Chuckwallas, Genus *Sauromalus*." *Transactions, San Diego Society Natural History*, Vol. 10 (1945), pp. 269–306.

——: "The Lizards of San Diego County with Descriptions and Key." *Bulletins, Zoological Society San Diego*, No. 25 (1950), pp. 1–63.

Smith, Hobart M.: *Handbook of Lizards. Lizards of the United States and of Canada*. Ithaca, New York: Comstock Publishing Co.; 1946.

—— and Edward H. Taylor: "An Annotated Checklist and Key to the Reptiles of Mexico Exclusive of the Snakes." *United States National Museum*, Bulletin 199 (1950), pp. 1–253.

Smith, Malcolm A.: *The Fauna of British India, Including Ceylon and Burma. Reptilia and Amphibia*. Vol. 2.—*Sauria*. London: Taylor and Francis; 1935.

——: *The British Amphibians & Reptiles*. The New Naturalist. London: Collins; 1951.

Snyder, Richard C.: "Bipedal Locomotion of the Lizard *Basiliscus basiliscus*." *Copeia* No. 2 (1949), pp. 129–37.

Stebbins, Robert C. and Harry B. Robinson: "Further Analysis of a Population of the Lizard *Sceloporus graciosus gracilis*." *University California Publications Zoölogy*, Vol. 48 (1946), pp. 149–68.

Taylor, Edward H.: "A Taxonomic Study of the Cosmopolitan Scincoid Lizards of the Genus *Eumeces* with an Account of the Distribution and Relationships of Its Species." *Science Bulletin, University Kansas*, Vol. 23 (1935), pp. 1–643.

Waite, Edgar R.: *The Reptiles and Amphibians of South Australia*. Adelaide: Harrison Weir; 1929.

Walls, Gordon L.: "The Vertebrate Eye and Its Adaptive Radiation." *Cranbrook Institute Science*, Bulletin No. 19 (1942), pp. 1–785.

Zangerl, Rainer: "Contributions to the Osteology of the Skull of the Amphisbaenidae." *American Midland Naturalist*, Vol. 31 (1944), pp. 417–54.

Index

✸

j

Index

xi

A NOTE ON THE TYPE

This book was set on the Linotype in JANSON, *a recutting made direct from the type cast from matrices made by Anton Janson. Whether or not Janson was of Dutch ancestry is not known, but it is known that he purchased a foundry and was a practicing type-founder in Leipzig during the years 1660 to 1687. Janson's first specimen sheet was issued in 1675. His successor issued a specimen sheet showing all of the Janson types in 1689.*

His type is an excellent example of the influential and sturdy Dutch types that prevailed in England prior to the development by William Caslon of his own incomparable designs, which he evolved from these Dutch faces. The Dutch in their turn had been influenced by Garamond in France. The general tone of Janson, however, is darker than Garamond and has a sturdiness and substance quite different from its predecessors.

The book was composed by the Plimpton Press, Norwood, Massachusetts. Printed and bound by The Book Press, Brattleboro, Vermont. Photographs reproduced by Capper Engraving Company, Knoxville, Tennessee.